THE DECORATIVE TWENTIES

THE DECORATIVE
TWENTIES

Martin Battersby

✳ Walker and Company, New York

Acknowledgements

The author would like to express his gratitude to Condé Nast Publications for their courtesy in allowing him access to their files of *Vogue* and *House and Garden* which yielded much valuable and often surprising information; and to Miss Greenhill and the staff of Brighton Reference Library for their unfailing assistance and patience.

First published in the United States of America in 1969 by Walker and Company, a division of the Walker Publishing Company, Inc.

Library of Congress Catalog Card Number: 71-84213

First published in Great Britain by Studio Vista Limited
Blue Star House, Highgate Hill, London N19

Set in 10pt Aster, 1½ pts leaded

Printed in the United States of America

Contents

Introduction

The popular conception of the years between the Armistice and the Wall Street crash as a period of hectic gaiety, of short skirts and Oxford Bags, of jazz, gin and drugs has been fostered by contemporary entertainment to such an extent that it comes as a shock to find, in the books and periodicals dealing with the decorative arts of the time, constant references to the hard struggle of artists and designers to maintain even a reasonable standard of living. References to the difficulties facing creative workers began to appear in the editorial comments of *The Studio* and its companion volume *The Studio Year Book of Decorative Art*, neither of which had hitherto shown any concern about the possible plight of their contributors or readers — if indeed there had been any need to do so. An editorial in *The Studio* of 1922 commented that ' it is no secret that artworkers of practically all denominations are experiencing a very bad time just now and in view of the depressed condition of trade generally and the enormous burden of taxation which the country at large has to bear this is not at all surprising.'

Artworkers were of course, not the only people affected but naturally *The Studio* was concerned about their welfare, for upon them the existence of the magazine depended. All classes were affected with one exception — the ' New Rich ' — for the signing of the Armistice found the Allied nations profoundly disillusioned, exhausted from the struggle and nearing bankruptcy. The pomp of victory parades in London and Paris could not conceal the fact that the flower of youth in both countries had been mown down. The habits and customs of the pre-war years were gone, and faced with the uncertainties of the future, the older generation mourned for the comfort and security of the pre-war Edwardian years, forgetting that they too had had their darker side. The younger generation, the ex-officers with small gratuities, and other ranks returning to Civvy Street and unemployment, the widows and fiancées of those who did not return, these found themselves in a changing world and plunged, if circumstances permitted, into a mood of feverish gaiety in an attempt to stifle suspicions that their sacrifices had been in vain and millions of lives wantonly thrown away for no result.

Germany, it was true, lay in ruins, utterly broken and no longer a danger to the peace of Europe — or so it was thought. But France, technically on the winning side, was little better off. For four years northern France had been devastated as the armies fought to the death, churning the landscape into a wilderness of blood-stained mud. A vast belt of desolation lay where towns, villages and factories had been. The economic structure of the country was in a serious condition. England was equally depleted of manpower and money by the years of war, while labour unrest and wide-spread unemployment caused the Government grave concern.

Against this sombre background emerged two new classes, the New Rich — the exception already referred to — and the New Poor. The former were the cause of bitter comment. From fairly humble beginnings at the outbreak of hostilities, they had, by various means (in some cases by alleged trading with the enemy countries through neutral channels) profited to such an extent that at the Armistice they were not only millionaires but often titled into the bargain. In the novels of E.F.Benson and Michael Arlen, these ' New Rich ' were satirized, none too kindly, for the hard-faced ruthlessness of the men and the vulgarity of their wives, whose social ambitions were pitilessly exposed. Armed with their newly acquired wealth and their titles, the wives hoped to enter Society by lavish entertainments in their houses in London and the country. ' The present possessors of great wealth ... of a different and on the whole a less cultured class ', as a writer in *The Studio* referred to them, were in fact regarded as blessings by the luxury trades, where their lavish spending saved many a firm from bankruptcy in the post-war years. They naturally gravitated to the

1 Barbara Greg woodcut book illustration

best-known firms when it came to redecoration and the furnishing of their new homes and the traditional period schemes with which they were presented were very much to their taste, giving them the feeling of living in 'traditional' surroundings.

The New Poor, far greater in numbers than the New Rich, only began to receive attention when the latter's spending mania had exhausted itself. Once the New Rich had provided themselves with houses, furniture, paintings, they started spending their money in other ways and the furnishing and decorating firms were forced to cater for a less affluent public. The words 'deferred payments' began to appear in small print in advertisements — by 1930 these same words were often in type as large as the name of the advertiser. The interiors illustrated in these advertisements show the current taste in England, pastiches of the Tudor or Georgian periods or rooms in the Chinese taste. It was not until the late 1920s that new influences from the Continent were allowed to disturb the preoccupation with historicism.

In marked contrast to London, Paris was the centre for an extraordinary outburst of creative energy in the decorative arts. In addition to the artists and designers established before the Great War, a new generation of talented and original creative workers in the field of furniture, glass, bookbinding and decorative metalwork emerged, all of whom were given opportunities of displaying their work in the 1925 Paris Exhibition. Hard on their heels came another generation of designers who advocated 'modernism'* in their work in that a preoccupation with the machine and its forms was expressed by the use of new materials, glass, metal and bonded wood.

Art Nouveau was essentially an artificial and imposed style, valuable in that it had broken the long domination of historicism but at the same time capable of little development beyond ever more extravagant fantasy. Commercialized by the 1900 exhibition it soon deteriorated in quality and among the first exponents of the style to react sharply against it were Léon Jallot, the director of Bing's workshops, Maurice

---

* The term 'modernist' has been used throughout this volume to denote furniture and other artifacts which were made in the period after approximately 1925 and which were designed in the new style with no allusions to the style of any former age. Not only was this term used at the time — with occasional alternatives of cubistic or futuristic — but the justification for its use is explained by J.C.Rogers in his book *Modern English Furniture* (1930). 'The expression 'modern furniture' covers the industry's whole output, irrespective of design or style, and without more precise definition it may mean replicas of antiques or pieces of really modern design in which the author has sought to express his own ideas rather than to copy the work of craftsmen long since dead. Furniture that is new solely on account of its recent construction is not justifiably entitled to the term 'modern' and owing to such loose application, the word 'modernist' has therefore been frequently used of late to distinguish work that is new in form as well as material.' The word 'modernist' was in use in France as early as 1922.

Dufrène and Paul Follot, both of whom had contributed to La Maison Moderne. In their view the future for the design of furniture and interiors lay in a reappraisal of the traditions of the late eighteenth century and an adaptation of their forms to the needs of modern life. Together with André Groult they may be considered the progenitors of Art Déco which lasted from approximately 1910 until 1925, the year of the important exhibition of the decorative arts in Paris which at once gave the style its name, demonstrated the culmination of the style and, in the same way that the 1900 Exhibition had sounded the knell for Art Nouveau, saw its passing. From the Ballets Russes which made their first appearance in Paris in 1909, designers borrowed a spectrum of vivid, intense colours while the exhibition of decorative art from Munich held at the Salon d'Automne in the following year had a decisive influence on the decorative idioms of the style and the formalized floral motifs so characteristic of Art Déco can be traced back, via Munich and Vienna, to those of Charles Rennie Mackintosh, whose work was so much admired in those two cities.

The war years necessarily interrupted the development of Art Déco but in 1919 an outburst of creative activity resulted in the formation of a number of organizations which furthered its cause. La Compagnie des Arts Français was founded in 1919 by Louis Sue and the painter André Mare who, in company with a number of painters, sculptors and textile designers, created interiors and furniture based on traditional forms and decorated with swags of drapery, garlands of flowers and sculptured reliefs with a neoclassic flavour. Emile-Jacques Ruhlmann, who had caused a stir at his first exhibition in 1913, opened the business in 1919 as an outlet for his elegantly luxurious furniture. In the same year René Joubert founded Décoration Intérieure Moderne, more generally known by the initials DIM, and their furniture was the first of modern French decoration to be shown in England in 1928. The two veterans of Art Nouveau, Paul Follot and Maurice Dufrène, took influential positions as heads of the decorating departments at two major Parisian department stores. Follot with his associate Laurent Malclès became the director of 'Pomone' at the Bon Marché in 1923, two years after Dufrène had founded 'La Maîtrise' at the Galeries Lafayette.

By 1925 two other influences can be observed, those of cubism and Negro art. There had been an exhibition of cubist art in Paris in 1911 but it was not until after the war that the graceful femininity of much of Art Déco ornament became tempered with the more angular forms inspired by cubist painting — the beginnings of a transitional phase between Art Déco and modernism. Negro art had been collected by a coterie of painters since approximately 1905 and had had a strong influence on the young and comparatively unknown painters of the cubist school, but it was not until 1922 when there was an exhibition of French Colonial art that the exoticisms of African sculpture became acceptable to a wider public.

The decline of Art Déco was due partly to an inevitable change in fashion and partly to the work of new designers whose work began to attract attention — not always favourable. For political reasons Germany had no exhibit at the 1925 exhibition and thus the work of the Bauhaus founded in 1919 was known only to a limited few in France but the angularities of the USSR Pavilion, designed by Malnikov, aroused considerable interest, as did the exhibit 'L'Esprit Nouveau' designed by le Corbusier and Pierre Jeanneret. The stark simplicity of the new school, the avoidance of any unnecessary decoration in favour of spatial concepts as personified in the work of le Corbusier, Jeanneret, Charlotte Perriand, Robert Mallet-Stevens and Djo-Bourgeois repelled many by its austerity and apparent lack of comfort, but in spite of the hostility of the adherents of Art Déco, it gradually won acceptance in a modified form.

If a disproportionate amount of space throughout this book seems to have been

2 M. Dufet advertisement for Chez Fernande Cabanel, 1922

devoted to the decorative arts of France in preference to those of England, it must be stated that this is not due to any feelings of Anglophobia or Francophilia on the part of the author. The explanation is simply that the amount of information regarding French work during the period under examination is extremely plentiful while that concerning English work is scanty. In addition, the activity among all branches of the decorative arts in France, from dressmaking to wrought-iron work, was intense in the years immediately following the Armistice of 1918. It was as though it were necessary to reassert French eminence in matters of taste as soon as possible and to demonstrate to the world that though France had emerged from the four year struggle profoundly shaken and near bankruptcy, her creative energies were undiminished and unceasing and could be brought into effect to give proof of her versatility and originality. Similarly in 1945, at the end of an even worse war, one of the first exports from France was the ' Théâtre de la Mode ', a combined effort on the part of the dressmakers, designers and writers and a demonstration that even after the miseries and hardships of occupation, French supremacy in fashion was still unrivalled.

There was also, during the 'twenties, more encouragement for designers and craftsmen in France and equally more opportunities for exhibiting their work. Twice a year at the Salon d'Automne and the Salon des Artistes-Décorateurs elaborately mounted displays of the work of the leading interior decorators were held and during the year innumerable smaller exhibitions of glass, ironwork, bookbinding, ceramics and textiles gave the public the opportunity of seeing the latest creations. The International Exhibition of Decorative Art held in Paris in 1925, the first and the biggest exhibition ever devoted to this subject, was an assertion of French genius in this field and the greater part of the exhibition was given over to French work in every branch of the decorative arts — from complete interiors to children's toys.

It must be admitted that the post-war years in England were not, in comparison, a brilliant period in the history of British minor arts. Shackled by tradition wrongly applied — in that it looked back to the past for inspiration instead of developing — and hampered by the lack of an informed and interested public, designers were working in a vacuum of indifference, in spite of the efforts of a very few associations and private persons. As a consequence of this complete lack of encouragement, there were no designers in England whose work could rival that of Lalique or Marinot in glassworking, Ruhlmann, Follot or Herbst in the design of interiors and furniture, Edgar Brandt in ironworking, Pierre Legrain or Rose Adler in bookbinding — the list could be continued indefinitely. Any lessons that London could have learned from Paris were ignored and, just as the followers of the Arts and Crafts movement in England had regarded the contemporary French Art Nouveau with feelings ranging from an ignorance of its existence to puritanical suspicion of its imagined decadence and immorality, so twenty years later the little that was known of French work was viewed with either suspicion or a carping criticism based, as criticism so often is, upon insufficient knowledge. As an example of this, the statement by Marriott Powell may be quoted from the official report from the Department of Overseas Trade in which he comments on the French exhibits of glass in the 1925 Exhibition. Referring to the display of *pâte-de-verre* (see page 71) by François Decorchement he stated that the process of making this type of glass was invented by Decorchement, was a closely guarded secret and that this secret would die with the inventor. That an important piece of *pâte-de-verre* by the sculptor Henri Cros (who had rediscovered the ancient techniques of making this type of glass) had been a major exhibit in the 1900 Exhibition in Paris and had caused considerable comment, that since then Dammouse, Despret, Schneider, Argy-Rousseau and others had been producing in considerable quantities *pâte-de-verre* some of which was on sale in England — all this

3 F.C.Bayliss Smith's Tea Room, Paris

seems to have escaped the notice of Powell, who was considered sufficiently an authority on the subject of glass to be asked to report in an official capacity. The only exception to this attitude was that the superiority of French dressmaking was recognized in England, but at that period fashion as a decorative art was ignored by designers or craftsmen working in other fields in England; in any case this was cancelled out by the fact that English tailoring was the best in the world.

A comment by a writer in *House and Garden* for 1921 struck an unusual note for the period by its praise of French design. It was noted that 'in every town [in England] shops filled with every sort of second-hand junk have multiplied and people utterly deprived of taste proudly display their latest " finds " and throughout the middle classes an " old " thing has become synonymous with a thing that is beautiful and desirable... at present most of the good designs come from France. The French are less conservative and more eager to be up-to-date. Some sorts of social success positively depend upon a gift for inaugurating fashions.'

The exchange of information about developments or achievements in the decorative arts was negligible and mostly one-way. *The Studio* in its monthly issues and in the *Year Books of Decorative Art* illustrated examples of French work but these were often five or more years out of date and in some of the annual volumes French decorative art is not to be found while that of Austria and Hungary is given space. Equally, work by English designers or craftsmen was rarely, if ever, noticed in French periodicals specializing in the decorative arts and it is unlikely that the editors of these magazines would have considered the English Tudor-inspired interiors of any great interest to their readers — in spite of the aggressively Elizabethan decorations of Smith's Tea Room in the rue de Rivoli. Some contemporary French wallpapers were, however, to be found for sale in London and were commented on with faint praise by magazines while Lalique glass had considerable popularity in England; but it was not until the 1925 Exhibition that any active interest was shown in French work. Even than it was three years before Shoolbred's held an exhibition of furniture by DIM (Décoration Intérieure Moderne) and other French designers and it was not until 1929 that Waring and Gillow took the step of opening a depart-

4 Marcel Renard *La Soie* pottery figure, Paris Exhibition, 1925
Atelier Primavera oval bowl; circular box
Henri Simmen vase

ment for the sale of French modern furniture under the direction of Paul Follot and Serge Chermayeff. These gestures may not have been from an altruistic desire to proselytize on behalf of French culture so much as attempts to provide stimuli to waning business. The post-war boom in decorating brought about by new-rich clients was coming to an end, no new clients were coming to take their place and the growing economic stresses were beginning to make their mark in a decided falling-off of business. There was also a new threat to their stability in the emergence of the individual interior decorator, not as yet a serious enough threat to cause concern but one which would increase in the following decade and in some cases result in the disappearance of old-established firms. As they worked from their homes or from small shops leased at low rentals these designers could undercut the big firms as their overheads were in some cases minimal. Very often belonging to the ranks of the New Poor, ruined by the war or with their incomes reduced by taxation, they were more anxious to please their clients, as they depended upon personal recommendations, and as they exploited their own personal taste could create more original and unconventional interiors — 'amusing' was the contemporary word — at considerably less cost than that charged by the big firms. Those not endowed with financial acumen soon ran into money difficulties and found themselves in the bankruptcy courts, but the survivors proved serious rivals to large businesses and in the depression years of the 1930s took their clientele away from them almost entirely. With their success or failure depending upon their originality the decorators were more open to influence from abroad and thus there was a greater awareness of trends in France and the Continent during the 1930s than there had been in the previous decade.

THE
DECORATIVE
ARTS
IN FRANCE

5 C. Saupique *Le Café* decorative panel, 1924

6 P. Turin bronze commemorative medal for the Paris Exhibition, 1925

The 1925 Paris Exhibition

The Exhibition of Decorative and Industrial Arts held in Paris in 1925 — exactly halfway through the period under examination — was unique in several respects. Firstly it was the first exhibition on an international scale for over a century in which the applied arts were the sole reason for the exhibition. There were none of the displays of scientific, mechanical or agricultural progress which were the usual features of so many exhibitions before and since, particularly so in the case of the British Empire Exhibition (opened in Wembley in the previous year), where the decorative arts played only a minor role. Secondly the exhibits were required to be representative of contemporary life and feeling and nothing directly copied from or inspired by any decorative style of the past was admitted. Thirdly it could be said that the exhibition had taken one hundred and thirty years to bring about.

The French Revolution had led to the dispersal of the corporations of designers and craftsmen, partly by the disappearance of their aristocratic patrons and more because they were likely to be possible centres of reactionary agitation against the revolutionaries on account of their long association with and dependence upon the ancien régime. However, a number of the more farsighted revolutionary leaders, more concerned with the artistic future of the new authority than with the political manoeuvring which brought so many of their number to ignominious deaths on the scaffold, felt that some show of reassurance should be made if the economic future were to be maintained on a firm basis. And so a 'Public Exhibition of the Products of French Industry' was organized by François de Neufchâtel and it was opened to the public in August 1798. Despite the appeal of the organizers and even of Marat himself that in the glorious future toward which the Revolution was the first step, industry should march forward hand in hand with science and art, the painters and sculptors to whom it had been addressed remained aloof and unco-operative and continued to shun both science and industry for the next hundred years or so. The main reason for this was due to the different methods of training artists and craftsmen. An aspiring painter would be apprenticed to the studio of an established artist from whom he would learn only those crafts directly concerned with the preparation and execution of a painting, the same thing applying to sculptors, and whether he made a success of his career depended almost entirely upon his skill, imagination and initiative. On the other hand, French craftsmen in the eighteenth century were only allowed to practise their acquired skills when they had proved their proficiency after serving a long apprenticeship. Thus the gap between the 'fine arts' and the 'applied arts' was firmly fixed. An artist could, if he so wished, exercise his talents in any branch of the 'fine arts' whether painting, sculpture, engraving, architecture ... but to encroach on the territory of 'craftsmanship' was to encounter the opposition of the guilds and associations of craftsmen.

The French Revolution and the turbulent events of the succeeding years were not fruitful grounds for a closer relationship between artists and craftsmen and if anything the gap was widened. The ancien régime, whatever its failings, had maintained a high standard of taste in its surroundings, and by its patronage the craftsmen of France had produced masterpieces of refined and fastidious taste in interior decoration, furniture and all branches of the decorative arts. The disappearance of these enlightened patrons was not compensated by the rise, at the end of the eighteenth century, of a new-rich class who followed the artistic dictatorship of Percier and Fontaine, the official designers to the Napoleonic court. Gustave Geffroy, writing in 1900, pointed out that a contributory factor to the beginning of the decline in taste during the nineteenth century was the carnage of the Napoleonic military campaigns and the consequent sapping of the 'creative force' of France — an argument which perhaps loses some validity when it is considered that the same lowering of taste took place in England at the same period. Although admittedly engaged in the Napoleonic War, for England the losses of manpower were not so great as those suffered by France who was fighting on many fronts.

The tradition of patronage broken, manufacturers and craftsmen faced with increasing demands for consumer goods in the first half of the nineteenth century found themselves lacking in any form of guidance in the field of design, a situation which was complicated by the growth of mass production by machinery. In too many cases the manufacturers were too intent on large, easily earned profits to be willing to make any expenditure for the services of designers — even if they had been available. In consequence, after every international exhibition the artistic standards of the French exhibits were severely criticized in the official reports, the usual complaint being that the objects on display were not expressive of contemporary French life, were encumbered with ill-drawn decorative motifs borrowed from every historical style and applied with no purpose or design. In time the volume of this criticism began to take effect, particularly after the Great Exhibition of 1851, when the low standard of the Sèvres exhibit in particular was evident even among the hotch-potch of historical pastiches which made up the majority of the exhibits. To ameliorate the situation, L'Union Centrale des Beaux-Arts Appliqués à l'Industrie was formed and in 1882 this was to be transformed into L'Union des Arts Décoratifs and the Musée des Arts Décoratifs was founded with the funds raised from the proceeds of a lottery. This was, to begin with, little more than a collection of antiques of decorative interest, had no permanent home and no interest was shown for some years in the acquisition of contemporary works of art. The practical application of art to industry by the training of young craftsmen had no official sponsorship until 1899 when a chair of art applied to the crafts was established at the Conservatoire des Arts et Métiers. It was necessary, in addition to these steps, to awaken the interest of the general public, for without this support and collaboration any efforts would inevitably fail, and with this end in view, the magazine *Art et Décoration* was launched in 1897.

There were high hopes that the result of so much effort on the part of well-meaning individuals would be seen in the Paris Universal Exhibition of 1900. But something went wrong. A previous exhibition (held in 1889), had been criticized on the grounds that while the buildings such as the Eiffel Tower, the Galerie des Machines and others were ahead of their time in the use of metal and glass, the exhibits housed in these pavilions were pastiches of styles ranging from 1600 to 1800 — the exceptions being glass by Gallé and Rousseau and pottery by Dammouse and Delaherche. In 1900 the reverse was the case. The exhibits were original — too original for the taste of many visitors — but the buildings were composed of a medley of historical styles, made of plaster or stucco which masked the iron framework. The over-all effect was lively and attractive but the general opinion was that an opportunity had been missed.

Undeterred the reformers continued their struggles. In 1901 a group of younger designers, including a number whose names are linked with Art Nouveau — though they were soon to abandon the style — banded together to form 'La Société des Artistes-Décorateurs'. The exhibitions staged by this fraternity grew increasingly influential as a result of its attempts to awaken public interest in contemporary design — despite the hostility from such interested parties as the numerous antique dealers in Paris who could see their livelihood seriously threatened. Long after most countries in Europe had established their museums of the decorative arts France, in 1905, established the Musée des Arts Décoratifs in its permanent home in the Pavillon de Marsan, one of the wings of the Louvre. It is interesting to note that

Rodin's masterpiece *Les Portes d'Enfer* had originally been commissioned for the entrance to the museum at a time when it was to be housed in a building on the site of the Gare d'Orsay.

In 1902 the Italian organizers of an exhibition at Turin had stipulated that the exhibits must be original works displaying a marked tendency to an aesthetic renewal of form and that imitations of historical styles or industrial products lacking in artistic inspiration would be refused admittance. An exhibition with the same regulations was proposed by a M. Couyba in 1907 but it took four years before the idea was put to the French Senate and another year before plans were finalized for an exhibition in 1915.

A curious and unconsciously prophetic report had appeared in the German press in 1912 that the Universal Exhibition was to be postponed until 1920 ' because of the fears entertained in France regarding Germany's ascendency in the field of industrial art and the menace thereby involved to France's erstwhile unassailable lead among the nations in this field.' By delaying, it was alleged, the French hoped to redress the balance by a drastic reorganization of the technical schools. The report was both confirmed and denied but neither country could have foreseen that any postponement would be due to a struggle more deadly and ruinous than one to determine artistic superiority. The Munich Exhibition of Applied Art held in Paris in 1910 had been bitterly attacked by French critics but during the six weeks of its duration had attracted large crowds — large enough to warrant regulation by the police, an unknown occurrence. It had resulted in record sales and had a disturbing effect upon French artists and designers whose inborn conviction of French prominence in the decorative arts was shaken. Thus there may have been some grounds for the rumoured reasons for the postponement of the Universal Exhibition. Paul Poiret, travelling in Germany and Austria at this time, was extremely impressed by the contemporary work of Bruno Paul, Josef Hoffmann, Dagobert Peche and others with the result that on his return to Paris he founded the influential Atelier Martine in 1912.

The outbreak of war in 1914 caused the indefinite shelving of the project but soon after the Armistice, four years later, the idea was revived in the hope of boosting French morale which was at a low ebb. The detested enemy Germany had been humiliated and ruined but France herself had suffered losses in manpower and property and her former ally Russia, upon whose might so many hopes had been pinned a short twenty years before, was torn by anarchy and revolution. How better to show the world that France was unshaken in spirit than by a display of some of her greatest assets — her style and elegance, her mastery of the arts and her superb craftsmanship. The four years of the Great War had, however, caused an almost total suspension of any development of the decorative arts in France, as the majority of artists and designers were enlisted into the French army and large areas of French soil were completely devastated by the ravages of war. In consequence the tendency was, in 1919, to continue the trends prevalent in 1914, and to examine these trends it is necessary to turn the clock back some thirty years.

The extravagances of the ephemeral Art Nouveau did not find general favour even when that style was at its height in the late 1890s. More acceptable to the majority of well-to-do people wishing to redecorate their houses was a revival of the late eighteenth century styles of the Directoire and Consulate periods — simplified versions of Louis XVI furniture and decorations. The painter Paul Helleu is generally credited with being a prime mover in this revival. Much in demand as a fashionable portrait painter he invariably posed his sitters in surroundings which reflect his enthusiasm for late eighteenth century furniture and the simple and elegant furniture, usually painted in white or a delicate pastel shade and lightly picked out in gold, began

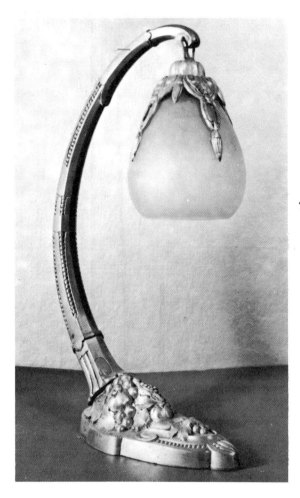

7 C. Ranc ormulu electric table lamp

8 Renouvin music stool, prior to 1925

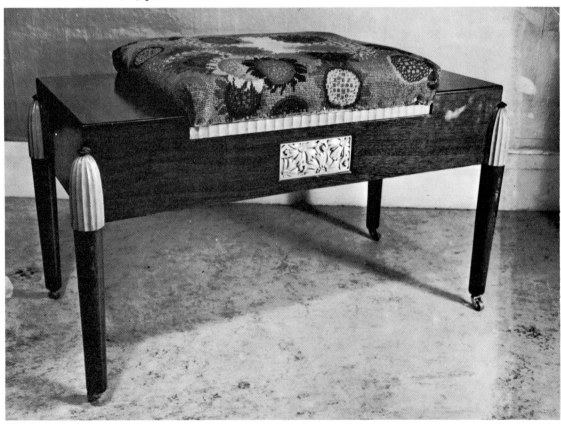

9 Gilt single chair, *c.* 1923

to be collected by the actresses and singers who posed for him, Cécile Sorel and Yvette Guilbert for instance. As is usually the case, the demand began to exceed the supply and reproductions of varying degrees of excellence soon began to appear — Madame Sorel remained blissfully ignorant that her 'antique' furniture was in fact younger than she was. The failure of Art Nouveau to fulfil the hopes of its originators and its virtual disappearance, with few exceptions, during the early years of the century, left the revived late eighteenth century style as the main decorative influence, much to the relief of the growing number of antique dealers in Paris who had always been antagonistic to Art Nouveau as a threat to their livelihood.

Marcelle Tinayre, in a series of articles written for *Femina* in 1912, gave in addition to some shrewd advice, a reflection of French decoration of interiors of the time. The series, six in all, concerned the decoration of a hypothetical small country house of the Louis XIII period which had been added to and altered during the eighteenth century and, in view of this, most of the advice concerns the use of period furniture about which the reader was warned as to the prevalence of fakes and 'antiques' and the common practice of unscrupulous dealers of placing these reproductions in farmhouses in the country districts for 'discovery' by enthusiastic amateur collectors. Genuine pieces of the Louis XV or Louis XVI periods were already becoming extremely rare and collectors were beginning to turn their attention to furniture of later periods such as the First Empire and Restoration. Giving advice about a problematical modern villa with no period associations the writer was asked in what style the decorations should be — in the absence of a modern French style. The reply was that there could be a modern style, beautiful and adapted to the needs of contemporary life (provided that the demand ceased for false antiques or furniture in the style of past periods) for there was no lack of skilled craftsmen and designers in France, and that, in fact, there were already signs of new developments discernible in the autumn exhibitions of the Salon.

10 Maurice Dufrène interior designed for La Maîtrise, 1928

These developments were the work of a number of designers who, after being involved in the Art Nouveau movement, began to produce original works which while not by any means slavish copies of antiques were in the spirit of the Directoire and Consulate periods and could be placed in the same room without too much disharmony, but were still unmistakeably products of the twentieth century. Foremost among these designers were Paul Follot, Maurice Dufrène and Clement Mère, all of whom had been associated with 'La Maison Moderne' founded by the German critic Julius Maier Graefe in 1898 for the purpose of making Art Nouveau available to all purses. Follot's work for this enterprise consisted of work in metal and leather in the Art Nouveau style and like Dufrène's metalwork, which included mounts for Tiffany vases, was characterized by its use of conventionalized leaf and plant forms combined with abstract arabesques. No work of Clement Mère is illustrated in the catalogue of La Maison Moderne issued in 1901, but it is safe to assume that his contributions were in a similar style. Léon Jallot, an associate of Bing's 'Art Nouveau' which closed in 1901 and the sculptor Armand-Albert Rateau were also among those who reacted sharply against Art Nouveau and, in the period around 1905, laid the foundations of the style which, with variations, lasted until

11 Maurice Dufrène boudoir, 1914

12 Maurice Dufrène Motor-
car decoration,
Paris Exhibition, 1925

13 P. Turin *Printemps* large silvered metal version of medal designed for the Paris Exhibition, 1925

the 1920s. This style, which has been known as ' Art Déco ' in retrospect was a com-bination of elements taken from the late eighteenth century and, after the advent of the Russian Ballet, a strong oriental influence expressed in the use of vivid colours — again a reaction against the delicate tones favoured by the exponents of Art Nouveau. Certain motifs were in constant use as decoration; garlands of highly conventionalized flowers, baskets of flowers, an elongated oval, an octagonal panel, together with an almost obsessive preoccupation with spiral forms. The treatment of flowers, and particularly roses, became highly individual and a close similarity between the geometrical roses used by so many French designers of the time and those originally invented by Charles Rennie Mackintosh and his associates can be discerned. Mackintosh's work was influential in Vienna and Munich in the early years of the century and it can be no coincidence that so many of the motifs used by French designers in the years before and after the war can be found in the Munich periodical *Die Kunst* for 1906.

14 Woodcut decoration from an advertisement, 1925
15 Sue et Mare oval mirror with gilded bronze frame, 1923

16 Coffee set in Limoges porcelain, *c.* 1923

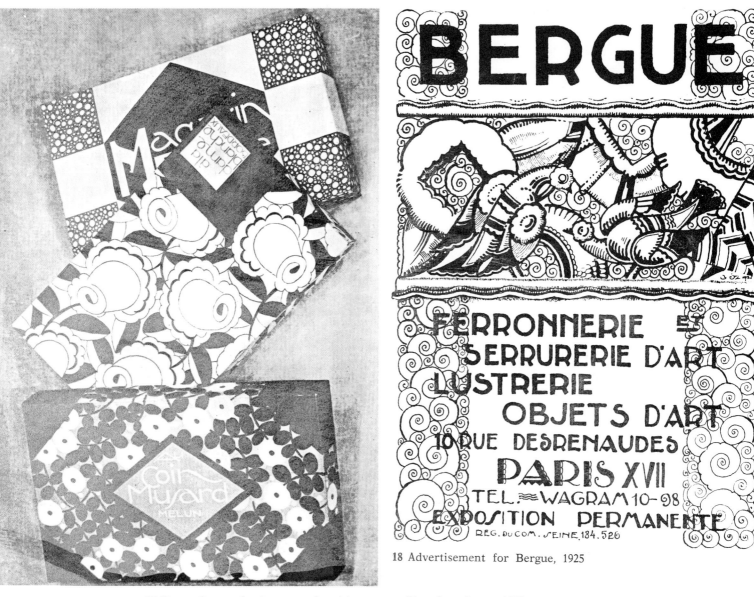

18 Advertisement for Bergue, 1925

17 Boxes for confectionery and writing paper, French, prior to 1925

It was in these terms, in this decorative idiom, that the Exhibition was conceived for its proposed date of 1915, and it is possible that a considerable number of the designs for the pavilions and even the individual exhibits were executed in readiness for completion by that date but not actually used for another ten years. Postponement followed postponement for even after the decision was made in 1919 that plans should proceed there still remained difficulties to be overcome before a definite date could be fixed; difficulties arising from the depleted economy not only of France but of the various countries invited to participate. The British Government was offered a site for a pavilion and a grant was made for the erection of a building. Owing to the limited funds available, this was too small to house a really representative selection of British products — in any case the British Empire Exhibition at

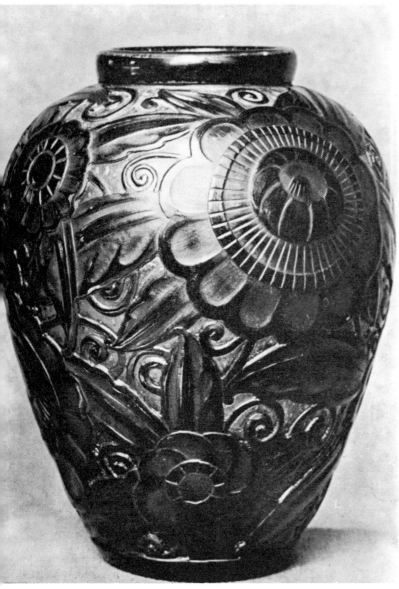

19 Daum glass vase   **20 A. Piguet** wrought-iron door

Wembley in the previous year had proved a costly venture and the advantages of exhibiting so soon after in Paris were not considered sufficient to warrant any further large expenditure of public funds. Any space occupied outside the official site would have to be paid for and British manufacturers were unwilling to incur this expense for the dubious benefit of displaying their products on the Continent, where so many of the countries had imposed heavy tariffs. Consequently many English skills, pottery, commercial printing, posters, theatrical art, carpets, dress fabrics — especially artificial silk (in the production of which England was foremost in the world) were either poorly represented or not represented at all. Great Britain had shown little of her contemporary work at the 1900 Exhibition and on this occasion she was represented by a meagre exhibit and that not of the best available.

Another difficulty, not mentioned in the official reports but commented on in the English press, was the refusal of a large number of French manufacturers to exhibit alongside their German counterparts. This was due less to a fear of artistic competition than to a hatred of their former enemy and an unwillingness to participate in anything that would give Germany a chance toward recovery. This impasse caused at least one postponement and it is significant that when the date was finally settled Germany was not among the list of European countries to exhibit. Other notable exceptions were Norway and the United States, while China and Japan were the only Far Eastern countries represented.

The site of the exhibition was that of the much larger 1900 Exhibition and included the Esplanade des Invalides, an area of the Right Bank, and, connecting the two areas on opposite sides of the Seine, the Pont Alexandre III, which was built

21 J. Leleu armchair, Paris Exhibition, 1925

over with a row of shops displaying the products of luxury firms. As in the previous exhibition, every tree growing on the site had to be preserved and each pavilion was surrounded by gardens and fountains fed from the nearby river. The pavilions were by regulation low in height and as none of them were intended to last longer than the duration of the exhibition, they were mainly constructed of plaster on wooden frameworks. Metal was only used as a decoration, ornamental grilles and gates, or in conjunction with glass as in Lalique's fountain in the form of an obelisk lit from the interior. The plaster construction was necessitated by the need for economy but had the great advantage that large decorative panels of relief sculpture could be incorporated into the architecture at a comparatively low cost, an opportunity that was used by architects in the majority of the French pavilions. Plain surfaces were embossed in a variety of textures, coloured or dusted with gold and silver powder.

22 Jean Puiforcat silver and lapis-lazuli dish and cover, Paris Exhibition, 1925

23 Pierre Patout entrance from the Place de la Concorde to the Paris Exhibition, 1925

Except for those pavilions which reflected the national characteristics of the countries they represented, the majority of the buildings were built in styles which had no historical connections. The simple masses were undecorated by the classic columns, architraves, mouldings and arches which might have been expected (a notable exception to this being the Italian pavilion whose classic bulk overshadowed the rather insignificant British pavilion). The monumental entrance gates were of a new conception, that of the Place de la Concorde comprising ten starkly simple pylons framing a bronze statue, *La Bienvenue*, in an identical pose to the controversial *La Parisienne* which had surmounted the entrance of the same site to the 1900 Exhibition. The Porte d'Honneur, sited between the Grand Palais and the Petit Palais incorporated huge panels of decorative ironwork by the master craftsman Edgar Brandt. The most successful building in the exhibition was undoubtedly 'Le Pavillon d'un Collectionneur', an adaptation by the architect Pierre Patout of the house he had built for the designer Emile-Jacques Ruhlmann, containing some of the finest pieces of furniture designed by Ruhlmann and, together with the surrounding garden, embellished with pieces of sculpture.

24 **Pierre Laprade** pavilion for Studium-Louvre at the Paris Exhibition, 1925

25 **Pierre Patout**, 'Le Pavillon d'un Collectionneur', Paris Exhibition, 1925

26 Jacques Ruhlmann study in ' Le Pavillon d'un Ambassadeur ' in the Paris Exhibition, 1925

The Art Déco designers

Emile-Jacques Ruhlmann

Undoubtedly the French decorator par excellence of the period was Emile-Jacques Ruhlmann. Classed in his lifetime with such great *ébénistes* as Reisener, Weisweiler and Rœntgen, his work was simpler than that of his eigtheenth century predecessors but no less costly in its perfection of detail, consummate craftsmanship and in the use of rare materials such as ivory, shagreen, tortoiseshell or lizard skin. Early in his career he had decided that his métier lay in supplying the richest people in the world with the most expensive and sumptuous furniture and this ambition he fulfilled. Mass production did not interest him; neither had he any philanthropic ideas of bringing art within the reach of the humblest. Only the best, regardless of the cost — and the cost in man-hours of achieving the perfection of finish he demanded was often prodigious — was of any interest to him and such was the beauty of his creations that, again regardless of the cost, he found willing clients and had more than enough commissions for decorative schemes to maintain a large workshop. Inevitably he became, in the period from 1919 to his death in 1933, a status symbol and the owner of an interior decorated in the unmistakable Ruhlmann style was recognized as being very rich and having good taste. Being above fashion, he was unaffected by the changes in fashion brought about by the 1925 Exhibition where his exhibit ' Le Pavillon d'un Collectionneur ' had met with unstinted and deserved praise, but whether his extravagant methods of working would have survived the financial crises of the 'thirties is a matter of speculation.

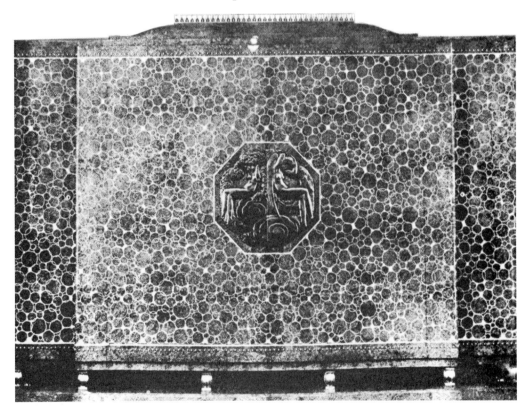

27 Jacques Ruhlmann cabinet, prior to 1925

31

If Ruhlmann's furniture was compared to that of Reisener his architectural decorations can be found to have affinities with another eighteenth century master — Claude Nicolas Ledoux — with whom he shared a taste for a monumental simplicity. An examination of photographs of interiors by Ruhlmann shows that he had little feeling for the small intimate room — he was at his happiest concocting schemes for public rooms at least twenty feet high with great waterfalls of crystal chandeliers, the plain walls relieved by panels of relief carvings or overscaled damasks. His bedroom `in the 1928 Salon des Artistes-Décorateurs, for instance, was the size of a film set and had a chandelier which, for size, would have been appropriate in Versailles.

28 Jacques Ruhlmann ebony and burr-walnut table, Paris Exhibition, 1925

29 Jacques Ruhlmann single chair and small table, prior to 1925

30 Jacques Ruhlmann the salon of ' Le Pavillon d'un Collectionneur ', Paris Exhibition, 1925

31 André Groult interior, 1921

André Groult

André Groult was foremost among the younger decorators who reacted against Art Nouveau about 1904. Sharing the view that Art Nouveau was too created a style, one which had been imposed on public taste rather than one which had logically developed from a preceding style, Groult held the view that the traditional forms and techniques prior to the introduction of mechanization could be adapted for twentieth century use, enlivened by a sense of fantasy and employing the talents of contemporary designers. This attitude pleased neither those who advocated a break with all reminders of the past nor those who felt that good design stopped short around 1790, while allowing in a grudging way that some 1830 pieces of furniture were not without virtue.

Groult's favourite collaborators were chosen for their ability to harmonize with his ideas for a revitalized Louis XVI style. Charles Martin, the painter and illustrator of éditions de luxe, created mural panels in harmonies of grey, blue and pink, of fêtes champêtres in modern dress as a setting for Groult's furniture which, in spite

32 Charles Martin *La Danse* painted panel

of its characteristically Art Déco embellishments of baskets of geometrical flowers, bunches of ostrich feathers, ropes and tassels, reproduced shapes reminiscent of Louis XVI originals. Laboureur designed wallpapers for Groult, but the artist most favoured by him was Marie Laurencin 'whose paintings began where music ended'. For him she designed wallpapers — notably a design of doves and ostrich feathers for a bedroom, the furniture covered in shagreen — and one or more of her paintings can usually be seen in the interiors Groult had exhibited at the Salon d'Automne or the Artistes-Décorateurs since 1910.

For the 1925 Exhibition Groult collaborated in the design of a number of pavilions, the most important contribution being the bedroom in 'L'Ambassade Française' — again with shagreen furniture and paintings by Marie Laurencin. He was too traditional in his outlook to be able to adapt to the change from Art Déco to the hard angular 'modernism' which the 1925 Exhibition brought about and the growing taste for simplicity was incompatible with his decorative ideals.

33 Edgar Brandt *Les Cigognes d'Alsace* wrought-iron and bronze decorative panels, *c.* 1923

Edgar Brandt

The famous smith Edgar Brandt, ' perhaps the most famous in the world ', continued the traditions established by Emile Robert, whose exhibits at the Union Centrale des Arts Décoratifs had re-established the broken links with the traditional craftsmanship of the eighteenth century. Since then there had been technological advances which placed at the disposition of craftworkers in iron such processes as mechanical chiselling, electric drilling, power-hammering and autogenous welding — by the last-named process different metals could be joined together, thus giving a richness of texture and colour previously unobtainable.

Brandt had contributed to the 1900 Exhibition but it was not until 1921 when he and his collaborator Henri Favier built a house to the latter's design in the rue Erlanger that his work achieved maturity and attracted public attention. Incorporated into this private house was a *salle d'exposition*, intended primarily for the display of Brandt's own work but later, in 1926, opened to the work of decorative artists in other fields than ironwork. The panels *Les Cigognes d'Alsace* dating from about 1922, replicas of which were installed in the interiors of the lifts at Selfridges in London, are brilliant examples of his work and show the repertoire of decorative motifs, spirals of square-sectioned rods and flattened scalloped bands combined with semi-

34 Edgar Brandt advertisement, 1925

35 Edgar Brandt *L'Oasis* five-fold screen, Paris Exhibition, 1925

naturalistic forms which were typical of Art Déco, as is the octagonal centre panel placed high in the centre of the composition. Like other smiths of this period Brandt made decorative use of hammer marks which were used to give texture to the plain structural elements in a design, and the spirals which are used to represent clouds in *Les Cigognes d'Alsace* can, by the addition of leaf shapes, be turned into roses or other flowers.

Brandt's work for the 1925 Exhibition, in collaboration both with Henri Favier and other designers, was one of the main attractions and almost requires a volume to itself if an adequate description is attempted. His screen in ' La Salle des Ambassadeurs ', made of iron, brass, copper and other metals was, as one critic commented, almost a kind of larger jewelry. The large grilles at the Porte d'Honneur were not in fact of iron, although copies of some Brandt had made for a commission in America, but due to financial reasons were copied in plaster which was painted to simulate wrought-iron. In addition to architectural metalwork Brandt made considerable quantities of iron furniture and decorative cases to conceal radiators, which were increasingly used as central heating became more common in the large apartment blocks built in the post-war boom.

Brandt was the most celebrated worker in metal but there were many others, Raymond Subes, Paul Kiss, Edouard Schenck, Baguès and Gilbert Poillerat, working in a similar manner and achieving high standards of craftsmanship.

36 Raymond Subes radiator case

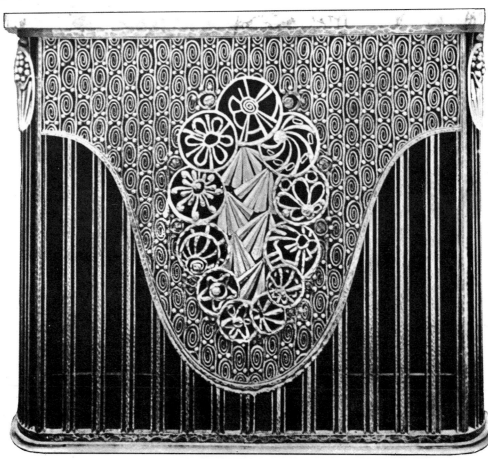

Jean Dunand

Jean Dunand was of Swiss origin but was brought at an early age to Paris where he spent most of his life becoming perhaps the leading exponent of metal and lacquer work. Essentially a craftsman, he was more interested in the work itself than the financial rewards it could bring, and in spite of the stream of commissions which kept him continually busy he never reached the degree of affluence which could have been expected. His early training was as a sculptor under the tuition of Jean Dampt, celebrated for his work in the Art Nouveau manner, but Dunand seems to have been untouched by the influence of that style and his inclinations lay more in metal work than in sculpture proper, though the experience gained by this early training was useful in later years.

Dunand had not yet perfected his individual style when he attracted attention by his first exhibition which took place somewhere about 1904. The vases and plates, each shaped by patient hammering from single sheets of copper, were unadorned and devoid of the rich surface textures and patterns of his later work. By 1910 his reputation had increased as his technical skill improved. The vases were still hammered from a sheet of metal but their graceful shapes were enhanced by patterns, simple but sophisticated, made by inlays of different and contrasting alloys, sometimes with the addition of lacquer. Blacks of varying degrees of intensity were

37 Jean Dunand lacquer furniture and screens, prior to 1928

38 Jean Dunand two hammered metal vases

obtained by oxidization, and other colours through chemical action by acids on the metal. Gold, silver, zinc, aluminium, steel — all were used for decorative effect in the vases, which were used by decorators, Ruhlmann particularly using vases of considerable size as dominating features in his rooms.

In 1920 Dunand was commissioned by a group of Americans to create a gift to Marshal Foch as a token of their gratitude and admiration. Dunand decided that the most appropriate form would be that of a decorative helmet, life-size, encircled by a crest of a cock's head. This was hammered from a sheet of bronze and enriched

39 Jean Dunand four metal vases and a covered box, prior to 1925

with damascened patterns in gold and silver. In June 1920 René Gimpel recorded in his journal a visit to Dunand's studio where he saw the completed helmet lying on a work bench beside another of aluminium and gold, which Dunand was making for Ida Rubinstein to wear as Cleopatra.

Not content with mastery over metal, Dunand became equally adept in the laborious craft of lacquer work and particularly the type produced in Japan. In some ways he set himself a harder task than that of the Japanese craftsman, for Dunand's work was on a larger scale and included large areas of unadorned lacquer where the least blemish or fault of craftsmanship would be instantly noticeable. The work was long and complicated. To achieve the effect he desired, that of a deep and lustrous mirror-smooth surface, as many as forty coats of lacquer had to be applied and, as the lacquer in drying tended to contract and could thus twist the wooden panel of a screen out of shape, another coat had to be applied on the reverse side to counteract the tension; both coats drying simultaneously ensured that the base remained true. The drying process presented complications, taking any time between three and four days, and paradoxically could only be satisfactorily accomplished in a room kept perpetually damp by means of streams of water flowing down the walls. Further complications were added in that the drying process could only take place in a darkened room and for some mysterious reason was affected by the moon's influence, the best result occurring when the moon was full. After each coat a process of careful rubbing down and smoothing to a perfect surface had to be performed before another coat of lacquer could be applied.

Only a dedicated craftsman such as Dunand could have produced so many screens, pieces of furnitures and other smaller items and his reward for this laborious work was a steady stream of commissions from decorators and connoisseurs. His screens and furniture were ornamented with decorations in gold and silver, either from his own designs or to the requirements of others, and usually had the rich black background described, though coloured backgrounds were often used.

From the Japanese he borrowed the technique of eggshell lacquer, the crushed shells being pressed into the lacquer before it was dry. The skill lay in ensuring that the fragments of eggshell were of a more or less uniform size and of even distribution so that the intervening lines of black lacquer, of the thickness of a hair, give the appearance of a fine mesh over the pale surface of the eggshells. Such a finish was copied by others and can be found on metal cigarette cases, though it is possible that Dunand may have done these as well.

Dunand was commissioned to execute lacquer panels in the smoking room of 'L'Ambassade Française' at the 1925 Exhibition. Gabrielle Rosenthal described this room as 'the most complete and the best created up to the present in the cubist manner. Conceived in a magnificently barbaric harmony of colour, it has a ceiling of silver leaf enlivened with touches of red lacquer which being on several planes, allows indirect lighting to fall upon the highly polished black furniture, on the off-white carpet and a large decorative panel of red lacquer with silver ornamentation.'

Dunand gave a number of exhibitions of his metal and lacquer in collaboration with Goulden, the enameller, Pierre Jouve, the painter and sculptor of animals, and Schmeid whose engravings and illustrations did so much to maintain the high standards of book production in the 'twenties. As a result of such an exhibition in 1929 Dunand received the accolade of critics and was hailed as the greatest craftsman of the age.

Gabriel Lacroix

If Jean Dunand was esteemed as the greatest craftsman of the time, Gabriel Lacroix was considered by the critic Ernest Tisserand as the 'prince of metal'. Prevented by ill health from producing a large body of work Lacroix only exhibited at the Salon des Décorateurs; his first entry, a figure of a seal, beaten from a single sheet of metal, caused an immediate sensation and gained the highest praise for the sensitivity of the modelling and the consummate craftsmanship. Thereafter he submitted each year a piece of sculpture of an animal or a bird, a tiger, a panther, a vulture or an owl, all of them meeting with the same unreserved admiration. His technical skills had been learned through years of work among the tin and copper smiths whose workshops were housed in the beautiful ancient buildings of the Marais district of Paris. Pewter, zinc, silver, gold and platinum, each with their different characteristics, were hammered by him into the most intricate shapes over wooden forms which he had first carved, the thin sheets of metal being moulded into the finished sculpture by the patient work of thousands of hammer blows coaxing the metal into a continuing form with no joins or breaks. Lacroix was an instructor in metalwork at the Ecole des Arts Appliqués and many of his pupils, benefiting from the rigid discipline he imposed, became noted silversmiths: Maurice Muller, in particular, exhibiting with success at the Salon des Décorateurs.

40 Motif of baskets of flowers, from *Die Kunst*, 1906

41 Motif of a basket of flowers in an oval panel, from *Die Kunst*, 1906

Eileen Gray

It was stated that Eileen Gray, an Englishwoman who had made her home in Paris, was the first to revive the art of lacquer, but as no chronological information was given by the writer making this claim on her behalf, the matter is open to doubt in view of the work done by Dunand and others in the same field. However, it is certain that Miss Gray achieved great skill in mastering the Chinese techniques of applying lacquer to screens, doors and furniture. Her belief was that lacquer should be seen as a new material, divorced from all associations with the Chinese coromandel screens or Louis XV furniture embellished with ormulu and used to express contemporary idioms of decoration. In her attempts to create interiors devoid of the least historical references and even of ornament derived from nature she evolved a personal decorative idiom based on geometrical shapes, carried out in 'les tons fauves et nocturnes' — a style so individual as to appeal only to a limited public but nevertheless anticipating the modernism of the latter years of the 1920s. Furniture or screens made before 1922, when an illustrated article by the Duchesse de Clement-Tonnerre on Eileen Gray's work appeared in *Feuillets d'Art*, have affinities with work done by others some eight years later. Eileen Gray also collaborated in the design of interiors with Jean Badovici.

42 Eileen Gray lacquer screen

Armand Rateau

Armand Rateau's individual style with its echoes of Minoan, Graeco-Roman, Syrian and Persian styles was seen by a wide public at the opening of the Théâtre Danou in Paris in 1922. Designed by the architect Bluysen, the decorations of the auditorium and its approaches were entrusted to Jeanne Lanvin, Rateau and Paul Plumet. The interior of the small auditorium — there were only ten rows of seats on the ground floor — was coloured in an unrelieved ' Bleu Lanvin ' a shade approximately that of cornflowers, and the decoration concentrated around the proscenium arch. Pilasters of lapis-lazuli were flanked by panels of gilded decorations modelled in high relief incorporating birds, monkeys and other animals sporting among exotic foliage, the centre panel over the stage having as its central feature two elongated female figures elegantly reclining amid more foliage — in the original design these were two peacocks which confronted each other but were probably replaced by human figures for superstitious reasons. The conventionalized marguerite which was Mme Lanvin's personal symbol played a prominent part in the decorations. These panels were set off by their ivory white backgrounds and the same colour was applied to the fronts of the two balconies which had appliqués at intervals in the forms of plumes of ospreys in gilded wires and crystal beads. The foyer and corridors were simply decorated in complete contrast with the walls covered in sheets of grey-white marble relieved with motifs in gilded bronze.

A little-known work by Rateau was the bathroom installed in the palace of the Duchess of Alba in Madrid in 1926. In the centre of a circular domed room a bath, carved from a single block of white marble, was sunk into the black and white marble floor. The walls were entirely covered with gold lacquer decorated with a grove of trees among which deer, squirrels, hares, pet dogs, pheasants and other birds can be seen. The furniture, also by Rateau, was of bronze with a green patina and consisted of a dressing table with a swinging circular mirror, an armchair, a chaise longue, a low tea table and a pair of lamp stands — the chairs and the chaise longue being covered with fur rugs when the bathroom was in use. These were replicas of those created for Jeanne Lanvin in Paris and the combination of bronze lacquer and marble warrants the contemporary description of the room as ' luxurious with striking modernistic decorations '. The walls and furniture have references to Persian and Graeco-Roman originals which are characteristic of Rateau's work and the room could be imagined as a setting for the heroine of Pierre Loüy's *Aphrodite.*

43 Armand Rateau bathroom for the Duchess of Alba, Madrid, 1925

44 Jean Dupas *Les Perruches* decorative panel, Paris Exhibition, 1925

The mural in France

Jean Dupas

A major decorative artist active in the 'twenties was Jean Dupas, whose work is unjustly now almost forgotten. A pupil of Carolus Duran and the much respected Albert Besnard, he won the Prix de Rome, and his painting *Les Pigeons Blancs* won a gold medal at the Salon des Artistes Français of 1922. As a result, his decorative panels of elongated women in fantastic dresses accompanied by birds (which he used as compositional devices for patches of light colour contrasted against a dark background) were in great demand and his talents called upon by the Sèvres factory, the London Underground (for posters) and commercial firms in France, England and America. His highly individual treatment of the women in his pictures he explained as a ' re-creation of nature according to his own temperament ', the simplification of the anatomy of his subjects into geometrical, elongated forms, the exaggerated dresses, hats and coiffures being given a formalized treatment which was intended to harmonize with the architectural surroundings. Ruhlmann was an admirer of his work which he used whenever possible — his panel *Les Perruches* (The Lovebirds) was the focal point of the salon in ' Le Pavillon d'un Collectionneur ' in the 1925 Paris Exhibition. In 1928 Ruhlmann collaborated with him again in the decoration of the Chambre de Commerce de la Seine.

José-Maria Sert

José-Maria Sert was one of the most prolific mural painters of this century although comparatively little of his work still remains *in situ*. His début as a painter was in 1900 when his murals formed part of the decorative scheme in the dining room of Bing's ' Art Nouveau ' exhibit in the Paris Universal Exhibition. Never part of the Art Nouveau movement in France, Sert had arrived from his native Barcelona only a short time before and it is possible that his work was a last minute substitution for that of another painter. From photographs which exist of the dining room it would seem that he was given little time to co-ordinate his scheme of decoration with the scale of the room or with the furniture by Eugène Gaillard for which his panels were meant to serve as a background. But in an immature way the characteristics of Sert's style were already to be seen, the use of bistre and gold, the boldly modelled forms and the largeness of scale. If anyone could be said to be born out of his time it was José-Maria Sert, a man who should have flourished in the eighteenth century. His masters were the elder Tiepolo, Veronese, Tintoretto and Goya — which makes his collaboration at Bing's 'Art Nouveau ' all the stranger — and his admiration for these artists continued all his life and can be detected in everything he did.

At his happiest when working on a large scale, it was not long before he was drawn into the circle surrounding Diaghilev, and in 1914 he designed the settings for *La Légende de Joseph*, his backcloth in the manner of Veronese forming a background for Léon Bakst's costumes and the dancing of the young Leonid Massine in his first important role as Joseph. Sert was the first non-Russian designer to be employed by Diaghilev and his imposing architectural compositions are in the same vein as those of Bakst. Two more ballets for Diaghilev followed, the costumes for *Las Meninas* in 1916 and four years later, the opera ballet *Astuzie Femminili*, the dances from which were presented in Sert's setting and using his costumes as *Cimarosiana* in 1924. But his work was not confined to the theatre, for at intervals he was engaged upon a vast decorative scheme for the cathedral of Vich, paintings which were destroyed in the Spanish Civil War. According to Jacques-Emile Blanche the first version of this giant undertaking was half finished and then, for some undisclosed reason, abandoned in favour of an even more elaborate scheme. Misia Sert, the wife of the painter, has left it on record that Sert was engaged on yet a third series of paintings for the rebuilt cathedral up until the time of his death in 1947.

Throughout the 'twenties Sert, helped by two assistants, worked indefatigably not only on the panels for the cathedral, some of which were exhibited in Paris in 1929, but also upon almost innumerable commissions for murals in private houses, smaller decorative panels and screens. ' Sert pilfers wherever he passes ' wrote René Gimpel in his journal and there were few technical devices of perspective and trompe l'œil which he did not press into service. Painted in black or sepia on backgrounds of gold or silver leaf and enlivened with touches of brilliant vermilion or emerald green, his vast compositions *The Travels of Sinbad the Sailor* or *The Exodus from Egypt* were conceived on a heroic scale employing every trick of exaggerated perspective; vast staircases down which troop crowds of fantastically dressed characters; tight ropes strung between baroque obelisks and supporting Chinese jugglers and harlequins; perspectives of palm trees and fountains; life-size elephants and camels with trappings decorated with golden tassels and fringes; eighteenth century balloons in dizzy perspective. The Sinbad murals, painted for Josiah Cosden and decorating the ballroom at Playa Riente in Palm Beach, were so overwhelming with fantastic creatures that the servants were reputed to have refused to carry out their duties as they were so terrified by the wild life Sert had created.

The murals for the ' Marquis de S.' at Madrid were more restrained and were brilliant essays in the art of trompe l'œil. Rejecting his usual gold or silver background which here would have lessened the realistic effect he desired, Sert painted, against a vermilion background, panels of seeming white drapery which appeared to be painted with scenes of Spanish life at the time of Goya — these were carried out in tones of carmine and each piece of drapery had a decorative border, also in carmine.

On occasion, Sert painted on the back of large sheets of plate glass — something needing a sure touch as the highlights of the composition have to be applied first and the shadows and modelling gradually painted until the complete composition can be seen from the front. When this work, usually in black or sepia, was completely dry the rest of the glass was covered in gold or silver leaf and the final result was of an antique mirror, painted with decorative compositions — similar to Chinese glass paintings but on a far larger scale. A ballroom for Sir Philip Sassoon was done in this manner, the subject being scenes from the Old Testament on a gold background. Sert's work, mostly done for the private houses of rich people, was almost unknown to the general public. One commission which could be seen, however, was that for the entrance of Radio City in New York.

Etienne Drian

Another decorative painter active in the twenties was Etienne Drian; less showy and spectacular than Sert his clientèle lay more among the rich with less flamboyant tastes. A self-taught artist, he first exhibited in the Salon de la Nationale at the age of fifteen and after a period as a fashion designer found his vocation as a decorative artist through his contributions to the luxurious fashion magazine *La Gazette du Bon Ton* from 1913 to 1915.

In contrast to the current style of fashion drawing, as practised by George Barbier, Iribe, Georges Lepape and Erté, which depicted the models in a decorative and unrealistic manner, Drian's women were more lifelike and show influences of Boldini and Toulouse-Lautrec. His ability to record elegant women led to his becoming a latter-day Helleu and there were few society women whom he did not depict in drawings in sanguine crayon. His painted screens and decorative panels were much in demand in the 1920s and the subsequent decade. There are two particularly representative panels which portray Lady Mendl and her Pekinese and Miss Anne Morgan and her borzoi (a breed of dog favoured for its decorative qualities in the 'twenties). These panels were painted in sepia on gold backgrounds, and showing the sitters posed against the great staircase at Versailles they occupied prominent positions in the Galerie des Glaces at the Villa Trianon, Lady Mendl's house at Versailles.

A noticeable characteristic of the majority of French interiors during the 1920s and particularly those exhibited at the Salons, is that almost complete absence of any display of easel paintings — a trend which became even more marked after 1925 when the tendency was toward an even greater degree of simplicity and the abandonment of any unnecessary ornamental features. Mural paintings or large decorative panels often form an integral part of the decorative scheme and painted screens were often used, but easel paintings by contemporary artists do not seem to have been in favour with the interior decorators, possibly because they might divert the attention away from the furniture. The exception to this was Marie Laurencin whose delicate portrayals of girls with fawns or guitars appear in many interiors by André Groult, Louis Sognot and Marcel Guillemard, adding a slightly decadent note to the décor. In the case of the decorator Jean Michel Frank, much in vogue in France and the United States toward the close of the decade, it would have been almost a sacrilege to have suspended a painting on the luxurious wallcoverings of vellum or straw mosaic which he used. It was not until the 1940s that it became fashionable to cover one or more of the walls of a room with a mosaic of assorted paintings, drawings and prints.

The new modernism

The reasons for the decline of Art Déco can be attributed to a variety of causes. It had been the predominating decorative style in France since approximately 1910 and there was a natural desire for a change. Cubism in a modified form had become acceptable as a decorative idiom and after the exuberance of Art Déco, the clean lines and more muted colours of modernism made a refreshing change from floral baroque idioms which had been too much worked over and finally, economic factors were limiting the market for expensive furniture or decorative schemes.

The new anti-decorative feeling can be seen in retrospect as a combination of many factors: German and Russian films, with their new approaches to photography and a use of mobile cameras to express emotion by movement and eccentrically angled shots; an absorption with 'the machine' which led to the organization of the Machine Age Exhibition of 1925 by Jane Heap, an administrator of the avant-garde magazine *The Little Review*, and, not least, of all the technical improvement in materials which made possible the cheap manufacture of simple, unadorned furniture. It is tempting to attribute the origins of this new approach to the work of the Bauhaus but to do so is perhaps to overestimate its influence on contemporary design outside Germany. That the work and ideals of the Bauhaus were known and admired by a small coterie of the younger French designers is certainly quite

45 Djo-Bourgeois interior, *c.* 1927

46 Robert Mallet-Stevens modernist interior, 1927

evident from the work of le Corbusier, Pierre Jeanneret, Charlotte Perriand, Jean Puiforcat, Raymond Templier, René Herbst, Mallet-Stevens and Francis Jourdain, but they encountered the incomprehension of the public and the hostility of the critics during the late 1920s and it was not until the early 1930s that they were able to overcome prejudice and gain a limited recognition.

Today, when the bookshops are flooded with volumes, illustrated in colour, dealing with practically every period, past and present, of the history of art, it should be remembered that forty years ago there was no such plethora of information. Not only were there comparatively few books published on the arts but their subject matter was limited to the arts of the past and contemporary, especially avant-garde, work generally ignored. Only *The Architectural Review* and *The Studio* (both in its monthly editions and the annual year books of decorative arts), recognized the existence of any new work or ideas on the Continent and it is certain that many designers of the time were ignorant of the very existence of the Bauhaus or if aware, regarded it as an object of derision. The same prejudice against German ideas which had led to the exclusion of an exhibit from that country in the 1925 Exhibition, militated against any general acceptance of the Bauhaus doctrines and the French have never, in any case, held German taste in any great esteem; or, for that matter, English taste.

Pierre Chareau

Pierre Chareau was an innovator whose influence had considerable effect on the development of interior decoration from the time of his first appearance as an exhibitor at the Salon d'Automne in 1919, when the austere simplicity of a bedroom he had designed contrasted sharply with the general trend. Its plain unadorned walls covered with beige unpatterned silk, contrasting with the dark grey silk, equally bare of design, which covered the bed served as a setting for the pictures by his collaborator, the painter Jean Lurçat. A contemporary critic declared that ' he had opened the windows letting in fresh air to dispel the stale sweat of the Ballets Russes and replacing the tarnished and dusty shades with fresh harmonies of royal blue and grey, lemon yellow and grey or the tones of pearl, rose and blue beloved of Marie Laurencin '.

The design of his furniture was characterized by a lack of any superfluous ornament, the form being emphasized by the rich surface texture of the rare woods he employed. He was responsible, along with Lurçat and Hélène Henry, the textile designer, for the study in ' L'Ambassade Française ' in the 1925 Exhibition and in 1928 Chareau, René Herbst, Mallet-Stevens and François Jourdain founded the Union des Artistes Modernes, influential in directing the course of design in the 'thirties.

Jean Michel Frank

A complete contrast to the austerity of many interiors of the post-1925 period — those of le Corbusier for instance — were those created by Jean Michel Frank, who also avoided any unnecessary ornament, reduced the decoration to the simplest elements but at the same time achieved an effect of the greatest luxury. Even colour was banished from his interiors, all that is except the natural tones of the materials used, beige, honey, ivory and subtle shades and variations of white. His rooms were settings for people, not for paintings, sculpture or works of art of any kind and an absence of these is noticeable in contemporary photographs of his interiors.

Frank had two favourite wall treatments, either covering them from floor to ceiling with carefully chosen squares of parchment or vellum which gave a golden glow to the room, or covering the walls in split straws which were glued with enormous patience vertically side by side, the different lengths of straw and the different tones giving an effect of a rich watered silk. There must have been one or more craftsmen specializing in this tedious work as Paul Poiret used the same method of decoration in a dining room on the liner *Ile-de-France* but in this case the straw was arranged in designs of palm trees and tropical vegetation, carried out in brilliant shades of red, blue and green. The walls and the furniture were unadorned by any mouldings, the latter being reduced to the bare essential shapes, but the simplicity of form was more than compensated by the richness of the surface texture of gold lacquer,

47 Jean Michel Frank interior, prior to 1929

snakeskin, undyed leather or parchment. Chairs, armchairs and settees were similarly simple but elegant in form but the finely executed unholstery was carried out in suede, silk, velvet, or a heavy plain silk in muted tones of ivory and brown. The curtains were invariably plain with no fringes or trimmings of any kind, hanging in unbroken folds of heavy neutrally-coloured silk ceiling to floor. The lighting was usually from indirect sources or bulbs concealed behind lumps of uncut crystal or quartz mounted on ormulu bases or hidden behind small screens made of thin sheets of alabaster.

The restrained luxury of Jean Michel Frank's interiors combined with the absence of any dated ornamental features resulted in a timeless quality — not being in fashion they would never go out of fashion, and the beautiful rooms he created enjoyed a deserved success in Paris and in California. Frank could, on occasion, work with simpler materials, for instance the apartment he helped Elsa Schiaparelli to furnish at the outset of her career as a dressmaker in Paris. As there was little money available, Frank had the walls painted white, designed a large couch covered in orange leather which contrasted with the brilliant green of two divans flanking the fireplace. Two small chairs covered in the same white rubberized fabric as the curtains, and black square tables, were the only other pieces of furniture. When Chanel, whose apartment was lined with antique mirror and filled with Chinese coromandel screens and eighteenth century furniture, visited Schiaparelli, the latter recorded that Chanel 'at the sight of this modern furniture and black plates, shuddered as if she were passing a cemetery'.

The glass house of Antoine, the coiffeur

1927 saw the completion of an extraordinary residence, the result of the collaboration between Antoine, the hairdresser and Madame Lipska, the decorator. Penniless and unknown, Antoine had arrived in Paris in 1901 from Poland, his only assets being a determination to become a famous hairdresser and a shrewd sense of the value of publicity. Within five years he had become sufficiently skilled to have the famous actress Eve Lavallière among his patrons and in a moment of amused indulgence she allowed him to cut off her hair while preparing it for a special occasion, knowing that if his idea for a striking coiffure was a failure she could always conceal her short hair under a wig. Happily the sacrifice was justified and thus in 1906 Antoine achieved his first success by inventing the first bobbed hair, an innovation he refused to repeat for another six years.

Shortly after this he opened his own establishment in the rue Cambon — with Jean Cocteau and Gabrielle Chanel as neighbours — the main salon being decorated in peony red with a carpet of the same colour (women's hair was not cut at this period so the problem of sweeping up discarded hair-cuttings did not arise) while the lighting was from Chinese vases which were adapted for electric light. The red walls were hung with paintings by Antoine's obscure and unknown artist friends — Kisling, Modigliani, van Dongen and Jean-Gabriel Doumergue. This salon became known to his clients as 'The Fountain' because of the five washbasins which were installed — a novelty at a period when it was not the custom for hairdressers to wash their clients' hair, only to dress it.

During the post-war years Antoine became the most celebrated and sought-after hairdresser in Paris, a position he had achieved by a mixture of showmanship, carefully calculated bizarre behaviour and a talent for enhancing the looks of his devoted clientele. The premises in the rue Cambon had become inadequate to deal with his many patrons and consequently four floors of a building in the rue Didier were taken, providing sufficient space to accommodate the hairdressing salons and a private apartment for Antoine and his wife. The move to a new address with all the attendant publicity gave Antoine the opportunity of turning into reality the fantasies he had dreamed for years and incidently to indulge his passion for glass in all its forms. The existing building was ruthlessly altered; floors were removed to give greater height to the rooms and the exterior walls were replaced by vast sheets of plate glass treated in such a way that while the occupants could see out, nobody could see in, thus dispensing with the need for curtains. The staircases were ripped out and replaced by others made entirely of glass — the problem of preventing Antoine's guests from slipping on this staircase was solved, after many experiments, by using glass slabs which had tiny bubbles of air introduced by a special process which resulted in a slighly roughened surface. For some time, it was Antoine's proud boast, the St Gobain factory was turned over entirely to the production of glass for his house. Not only the was the building itself of glass but the decorations and the greater part of the furniture; only the floors were of the conventional parquet but these were put to use in an ingenious manner. Each section of parquet formed the lid of a box sunk in the floor and in these compartments were stored household necessities and anything not in immediate use, a careful plan having been made of the contents of the boxes on each floor.

48 Madame Lipska and **Henri Martin**, office in the glass house of Antoine

49 Christofle vase; wrought-iron guéridon, *c.* 1923

The drawing room of the private apartment, which was two stories in height, was decorated with panels of sapphire blue and ruby red glass and was described as having a cupola of ruby glass supported by crystal columns. In this room was placed the glass coffin in which Antoine habitually slept in preference to his more conventional bed and in which he was often photographed surrounded by white lilies. This macabre notion, which was widely publicized, was reminiscent of Sarah Bernhardt who took a coffin with her on her tours and was reputed to sleep in it, but Antoine's claim was that the high glass sides of his coffin protected him, from the harmful electric rays in the atmosphere while he was asleep. An organ with glass pipes, glass dining tables and chairs from designs by Madame Lipska contributed to the icy glitter of Antoine's residence, the cold austerity being softened by the huge bunches of white lilies which were replaced daily.

The completion of this crystal palace was marked by a White Ball, the invitations to which were engraved on sheets of glass and delivered, wrapped in parchment, by hand. The 1400 guests were requested to wear white and were received by their host and hostess — Antoine in a white satin tail suit with his hair powdered to match, Madame Antoine in a white dress by Vionnet. Much to his chagrin Antoine had been unable to persuade his wife to share his enthusiasm for glass and her rooms were furnished in more conventional style, the walls being covered in quilted peach satin.

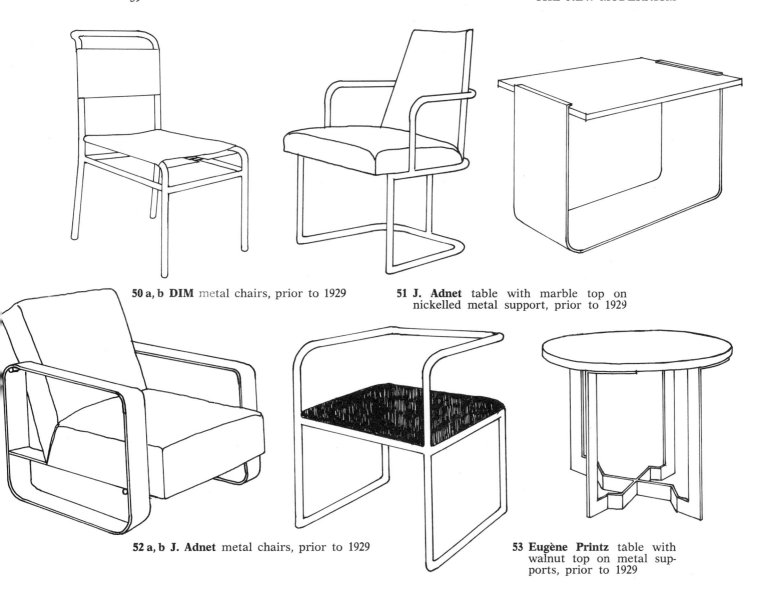

50 a, b DIM metal chairs, prior to 1929

51 J. Adnet table with marble top on nickelled metal support, prior to 1929

52 a, b J. Adnet metal chairs, prior to 1929

53 Eugène Printz table with walnut top on metal supports, prior to 1929

Metal furniture

Metal furniture was said to be one of the most controversial issues in French life since the Dreyfus case — the critic Ernest Tisserand remarking that it was worse than politics for arousing anger and that a well-bred woman who would not dream of criticizing the choice of paintings in a friend's house would, at the sight of a tubular metal chair, lose all semblance of self-control and express her opinion so forcibly that any further friendship would be impossible. This reaction was all the more surprising as metal furniture in some form or another had a history reaching back to antiquity, from Roman couches and tables to the steel and ormulu models of the Louis XVI period. Possibly there was an association with the brass bedsteads of the nineteenth century, themselves the ancestors of the tubular furniture of the 'twenties and certainly an association, less easy to eradicate, with surgeries and operating theatres, the latter constantly being quoted as being more suitable places for steel furniture than drawing rooms.

The wrought-iron furniture of Edgar Brandt and Raymond Subes and the bronze couches and tables of Armand Rateau were regarded more as works of art than pieces of furniture and could thus be admired in a different context, but the stark austerity of the steel or nickel plated chairs, revolutionary in design and apparently lacking the support offered by four legs, was another matter altogether. An early attempt to reconcile the public to the new furniture was by painting and graining it to resemble wood and the question of noise — a frequent source of complaint by its detractors

— was solved by ingenious salesmen who carefully filled all the drawers in a desk they were trying to sell with sound absorbing objects to avoid the tinny sound which, once heard by the customer, tended to ruin the sale.

It was hoped that metal furniture would prove to be the solution to two problems. Firstly the shortage of timber was still acute even after six or seven years of peace and tubular steel would be ideal for quick and inexpensive mass production, superior to the other materials such as cork, glass, ebonite and similar compositions with which experiments were being made. Secondly the growing use of central heating was proving disastrous to wooden furniture old and new, while metal furniture was impervious to the destructive effects of changes in temperature and dry air. But efforts to popularize it met with strong opposition from those involved in the production of wooden furniture. The organizers of the 1928 Salon des Artistes Décorateurs faced considerable pressure from the Chambre Syndicale d'Ameublement to request exhibitors to submit only furniture made of wood — metal to be used only in the traditional manner for ornamental purposes — a request which was, incidentally, ignored by a majority of the decorators.

The Salon of the following year featured furniture in nickel plate, aluminium and painted metal by Adnet, Joubert et Petit, and Eugène Printz, and writing about this exhibit Ernest Tisserand commented: 'In 1925 we do not remember having seen a single piece of furniture made of metal and we will not enter into any controversies as to whether the first piece was made in Germany or France, if the first cupboard with a metal framework was signed by Ruhlmann or Leleu, if the tubular chair was first seen in this store or that; metal furniture has appeared simultaneously in so many places at the same time that it can be considered a collective production, the invention not of separate individuals but of society as a whole'. Perhaps Tisserand was genuinely unaware that the first tubular chair was the creation of Marcel Breuer in 1925, when the twenty-three year old Viennese was the director of the Dessau Bauhaus furniture workshops or that Breuer had developed the idea into the cantilevered model of 1928 working along the same lines as Mies van der Rohe who had produced a similar model the year before. On the other hand it is unlikely that such a knowledgeable critic as he could have been unaware of the developments in design in Austria and Germany, even if for chauvinistic reasons he implied that the credit for such innovations belonged to French designers such as Pierre Chareau, Djo-Bourgeois and René Herbst. It should not be forgotten that French manufacturers had threatened to boycott the 1925 Exhibition if their German counterparts were invited to participate and that the work of German painters, sculptors and designers was rarely featured in French periodicals dealing with the arts during the 'twenties.

Whatever the arguments may have been as to the origins of metal furniture, the fact remains that during 1926 and 1927 a remarkable upsurge of interest in its possibilities was manifested among French, German and Austrian designers and those, moreover, with too much integrity and pride in their own originality to steal ideas from others. The fact that so many models bore a close resemblance to each other was explained by a writer in *The Studio* for 1929: 'Metal affords too few opportunities for personal expression to continue its appeal to the creative spirit... things have come to this pass that chairs by Herbst, Djo-Bourgeois or Charlotte Perriand are almost indistinguishable'.

The reason for the simultaneous interest in several quarters was undoubtedly due to the common denominator — the firm of Thonet. Founded by Michel Thonet in the early years of the nineteenth century, the firm had gradually developed a type of simple but elegant furniture (with the added advantages of cheapness and great strength) in which beechwood circular in section was bent under steam pressure

54 Lucie Renaudot design for a smoking room, *c.* 1926

with results which anticipated both in design and construction the tubular steel chairs of the 'twenties. Thonet furniture was in constant demand and vast quantities were exported from the various factories to most parts of the world. For such an organization the transition from the bending of wood to the shaping of metal tubing of a similar section was a comparatively simple matter, and by 1927 Thonet was making metal furniture to the designs of le Corbusier (who had previously used their wooden models in a number of houses he had built) Guyot, Mies van der Rohe and Marcel Breuer. With so many representatives scattered over Europe, many other architects and designers would be likely to come into contact in a short time with examples of Thonet's new products and thus be stimulated to explore its techniques.

The main concern of designers and manufacturers determined to popularize metal furniture was to erase the clinical associations with which it was linked in the mind of the public and to invest it with as much of an air of luxury as was compatible with its comparatively low cost. Some of the means used to do so could be seen in the successive Salons des Artistes-Décorateurs and other annual exhibitions, where the equivalents in furniture of the model dresses from the great couturiers, were shown to the public. Exhibited were examples of metal-supported dining tables with tops of

55 Georges Champion interior designed for Studios Gué, *c.* 1926

56 DIM dressing table in plate glass and metal, prior to 1930

black glass, tops of richly veneered wood which had to be protected from heat and scratching by a sheet of plate glass (paradoxically one of the objections to metal tops was the coldness to the touch) tops of marble or of thick rough-cast glass. Chairs when exhibited were covered in leather or fur and the metal frame was so designed as to minimize contact between it and the occupant of the chair. One reason for this, apart from the chilly feel of the metal, was that the nickel plating in the cheaper models could easily be scratched and worn away leaving an unsightly patch of the basic metal — the considerably more expensive stainless steel was impervious to wear. The problem of the rigid, and to some people extremely uncomfortable, back to most of the chairs was solved by René Herbst who filled in the backs of his chairs with horizontal metal springs which were covered in rubber, giving the appearance of rigidity but relaxing under pressure. Michel Dufet's furniture, completely sheathed in polished zinc relieved with geometrical decoration in red lacquer, was criticized by Maurice Dufrène with the words ' One cannot help looking for the connecting rods and engine '. This not unjustified comment came oddly from Dufrène, himself an ardent advocate of the new metallic, modernist school, and engaged in designing rooms with walls of plywood covered in sheets of copper or aluminium and furniture with harsh austere outlines of metal tubing. The most effective use of metal was in conjunction with thick plate glass, for instance the dressing table by DIM which in its complete break with traditional forms has the appearance of a piece of abstract sculpture. Pierre Legrain's stainless steel and plate glass piano, however, may be reckoned as an honourable failure.

57 Pierre Legrain glass piano

58 René Lalique glass clock; and motor-car mascot
Sabino glass vase

59 René Lalique vases of opalescent glass, *c.* 1925

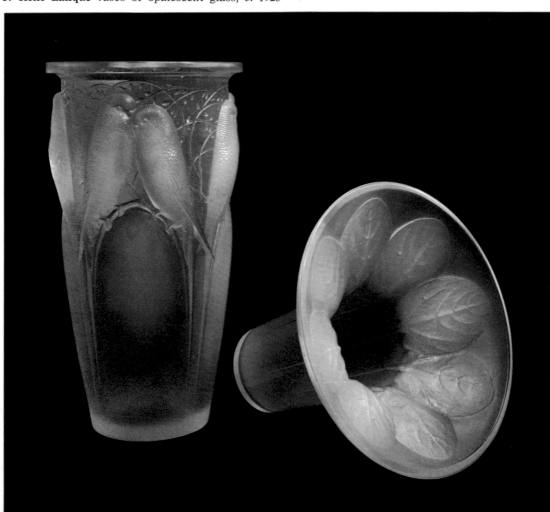

Glass

René Lalique

René Lalique's unique talents had brought about a revolution in the design of jewelry in the 1890s and for a few years he produced jewels which, justly esteemed for their qualities of design and craftsmanship, made him one of the leading figures in the field of Art Nouveau. It is on record that he became so concerned about the inferior imitations of his work that were being put into circulation that on one occasion he refused to allow the correspondent of an English magazine either to see or to reproduce some of his latest creations for fear that debased versions might appear on the English market. This anxiety was no doubt the reason for his gradual abandonment of designing jewelry in favour of glass (he had experimented in incorporating glass into his jewels, combining it with precious stones and using multi-coloured or opaline glass motifs to enhance the glitter of precious stones) and on his removal in 1901 into sumptuous premises built mainly to his designs and situated in the Cours-la-Reine his interests turned increasingly to the production of designs to be carried out in glass rather than to jewelry.

Like most of his contemporaries Lalique participated in the reaction against Art Nouveau which, as a movement, had effected a break with historicism but which had both failed to maintain the interest of discriminating collectors and patrons and had become cheapened by commercialism, and he shared the common problem of finding a new decorative idiom of self-expression. For a short period he worked in collaboration with the sculptor Gaston Lachaise, creating a number of designs incorporating the human figure, usually nude, and executed in moulded and lightly tinted glass in shades of brown, blue and peach colour. Animals and insects surrounded by decorative foliage were applied in relief at this period to vases and other objects.

Lalique found one solution to the problem of preventing his designs from being pirated by mass production when in 1908 he was invited by François Coty to design scent bottles. He fell in with this suggestion with enthusiasm.

The recent discoveries of chemical ingredients which, to a great extent, could replace the rare and costly essences which had hitherto been necessary to fix scents, meant that perfumes could be produced in greater quantities and in a wider range of varieties. The current taste in the early 1900s for everything reminiscent of the Arabian Nights created a demand for heavy, musky scents other than the versions of sandalwood and patchouli so favoured by the courtesans of the previous century. Scent manufacturers were beginning to feel the competition offered by dressmakers (Paul Poiret for example) who found a highly profitable side-line in selling perfumes.

Coty had the idea of marketing his products in beautiful bottles which could be packed in matching containers — at this period there were few aids to beauty being manufactured beyond perfume, toilet water, eau de cologne and face powder, so that the entry of couturiers into the field of scent presented a serious challenge which could only be met by appealing to the eye of the customers. Lalique's collaboration with Coty was extremely successful from the start; his bottle *La Libellule* (an echo of Art Nouveau when the dragonfly was a favourite decorative motif) proved to be responsible for increases in the sale of scent while his idea for a box for facepowder, covered in a repeating design of powder puffs in orange, black, gold and white, is still in use sixty years later and has become identified with the name of Coty.

In his search for new uses for decorative glass, Lalique invented lamps composed of circular or semicircular sheets of glass, about an inch in thickness, with a design deeply etched by acid on the back. This was mounted on a bronze base of sufficient bulk to give a firm support while a small electric bulb was concealed in this base; the light from this shone up through the thickness of the glass illuminating the

60 René Lalique *Suzanne* 1922; bottle with panels of nude female figures in low relief; packaging for Coty facepowder

61 Group of scent bottles and scent sprays dating from 1920 to 1930

62 René Lalique decorative lamp,
Paris Exhibition, 1925

63 René Lalique glass lamp

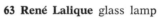

64 René Lalique dining room for 'Le Pavillon de la Manufacture Nationale de Sèvres' Paris Exhibition, 1925

incised design with a mysterious effect. This technique was used in a quite charming clock set in a circular slab of glass with two nude figures surrounding the clock-face, the male figure being cut in intaglio, the female in cameo, the different treatments of the figures emphasizing their characteristics when the light in the bronze base was switched on. *Suzanne*, dating from 1922, is another variation of this kind of lamp, the figure being of moulded opaline glass. The technique of acid-etched glass was used for the stoppers of elaborate scent bottles — probably intended as exhibition pieces — in which the stoppers (in some cases bigger than the bottles) curve down to enclose the bottles and are engraved with designs of flowers.

René Lalique was praised by a number of contemporary critics not only for the unusually high standard of design and finish of his works but also for his desire to give the public the benefit of his designs by manufacturing large editions of vases, lamps and so on when he could have had the same financial rewards by creating individual pieces which would have been sought after by collectors for large sums of money — as he had done at the turn of the century when he was pursuing his career as a jeweller, when he rarely if ever duplicated a piece of jewelry. In a different career as a *verrier* his aims were purely commercial, aiming to sell as many copies of his creations as possible. Consequently most of his work was mass-produced, and beyond the concept of the original model Lalique could not have played any active part in the making of his products except supervising their manufacture — unlike Marinot, for instance, each of whose glass vessels was a unique piece personally made by him. In view of the wide range of objects bearing Lalique's signature or stamp it is remarkable what a high standard of design was maintained; for there are few pieces, especially those dating from the 'twenties or before, which can be faulted for quality of design or originality — an originality which never becomes eccentricity.

The 1925 Exhibition gave Lalique many opportunities to demonstrate his versatility and imaginative range — examples of his glass and of Edgar Brandt's iron-work, often in conjunction, were to be found distributed throughout the various French pavilions of the exhibition. Apart from the various decorative fountains and screens which Lalique had made, the exhibit which created the greatest attention was the dining room made in collaboration with the Manufacture de Sèvres. Primarily a room designed for exhibition purposes and therefore released from practical considerations (the absence of any sound-absorbing materials such as curtains or carpets would have rendered the room intolerable in everyday life) it was a spectacular and original scheme with walls of grey-veined beige marble incised with scenes of a boar hunt in a forest, the lines of the design inlaid with silver or white composition. The floor and a long serving table were of the same marble as the walls, similarly engraved with patterns of leaves. The ceiling was coffered in a manner reminiscent of those to be found in Italian Renaissance palaces, the coffers

65 A. Hunebelle circular dish, *c.* 1927

and beams of glass moulded into designs characteristic of Lalique's style; the lighting was concealed in these panels. The simple but massive dining table designed by Bemel served to display a setting of Sèvres porcelain and wine glasses and candlesticks in moulded glass by Lalique.

The output from the Lalique workshops was considerable, some of the more popular models being reproduced in large numbers. There was a need to supply the constant demand in France and, in addition, as conditions improved a flourishing export market came into being. Lalique glass was completely unlike any glass made previously and its originality and decorative quailties made it suitable as gifts on such occasions as weddings and anniversaries. Lalique glass — along with that of Decorchement, Argy-Rousseau, and Goupy — was on sale at The Crystal Shop in London; later the Brèves Galeries were extensively advertised as being the agents for a number of models by Lalique.

It was thus inevitable that, just as his jewelry had been imitated and even plagiarized a quarter of a century before, Lalique's glass should be similarly treated. In fact, it was an indication of his success and the esteem in which his work was held, that so many firms should be making glass in styles which so closely resembled his. So far as is known no actual fakes were produced purporting to be original work from the Lalique establishment but a great deal was produced which at first glance could be mistaken for it; upon examination, however, the distinctive touch which is so characteristic of his work is lacking. The moulded opalescent glass which Lalique increasingly manufactured (it is often wrongly stated that this type of glass was his invention and that the secret of its manufacture died with him) was imitated with some conviction and can be found with the stamped signature 'Etling, France' and that of another firm, 'Ezan' — both these firms producing a wide variety of decorative vases and flat bowls to be used as hanging ceiling lights. Genet et Michon, specializing in lighting fixtures, incorporated pressed and moulded glass panels (some of which came close to plagiarism of Lalique designs) into wall brackets, chandeliers and strip lighting which replaced cornices in many rooms. André Hunebelle had a certain reputation as an original designer of glass and apart from each article bearing the impressed signature 'A. Hunebelle', his work shows definite traces of Lalique's influence. He created a number of vases and bowls of slightly frosted glass decorated with the spirals and formalized flowers characteristic of Art Déco but after opening a shop in the rue de la Boëtie in 1927 his designs followed the new fashion for geometrical compositions inspired by cubism, using a glass which was semi-opaque and only slightly opalescent. Sabino — sometimes referred to as Sabino-Marino — made vases, light fittings and furniture of glass in both white and a smoky-coloured glass, the latter being fabricated of units of pressed glass panels mounted on an invisible foundation and again there is a close resemblance to the work of Lalique.

Maurice Marinot

The glass of Maurice Marinot stands in a class of its own, each piece attaining the status of a work of art. A generation earlier, Emile Gallé had used glass in ways never before imagined, contributing all his acquired knowledge of chemistry, botany and geology to the creation of glass vessels which synthesized the poetry and beauty of nature which were the ruling passions of his life. René Lalique abandoned a career as the most celebrated jeweller of his time to devote his life to creating beautiful glass objects and to bringing them within the reach of the greatest number of people. Similarly, Maurice Marinot gave up a career as a painter to dedicate his life to the realization, through the medium of glass, of his visions of light and colour.

Marinot was twenty-nine years old, a painter sharing the ideas of the Fauves and the same scorn and derision which their works excited when, in 1911, he suddenly became possessed with the desire to turn his creative powers in another direction. From the moment when he first witnessed the process of glassmaking there was no hesitation although it meant that he had to start a long apprenticeship in this difficult craft. In spite of his poverty, he was prepared to make any sacrifice to achieve his ambition. Impressed by his single-minded zeal the Viard brothers assisted him by placing the facilities of their small glass factory at his disposal. His natural instincts as a painter led his first efforts into the direction of glass decorated with enamels, a technique which had been comparatively neglected since the end of the nineteenth century. Not sufficiently adept to make his own glass he decorated bottles, flasks and vases which were made by his more experienced fellow-workers to his designs, embellishing them with enamelled figures, flowers and garlands. But his perceptive eye was caught and his imagination fired by the appearance of glass that had been rejected through a fault in the composition of the glass or caused by a misjudgment in the blowing of the molten material.

Marinot began to question the accepted standards of symmetry of form and clarity of material, standards which necessitated the destruction in the factory of anything less than technically perfect. Where others saw impurities or bubbles in the body of the glass as faults, he saw possibilities of new and strange beauties of texture: irregularities of surface which ensured the rejection of the finished article he saw as virtues to be cultivated, exaggerated and controlled as a means of giving a play of light on the fissures and crackled textures. He found the bubble-thin, perfectly colourless glass wrought in symmetrical graceful shapes, incapable of serving as a medium of expression for his ideas. In so doing he set himself an even harder task. Impurities in the glass can appear by accident but to introduce them deliberately and govern their placing is another matter; the glass may well crack and distort by accident in the process of being blown but to bring about this effect at will meant learning a technique and then abusing it with intent. Consequently a great many of his efforts failed to achieve the results he envisaged and until he had complete mastery over his material he had to discard more than he finished until the desired effects were reached. For Marinot the thicker the glass — and consequently the more difficult to manipulate — the greater the opportunities for exciting and mysterious textures made by clouds of bubbles or particles imprisoned in its depths and as the glass became thicker so the shapes of his vases became heavier and more monumental. For even greater effect he made deep incisions in the surface of the finished vase with acid or with the wheel — incisions which were abstract devices for emphasizing form or which made decorative shapes resembling leaves or flowers. In other vases the molten glass was coaxed and manipulated into forms which resembled melting ice textured with the cracks to be seen in blocks of ice. Like Gallé and Lalique, Marinot

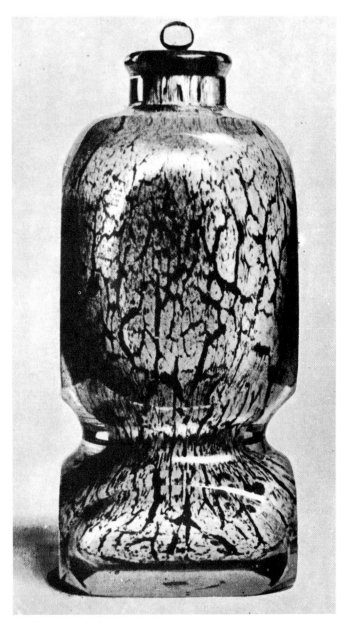

66 Maurice Marinot glass bottle

expressed his love of nature, not as they by literal copies or by using plants and flowers as decorative motifs, but by translating the textures of moss, lichens, bark into terms of glass. It has been estimated that in the twenty-six years during which he worked in glass (from 1911 until 1937 when he as suddenly gave up to resume his career as a painter) his output was approximately 2500 pieces, most of which are now in museums or private collections. His work found recognition at an early stage in his career and was sought after by connoisseurs.

Henri Navarre and Dumoulin made vases and bowls in a style similar to that of Marinot without however being held in the same esteem. The Daum factory produced a number of pieces imitative of Marinot.

Pâte-de-verre

Pâte-de-verre was a process of glass making which the French artisans had made particularly their own since its rediscovery by Henri Cros, a sculptor working for the Sèvres Factory. Intrigued by the possibility of polychrome sculpture and in particular that of the ancient Greeks he experimented for nearly thirty years until he recaptured the secrets of the ancient practice of *pâte-de-verre* which enabled him to create pieces of sculpture in which the colour was closely combined with the form and not something applied after the piece of sculpture had been finished. His great

67 Vase; glass by **Daum** ironwork by **Majorelle** 1920

bas-relief, some six feet in height, entitled *L'Histoire du Feu* was the centre-piece of the Sèvres exhibit at the 1900 Paris Exhibition and proved to be the inspiration for a generation of glassworkers.

The creative process of *pâte-de-verre* was lengthy. Powdered glass mixed into a paste with a volatile medium was applied in thin layers of the appropriate colours into a mould until the required thickness of the finished glass was achieved. The mould together with its application of the glass paste was then placed in a kiln and fired at a temperature sufficiently high to fuse the crystals of glass into one mass; upon removal from the kiln and after cooling the mould was carefully removed to reveal the object. As the firing was a hazardous process — the paste might not coalesce uniformly or the mould might disintegrate in the intense heat — the number of failures was high but when successful the glass had the appearance of tinted alabaster with a slightly waxy surface. The range of colours obtainable in the glass powders was unlimited and in consequence the most delicate as well as the most intense effects could be obtained.

The imposing dimensions of Henri Cros' masterpiece, which was of course made for exhibition purposes, were not emulated by those who came after him and it is rare to find a later piece of *pâte-de-verre* more than a foot or so in height. His smaller pieces, decorative masks and plaques of more modest dimensions, were technically more practical.

Argy-Rousseau's work was more commercial and he produced a greater range of objects for in addition to vases of various sizes he made lamps with shades, perfume burners, cigarette boxes and numerous small medallions, generally oval or circular and decorated with flowers in slight relief — these were intended to be used as part of belts or necklaces and have holes for cords or chains. Each piece is different in design as the process of making *pâte-de-verre* necessarily involved the destruction of the mould.

68 Marcel Goupy enamelled glass vase

Pâte-de-verre was also made by the glassworkers at Nancy and in particular by Schneider and by Walter, the latter working in collaboration with the sculptor Henri Bergé who used a punning signature with the initial of his surname making the outline of a sheep. Their bowls and dishes with decorations of small sprays of flowers or berries are thicker and heavier than the more fragile artifacts of Argy-Rousseau. Chandeliers with single shades for electric light bulbs and flat glass dishes framed in wrought-iron were made around 1920 often bearing the name 'Schneider'. The glass has the appearance of having been made of *pâte-de-verre*, being of a similar degree of opacity and shaded from a deep mauve to white or from red to orange; the large number of these shades in existence, however, their uniformity and lack of ornament, suggest that it is unlikely that they were made in the true *pâte-de-verre* technique and probably some means had been found of mass producing on a commercial scale by means of a simpler process.

The *pâte-de-verre* made by Daum seems to be comparatively rare but is not distinguished by any great individuality and cannot be compared with that from the workshops of the artist-craftsmen.

Enamelled glass

Enamelled glass by Decuper-Delvaux was described by a critic as 'modèles de verrerie d'une intelligence primesautière' a comment which is, to date, the only discoverable reference made by a contemporary. The stoppered bottle illustrated, signed on the base in gold 'Delvaux 18 Rue Royale Paris' is embellished in a typical Art Déco manner with bouquets of white rosebuds and blue ribbons enamelled on clear glass, while the ground of the vase decorated with formalized sunflowers in two shades of yellow with iron-grey centres and lines of gold spots is of a thicker glass textured with air bubbles. The small covered pot — probably part of a set intended for toilet

69 From left to right, vases by **Degne, Charder, Legras, Daum**

70 From felt to right, vase by **Delvaux**, vase by **Laroyer**, bowl by **Quénvit**

71 From left to right, vase inscribed 'Le Verre de France' bottle by **Delvaux**, bottle by **Nelia Casella**, bowl by **Delvaux**, vase by **Legras**

use — is of clear glass with a scattered floral design of deep blue and black. An addition to the technique of enamelling can be seen in the important vase signed by 'H. Laroyer'. The main body of the vase is of clear white glass and is decorated with four diagonal bands of cubist roses in black, white, grey and tango *, the bands joining and encircling the neck with a continuation of the floral pattern. To emphasize the design, the roses are linked by areas of glass which has been treated to give a texture resembling that found on the samorodok cigarette cases made by Fabergé.

Specimens of enamelled glass with the signature 'Quénvit' must be added to those about which no information has so far been found. Those examples which have appeared have the same background of mottled yellowish opaque glass. Some have fantastic flowers in bright orange and black enamel; an ashtray has three Poiret-like roses in turquoise blue set off by black leaves while the bowl illustrated has rather more elaborately drawn flowers, leaves and branches in off-white and black enamel, the wrought-iron stand having a similar design. From resemblance to textile designs known to be from the Atelier Martine it may be conjectured that these pieces were made by a pupil of Paul Poiret.

Le Verre de France

A considerable number of glass vases for flowers, bowls and lamp bases, some with a glass shade en suite are to be found bearing the incised inscription 'Le Verre de France' and at the time of writing no documentary evidence, in spite of intensive search and enquiry, has come to light which can give a clue as to the factory where this glass was made. The likeliest possibility is that it may be a byproduct of the Daum factory** as a description of the exhibit by Daum in the French section of glass in the 1925 Exhibition 'verres agatisés, verres camés à deux ou trois couches superposées' can be applied to this glass and to no other which was being manufactured about this time. In the majority of cases the ground is of a marbled or agate-like glass with a superimposed layer of thin clear glass which can be variegated in colour, either speckled or blotched with a darker shade or shading from a dark colour to a paler tone or another colour — the dark colour usually being at the base of the vase. This clear layer is cut away, probably by means of acid, to reveal the unpolished ground of the vessel. The designs are of conventionalized flowers, sometimes based on nature but often fantastic, fruit, butterflies, snails and other insects and a characteristic decoration applied to the bases and necks of vases consists of a stepped motif of elongated hexagons. Stylistically the ornament has lingering traces of Art Nouveau but there is a stronger quasi-oriental influence which, combined with the use of strong rich colours, orange, crimson, ultramarine and violet, would indicate a later date of the period between 1910 and 1925. The workmanship is not comparable to that of the acid-engraved work of the Art Nouveau period but the decorative effects are striking and original, though in some cases the colour combinations show a tendency to garishness.

* Tango, a shade of brownish orange was as popular in the 'twenties as Schiaparelli's Shocking Pink was a decade later. It was called after the dance introduced about 1910 — a dance which evoked the shocked comment of Princess Metternich ' In my time we only did that in bed'. It first appeared in a named version (for no colour can strictly be said to be entirely new) about 1920. Tango — unlike Shocking Pink — had no set shade or exact tone and could vary from terracotta to coral red. Dress fabrics, paint, carpets, enamels and the newly invented casein-based artificial materials were produced in the new colour and it remained as a standard colour in sample books of furnishing repps, velours and casement cloths for at least twenty years.
** It has also been hazarded that Le Verre de France was produced by Schneider at his factory at Epinay-sur-Seine.

Book production

Between the end of the 1914-1918 War and 1930, the level of production of French illustrated *livres d'art* reached a height unequalled at any time since the invention of printing in Europe. Although the acquisition of fine printed books with illustrations by the best contemporary artists did not exactly reach the fervour of tulipomania in seventeenth century Holland, the underlying forces were similar and had not the Wall Street crash of 1929 occurred, the enthusiasm for collecting would probably have resulted in as much speculation, and examples of limited editions could have changed hands for sums rivalling those reached by tulip bulbs three hundred years earlier.

Since the end of the nineteenth century the numbers of collectors of fine books had been steadily increasing. The formation of the ' Société des Bibliophiles Français' in 1820 had encouraged an interest in first editions or rare bindings; in 1874 the ' Société des Amis des Livres' was formed despite — and in the hope of improving — the extremely low standards of book production prevailing. In common with all the decorative arts, typography and book illustration were affected by the current taste for historical pastiche encouraged by technical advances in methods of reproducing different types of drawings and this malaise became more pronounced in the 1880s and 1890s. Apart from poorly designed type which gave an unpleasing ' grey' quality to the printed page, reproductions of wash drawings (made possible by the use of process blocks) had to be printed on coated or surfaced papers. Thus the unity of the finished book was destroyed by the need for one paper for the type and another for the illustrations — a volume entirely printed on surfaced paper becoming too bulky and heavy to handle, and, if exposed to damp, tending to turn into a solid mass when the coated surfaces stuck together. Few artists of talent could be persuaded to illustrate books when, owing to the methods of reproduction, they found themselves hampered by the need to modify their conceptions for technical reasons, and in addition, found that the finished result was a travesty of their original drawings. A change in this state of affairs was brought about by the example of William Morris and the practical application of his theories of book production as exemplified by the volumes from the Kelmscott Press. These radically altered conceptions of book production throughout Europe. When exhibited in France they proved the stimulus and inspiration for editors, typographers and illustrators, drawing attention to essential qualities of book production which had become neglected in the course of time — qualities which had remained valid, however, for five hundred years. Clarity of type, the balance of type and illustration, a harmonious spacing of margins; these had all been established for generations and were legacies of illuminated manuscript volumes, but during the nineteenth century had become overlooked and had not been replaced by any comparable improvements. Any technical advances emphasized the bad habits into which those responsible for the production of books, whether éditions de luxe or more commercial varieties, had fallen.

One of the first books in which a serious attempt at raising the standard of production could be seen was *Les Quatres Fils Aymon* which was published in 1883 and gave Eugène Grasset the opportunity to experiment in a revival of the principles of book design. Although this pioneering volume was at first received with indifference on the part of the critics and the public, a timely article drew attention to its virtues and it found its admirers, leading the way to further experiments in the same direction and Grasset, who had designed the type in addition to providing the illustration, became increasingly interested in creating other founts of type, Georges Auriol, Bellery-Desfontaines and Naudin followed where he had led and through their efforts the text, at least, of French books — commercial as well as limited or luxury editions — gradually acquired a new clarity and legibility. The editor Edouard Péllatan

launched a series of volumes in 1896 which raised typography to a higher level than
it had reached for nearly a century and once again it was realized that a page of
type, even without illustrations, could be a thing of beauty. Péllatan went further in
advocating the most careful choice of type for each book as he maintained that
there should be a subtle harmony between the physical shape of the letters and the
meaning conveyed by the words themselves.

William Morris had shown the path to be followed; a retracing of steps to an earlier
practice, by using woodcuts to serve as illustrations for his volumes. Péllatan and
the engraver Bracquemond became ardent advocates of his principles. In 1897 the

72 Raoul Dufy *La Carpe* illustration for *Le Bestiaire ou Cortège d'Orphée*
by Guillaume Apollinaire, 1911

73 Foujita illustration for *Amal et la Lettre du Roi* by Rabindranath Tagore, 1922

latter in his *Etude sur la Gravure sur Bois* stressed the importance of the unity of the printed page which, he wrote, ' should be obtained through the use of the woodcut — which should be a woodcut and not an imitation of an engraving or of photographic work '; adding that he required ' the wood to be cleanly cut leaving clear whites and rich blacks '. Woodcuts had the added advantage that they could be printed on the same paper as the text, unlike half-tone or process blocks. Bracquemond also stressed the importance of the editor — ' the architect of the book ' whose role he described as being similar to that of the conductor of an orchestra. On his shoulders rested the responsibility for the choice of paper, type, the artist who would create the illustrations or decorate the text, the choice of cover, in fact the whole conception of the volume and its success or failure depended upon his taste, knowledge and discrimination. In this context Bracquemond was referring to illustrated books which were reprints of accepted classics. Fortunately there were a number of editors who proved to possess these qualities — Léon Pichon, René Kieffer, Jacques Beltrand, Schmeid to name only a few.

The renaissance of book production had as a result an increase in the number of bibliophiles in France — the ' Société de Cent Bibliophiles ' was founded in 1895, followed two years later by the ' Société des XX '; 1904 saw the inauguration of the ' Société du Livre Contemporain ' and in the following year ' Le Livre d'Art '; that this enthusiasm was not confined to the capital was demonstrated by the formation of ' Le Cercle Lyonnais du Livre '. Members of these societies were given priority in subscribing to the limited editions published by the societies or by individual publishers, and consequently editors were more or less assured of the complete sale of an edition of an illustrated book which, in the majority of cases, disappeared into the libraries of suscribers and was unavailable to the general public. In fact the very existence of these books was unknown outside France and her French-speaking neighbours Belgium and Switzerland, and the very large exhibit devoted to illustrated books in the 1925 Paris Exhibition came as a revelation to many foreign visitors.

The size of an edition varied considerably and could be of any number between one hundred and one thousand. In some cases the edition was divided into different categories, and while the printed text and the illustrations were exactly the same in all cases, a few volumes, perhaps ten or so, were printed on extremely expensive paper with an extra set of loose illustrations signed by the artist; a larger number, generally about fifty, were printed on a less costly paper and a few extra illustrations might be added, while the rest of the edition was on a good quality paper and these volumes were intended for collectors of more moderate means. The varieties of paper were numerous, *japon, japon imperial, japon supernacré, hollande van Gelder, vélin de Rives, vélin pur fil à la forme blanc de Rives, vieux japon feutré, papier d'Auvergne, vélin de cuve de Marais, chine, feutre de Corée, chiffon Lafuma*. The cost of these hand-made papers was between ten and twenty per cent of the total of producing the book.

In contrast to these volumes de luxe, French publishers could produce series of illustrated books of good quality at a cost far lower than their English counterparts could hope to achieve. Ferenczi et Fils, for instance, issued ' Le Livre Moderne ', a series of novels which included new works by Colette and Henri de Regnier each illustrated with an average of sixty woodcuts by well known artists and with well designed type for the (1925) equivalent of fivepence. These were bound in paper and the original woodcuts reproduced from stereotypes. This and other series enabled anyone, no matter how limited his means, to own well designed illustrated books.

It was customary to use woodcuts, either monotone or in several colours, to illustrate the éditions de luxe during the 'twenties and if the blocks for these were not cut by the artists themselves, their drawings were translated by skilled crafts-

74 Picart Le Doux illustration for *L'Illustre Magicien* by Count Arthur Gobineau, 1920

men in terms of woodblock techniques without losing any of the essential character of the original designs. Other graphic techniques, etching, dry point, lithography or the *pochoir* process (a form of silk screen printing by means of which prints using anything up to twenty colours could be used) were employed to a lesser extent, but the technical accomplishments of the makers of woodblocks were such that Marie Laurencin's delicate watercolour drawings for *La Tentative Amoureuse* by André Gide were interpreted by means of colour woodblocks cut by Jules Germain. Colour drawings by Pierre Jouve (the sculptor and painter of animals who had made his debut at the age of sixteen with bas-reliefs for the main entrance to the 1900 Exhibition) for Kipling's *Jungle Book* were printed by means of colour woodblocks cut by Schmeid, himself an editor and illustrator of a number of beautiful volumes. Mention is made elsewhere of Raoul Dufy's woodcuts for Guillaume Apollinaire's *Le Bestiaire ou Cortège d'Orphée* the publication of which drew attention to his ability as a graphic designer. Picart Le Doux, the painter, illustrated a number of books with original woodcuts or by drawings reproduced by the *pochoir* process. Paul Véra, sculptor, painter and designer of tapestries and ceramics, extended his range into book illustration, using a characteristic blend of cubism tempered by decorative feeling. Guy Arnoux, an admirer of the Directoire period and influenced by it in his work in the pre-war years, drew scenes of contemporary life in the 'twenties. Dunoyer de Segonzac enlivened the pages of Valéry, Flaubert and Tristan

75 Maxime Dethomas
ilustration for
Les Folies Françaises by
François Couperin, 1920

Bernard with his spontaneous drawings. Kees van Dongen, the delineator of chic perversity, was a surprising choice for the illustrations for Kipling's *Trois Contes*. The talents of every artist of the day were enlisted to illustrate the volumes for which there was such a demand — Charles Laborde, Charles Guérin, Laboureur, Bourdelle, Pierre Laprade, Eddy Legrand, André Marty, Georges Barbier, Sylvain Sauvage, Robert Bonfils, Maxime Dethomas, Carlègle, Foujita — only a few of those whose work, sadly enough was condemned to remain unseen in the volumes which were too often left untouched on their owner's shelves. A study in any detail of the many illustrated books produced during the 1920s would require a volume to itself.

By 1927, however, there were signs that the demand for illustrated books was lessening, for collectors surfeited by the number of volumes produced were becoming more selective, consequently it became more difficult to market a book which fell below the highest standards. A periodical *L'Amour de l'Art* had a regular feature each month describing the latest productions and critical comment often drew attention to the fact that the search for new type-faces led editors to choose type that was more novel than legible or even pleasing to the eye; too many tricks were creeping into the typography itself, notably the omission of capital letters, which often led to confusion, and in addition the illustrator often failed to portray the mood and feeling of the text. Very often the same novel or volume of poems would be issued in an illustrated edition by different publishing firms and, of course, different illustrators.

By 1929 the boom had definitely ceased and the flood of éditions de luxe which had poured from the presses for nearly ten years had become a trickle. Many publishers were caught with unsold stocks and several were ruined while the illustrators whose work had been in such demand were forced to look elsewhere for commissions. There were still enough collectors to warrant the production of illustrated éditions de luxe during the lean years of the 1930s but the undiscriminating collecting fever had abated and publishers found that suscribers were not only greatly reduced in number but more selective in their purchases.

The owners of these éditions de luxe often had their most highly prized examples specially bound by the leading binders of the day, thus combining in one volume the finest specimens of paper, typography, illustration and binding. These individual bindings, tooled and inlaid with marquetries of inlaid leathers were naturally extremely expensive and to protect them from dust and fading due to exposure to light they had, in turn, to be kept in protective cases which were decorated en suite with the binding. Thus the books themselves became anomalies, too precious to be handled, let alone read, and condemned by their own value to remain locked in the libraries of their owners or lent on rare occasions to exhibitions.

Equally with other crafts bookbinding had a renaissance in the latter years of the nineteenth century when the work of Marius Michel raised the craft from the mediocre standards which had prevailed for fifty years or more. Descended from a family of bookbinders he was perhaps too firmly entrenched in the traditions of the seventeenth, eighteenth and early nineteenth centuries to be a true revolutionary, but through his work others were led to a reappraisal of the finest standards of workmanship and design.

The 1890s saw the emergence of a new school of binders who maintained that the cover of the book should prepare the reader for the contents by means of designs incorporating pictorial elements. This was not a new idea, having been used in cheaply printed books with paper covers decorated with lithographic illustrations of the contents, but the concept of applying similar designs to more expensive books destined for libraries, was considered revolutionary. The conventional tooled and gilded decorative motifs between the ' nerfs ' or ridges on the spine of the book and a geometrical or floral ornament, possibly the crest or monogram of the owner, enclosed in a tooled border on the front cover — elements which had become customary — these were abandoned in favour of a continuous design which spread across the front, spine and back of the volume. The nerfs, which would interfere with such a composition, were abolished completely, although their purpose was essentially functional. The disadvantage in that the complete composition could only be appreciated by opening the book flat was a source of criticism by tradition-alists. The conventional inlays of coloured leathers were elaborated and enhanced with inlaid motifs of metal, wood or some precious substance, giving rise to more criticism, in that these projecting ornaments could damage other books on the same shelf. The binders of the Ecole de Nancy, René Weimer, Victor Prouvé and Camille Martin were foremost in creating these unconventional bindings in the Art Nouveau manner and after the collapse of this style in the early 1900s, the break with centuries of tradition which they and their confrères in Paris, Gustave Dubouchet, Rapallier and Belville had brought about, remained, although the decorative idioms changed. In addition, the somewhat limited range of colour in leather bindings was extended to accord with the taste for brilliance which was prevalent in the years before and after the Great War. No longer was a shelf of fine bindings predominately brown with an occasional volume in sombre green or deep crimson:. grey, lemon yellow, rose pink, cyclamen, jade green, pale blue, mauve and black were used in new varieties of leather; silver and platinum were used in tooling as well as the usual gold while shagreen, vellum and panels of eggshell lacquer were incorporated to provide contrasts to the calf, morocco or goatskin.

The most celebrated binder of the 'twenties was Pierre Legrain who combined this career with one of designer of furniture and interiors. Legrain, like his less well known contemporary Paul Bonet, was not himself a craftsman, confining his part in the work to designing the binding, the execution of his design being entrusted to skilled craftsmen who were able to translate his ideas into reality. His first commissions were in 1917 from the couturier and collector Jacques Doucet (for whom he also designed interior decorations) and the success of these led him to open his own bookbinding studio in 1922 in collaboration with René Kieffer.

Legrain's bindings were invariably geometrical in style and his more elaborate conceptions taxed the craftsmen's skill and ingenuity to the utmost; his fondness for parallel lines and concentric circles of blind or gold tooling required the utmost accuracy and left no margin for error. An example of the technical demands he made upon his collaborators can be seen in the binding for Bernardin de St Pierre's *Paul et Virginie* (a work much favoured by publishers of éditions de luxe) with its

76 Pierre Legrain leather bookbinding for *Les Plus Beaux Contes de Rudyard Kipling*

decoration of conventionalized tropical foliage executed in inlaid leathers in several shades of green enlivened with blind and gold tooling — a design reminiscent of Edgar Brandt's screen in the 1925 Exhibition. A simpler binding of which, unusually, several versions appear to have been made, was for the *Croix de Bois* by Roland Dorgelès published in 1925, in which a ground of *tête-de-nègre* morocco was inlaid with a crucifix in black leather, contrasting with an inlaid metal background of palladium, the three shadows of the crucifix having been impressed and burnished to turn the leather almost black.

Legrain and Bonet are particularly characteristic of the cubist-inspired binders who concentrated on the use of geometrical ornamentation, eschewing the figurative and floral motifs used by René Kieffer (who worked on his own commissions apart from those he executed for Legrain), Cretté, Canap and Noulhac. Robert Bonfils, whose wood engravings decorated several éditions de luxe, designed romantic and decorative bindings — a mask and a mandolin on a background of rose morocco for Verlaine's *Fêtes Galantes* and the head of the saint in a nimbus of gold rays for *Le Martyre de St Sebastien*.

The 'twenties saw a remarkable increase in the number of women who became expert in book binding; the work of Rose Adler being shown in exhibitions along with that of her masculine rivals and attracting considerable attention with her harmonies of clear brilliant colours and inlaid cubist designs in silver and black. Geneviève de Léotard, Jeanne Langrand and Madeleine Gras were other names which feature in the many exhibitions of applied arts held in the 'twenties.

77 Georges Barbier *Lettre* illustration
to *Fêtes Galantes* by Paul Verlaine,
published 1928

78 Pierre Legrain leather bookbinding for
Paul et Virginie by Bernardin de St Pierre,
prior to 1925

79 Sylvain Sauvage illustration for
Contes Antiques by Pierre Loüys

78

77

79

Textiles

Since the seventeenth century the manufacture and export of woven fabrics, and in particular silk fabrics, had played a major part in the economy of France. In the financially difficult years following the 1914-1918 war, French manufacturers realized that if they were to maintain their superiority in this field, no effort must be spared and that high as the standard of technical development had become in the pre-war years it must be still further extended by an unceasing search for new varieties of weave combined with originality of design. Like most industries in France, that of silk weaving had suffered from the shortage of labour resulting from the casualties of the war but fortunately the centre of the industry had emerged physically unharmed by the conflict. There were in the district around Lyons no fewer than six hundred mills of major importance, while the number of smaller establishments — most of which concentrated on specialized luxury fabrics — and weavers working in their own homes on small hand-looms was beyond reckoning. In spite of the necessity of importing the raw material from abroad and the shortage of skilled weavers, such drive and energy was put into the task of restoring the industry that the exports during the year 1924 were double those of 1913 — a remarkable increase in view of the world-wide shortage of money and the heavy tariffs which some countries were imposing on imports. This increase could have been even greater had it not been for the competition of artificial silk, the manufacture of which had increased tenfold during the same period.

The increased demand for silk fabrics resulted from changes in fashion during the years immediately preceding the war, when silk began to replace woollen fabrics to make the long, flowing dresses reminiscent of the Directoire style, dresses which needed, as a fashion writer in *La Gazette du Bon Ton* commented, fabrics ' souples et brillants comme un eau reflétant le soleil ou les arbres '. The stiff silks of the taffeta variety, which had been specially treated to make the frou-frou sound considered seductively feminine in the latter years of the nineteenth century, were no longer desired and the ideal dress material had to be soft and flowing. New names for fabrics began to appear in the descriptive captions of fashion plates — charmeuse, marcelline, and organdie in addition to even more pliable versions of gauze, muslin, crêpe foulard and velvet. Crêpe de chine replaced linen, lawn or thin wool for underwear and a silk jersey fabric was being increasingly used for bathing dresses. These unpatterned dress fabrics made a considerable proportion of the increase in exports but an even greater proportion was in woven patterned materials used for dresses and for furnishing.

From the early years of the eighteenth century there had been a close collaboration between the silk manufacturers based in the district around Lyons and the distributors of their fabrics, whose warehouses were in Paris, and the former, realizing the importance of keeping in touch with the latest trends in fashion in the capital, made a practice of sending their designers to Paris at least once a year for a period. According to Joubert de l'Hiberderie writing in 1765, these designers were lodged at their firm's expense in the district near the warehouses for consultations about the forthcoming fashions with the retailers and in addition were encouraged to take advantage of the privilege, open to all French citizens (provided that they were respectably dressed) of attendance at Versailles where they could observe Court fashions and taste the atmosphere of luxury and elegance which prevailed there — despite the elementary sanitation. It was also their duty to attend theatres, concerts and the promenades of the raffish Palais Royal — in fact any place where they could test the pulse of fashion by observing its arbiters. Armed with the hints of changes in fashion they had observed in the elegant and sophisticated circles of the capital they returned to Lyons to materialize their impressions into designs for the next

80 Edouard Bénedictus moquette carpet

season's fabrics. As time went on and fashion began to change with ever-increasing rapidity and a demand for more exotic novelties, it was found more convenient to keep the designers based in Paris so that the smallest change in taste could be taken advantage of with the minimum delay. Designs were also bought from freelance designers and it became the accepted practice to commission sketches from artists even if they had no knowledge of the techniques of weaving or printing. There was no lack of competent technicians who could recast these suggestions, however slight, into a practical form without impairing the essential character of the idea.

Faced with increasing competition from abroad and demands from the home markets, manufacturers were only too willing to pay handsomely for that elusive but unmistakable style and elegance which had made Paris the unrivalled arbiter of fashion for so long.

The new techniques (introduced about 1920) applied to the weaving of plain materials were, of course, used in the manufacture of patterned stuffs and ingenuity was strained to the utmost in the never-ending search for new and exciting effects of texture and colour. The rage for oriental motifs in the pre-war years had led to a call for rich materials woven with gold and silver not, as had formerly been the case, resulting in a fabric of a harsh stiff texture. Now the demand was for gauzes, chiffons and lamés — sometimes combined with velvet — with designs in metallic thread and often printed with another design which contrasted but at the same time harmonized with that woven into the fabric. After the privations of the war years the demand for these rich metallic fabrics increased — especially those woven with silver which came into fashion about 1922 — and artificial silk was frequently used as a basis for the metal threads.

Another noticeable change in the post-war years was the lessening of the differences between dress and furnishing fabrics due in the main to the influence of Paul Poiret and his followers. Poiret was probably the first couturier to combine that career with one as an interior decorator and an elegant woman could wear a dress designed by Poiret in a setting from the studios of his Atelier Martine, her dress, curtains and upholstery — not to mention the enormous cushions which were an invariable feature of any Poiret interior — expressing a harmony of design which emanated from the same source.

Raoul Dufy's designs for printed fabrics were used indiscriminately by Poiret for dresses and furnishing. Designs for textiles, elaborately reproduced by the *pochoir* process and in some cases incorporating as many as twenty colours, were published in albums for the guidance of designers and with no indication as to whether they were intended for clothes or upholstery. Two authors of such albums may be cited

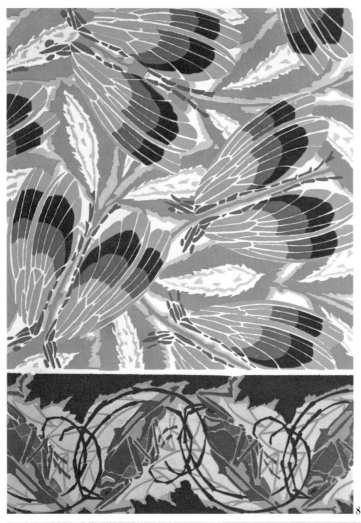

81

82

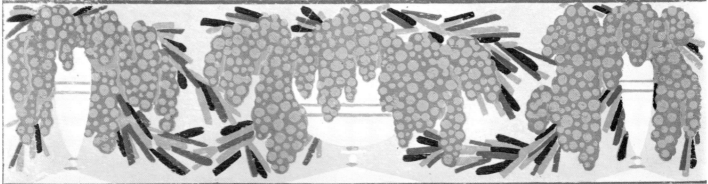

83

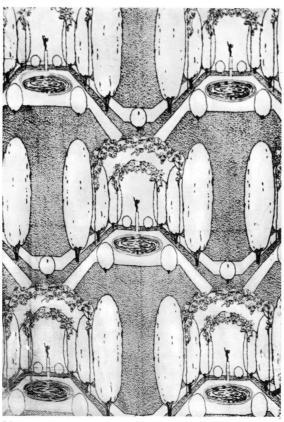

84   85

81 Séguy fabric designs, *c.* 1925
82 André Mare printed fabric border
83 Two designs for fabric or wallpaper borders
84 Jacques Ruhlmann printed silk, prior to 1925
85 Foujita printed silk

as outstanding among the many responsible for these productions — Séguy and Edouard Bénedictus. Séguy published *Les Fleurs et leurs Applications Décoratives* (1901), *Primavera* (1913), *Floréal* (1914) and *Samarkande* (1920). Bénedictus, specializing in designs for the use of artificial silk by the firm of Brunet, Meunie et Cie published three superb collections of designs during the 'twenties, *Variations, Nouvelles Variations* and *Relais*, the last appearing in 1930. Both these designers had started their careers with designs in the Art Nouveau manner and had adapted themselves to the various changes in taste which followed on the cubist-inspired motifs of the late 'twenties.

Their exact contemporaries, Maurice Dufrène and Paul Follot, had also started their designing careers during the Art Nouveau period, both having been associated with La Maison Moderne since its inception in 1898, but they, like so many other designers, reacted against Art Nouveau in the early 1900s and followed the various trends for designs inspired by Persian, Chinese and African sources. They were joined by younger designers such as Robert Bonfils, Madame de Andrada, Suzanne Lalique and Stéphany. Unfortunately, by the very nature of the material most of their creations have been worn out or have perished or faded and little actual fabric has survived of the many thousand designs of the period; the only way in which reminders exist are in black and white photographs or the coloured albums of Bénedictus, Séguy and others. A length of the grey and purple damask designed by Stéphany and made by Cornille et Cie for the salon of Ruhlmann's 'Pavillon d'un Collectionneur' in the 1925 Exhibition, is in the Musée des Arts Décoratifs — an imposing design on a large scale, embodying all the motifs used by eighteenth century designers, urns, doves, swags of flowers and strings of pearls, but treated by Stéphany in an unmistakeable twentieth century manner.

This rendering of traditional elements of design in a modern manner is particularly noticeable in printed materials which maintained the popularity they had enjoyed

86 Raoul Dufy *La Jungle* brocade in three colours, 1923   **87 Raoul Dufy** printed fabric

since the eighteenth century when printing of cotton and linen, known as *l'Indien-nage* was first introduced into France. Basically there were two methods of printing, by blocks or by rollers; the original block method, although cumbrous and slow, was used for the finely detailed *toiles de Jouy* until it was to a great extent superseded by the roller process invented in England by Thomas Bell in 1783 and introduced into France a few years later by Oberkampf who is said to have used for his rollers the melted-down guns captured from the Papal forces by Napoleon. Variations of this method — the metal rollers engraved with the design, rollers of wood with the design raised in metal motifs, etc, were used for different types of print during the nineteenth century but the popularity of these printed fabrics led to a general lowering of the standards of design and execution.

From 1908 to the outbreak of the war in 1914 the example of Raoul Dufy encouraged a number of younger designers to take a renewed interest in the craft and the industry itself, centred in Normandy, Alsace and the Ile-de-France, received a new impetus from the growing interest on the part of the public. In addition, a number of interior designers, Ruhlmann for instance, commissioned artists to design fabrics for their exclusive use in the decoration of houses for their wealthier clients and, with no necessity to economize on the cost, these materials were printed in the traditional manner, using wood blocks which were engraved with the design if not actually by the artist himself then under his close supervision. The slight variations of register and tone resulting from this hand-printing gave the fabrics a character and individuality impossible to obtain by machine methods and was much in favour with a discriminating clientele who were prepared to pay the necessarily higher cost of material printed by hand from hand-engraved blocks.

To those more familiar with Raoul Dufy as the delineator of the elegant leisured life of the period between the two wars, a world of casinos in the South of France, yachting, concert halls and racecourses, it may come as a surprise to find that he was in the 'twenties regarded as the foremost, if somewhat avant-garde, designer of textiles which were admired by a far greater public than his paintings and drawings. His illustrations to a volume of poems by Guillaume Apollinaire *Bestiaire ou Cortège d'Orphée* attracted the attention of Paul Poiret who invited him to collaborate in his newly formed design studio 'L'Atelier Martine'. After decorating Poiret's dinning room with painted panels of flowers the idea occurred to the couturier of using Dufy's talents in the graphic arts to decorate fabrics for dresses and for furnishing. With financial aid from Poiret and the assistance of a chemist named Zifferlein who

88 Raoul Dufy *La Pêche* printed fabric   **89 Raoul Dufy** *Les Moissonneurs* printed fabric

was responsible for the fastness and brilliance of the inks and dyes, Dufy founded a small printing studio. The extremely successful collaboration of Poiret and Dufy came to an end when the excellence of the prints came to the attention of M. Bianchini of the important firm of Bianchini et Ferier who approached Dufy with offers of opportunities for designing far wider than he could obtain with Poiret.

Dufy was tempted by the propositions made by Bianchini but felt that he was under a moral obligation to Poiret who had opened the door to success in this field in the first case. But Poiret who, to quote his own words, was ' too much of a grandee to prevent him from furthering his own career' brought the association to a close and Dufy in 1912 joined the firm of Bianchini et Ferier where he remained under contract until 1930. Already a master of printing from woodblocks, Dufy soon familiarized himself with the techniques of weaving and before long, a series of fabrics designed by him were in production: *Les Arums, Les Paniers Fleuris, Les Fruits, Le Losange de Roses, La Jungle, Longchamps*. The names of the designs are evocative of the period of Art Déco before the advent of the geometrical influences which gave Dufy less scope for his delineations of the good things of life and which probably led to the end of his association with Bianchini — his paintings were increasingly gaining recognition and this too may have influenced him to give up textile design. A four-fold screen, *Paris*, woven in tapestry after a painting by Dufy had been exhibited in the 1925 Exhibition and he also worked in this medium for coverings for furniture, the tapestry being woven by the Beauvais factory, but these tapestries were less interesting from the point of view of design than his printed toiles and woven damasks, being essentially woollen versions of his paintings, although executed with extraordinary virtuosity and fidelity to the original paintings.

In some of his fabrics — *Les Moissonneurs, Paris* and *La Pêche* — Dufy used the traditional eighteenth century format of a repeating group of figures in various occupations surrounded by arabesques or foliage and his example was followed by a number of other designers. Robert Mahias designed *Journée Orageuse* and *Mon Chapeau s'envole*, two charming compositions representing groups of people in costumes of 1920 posed in cloudy landscapes separated by garlands of conventionalized flowers; *Sauvagesses* by Drésa had befeathered American Indians in the eighteenth century manner amid garlands and urns of flowers; Paul Véra followed suit with *Saisons, Colombes* and *Les Divinités Champêtres* which he designed for the Compagnie des Arts Français, while from Ruhlmann's studio came a fabric adorned with a conventionalized formal garden with an arbour enclosing a statue. Prints from Poiret's

90 Robert Mahias *Journée Orageuse*
printed cotton

91 Robert Mahias *Mon Chapeau s'envole*
printed cotton, 1922

Atelier Martine, after the break with Dufy, tended to comprise flowers rather loosely drawn in brilliant colours, prints which were described by a contemporary as substituting lively effects of colour for refinement of composition. Foujita, André Groult, Francis Jourdain, and André Mare were other notable designers of printed fabric which did so much to awaken interest in contemporary idioms of ornament among the general public.

One of the most important exhibits in the textile section of the 1925 Exhibition was that of the firm of Rodier with a unique series of woollen fabrics intended for women's dresses. Inspired by the French Colonial exhibits at the Marseilles exhibition held in 1922, they drew upon decorative motifs from the indigenous arts of Cambodia, Annam, Guinea and Equatorial Africa — motifs which were not, however, disposed on the fabric in a conventional manner but were placed in such a way that when the dress was cut out from a length of material the motifs would form perhaps a band of ornament round the skirt hem or a decoration on the bodice and sleeves. Brilliant in colouring, they were enhanced by a plain white, cream or ivory background of soft wool. Each length of material was entrusted to a crafts-man who worked in his own home on a small Jacquard loom, hundreds of out-workers being employed in this way. These individual creations could be made more inexpensively in this manner, for the cost of setting up the complicated large factory looms for each piece would have rendered the finished work prohibitively expensive. These dress lengths of material, with the placing of the motifs arranged in collabor-ation with the couturier, proved so popular that no fewer than 20,000 new designs were produced in a matter of six years. This was in addition to the output of more conventional lengths of dress and furnishing fabrics woven in the usual commercial lengths by Rodier in the geometrical style fashionable in the late 'twenties.

Earlier in the 'twenties the ancient craft of batik was revived in Paris. As there was no way of replacing the craft by machine processes, the output was from small studios and each piece was of an individual design. Briefly the technique consists of covering parts of the fabric with a layer of wax before dyeing — lines or small details being drawn with the narrow spout of a small receptacle containing hot wax. After dyeing, the wax was melted away leaving the original ground colour and this process was repeated for each colour. Batik had been brought from the Dutch East Indies by the artist Thorn Prikker and a department of batik printing had been founded at the Harlem School of Decorative Arts. Madame Pangon, a pupil

92 Drésa *Sauvagesses* printed fabric

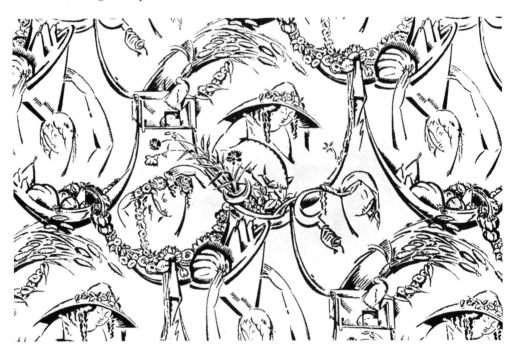

93 Paul Véra *Les Divinités Champêtres* printed fabric, 1922

94 Rodier woven fabric

of the school, brought some of her work to Paris in 1912 and its oriental richness of colour was immediately appreciated by Poiret and other designers whose imaginations were obsessed with the splendours of the Arabian Nights. Batik very soon acquired a French chic which almost obscured its Javanese origins, the limited range of colours — blue, brown, red, yellow and black — being extended into more exotic hues, while the wax masking was deliberately cracked to allow fine lines of colour to penetrate the backgrounds — something regarded as bad workmanship in Java. Batiks from the studios of Madame Pangon and her imitators were used for dresses, curtains, lampshades and cushions but after 1926 the fashion seems to have waned.

Sonia Delaunay

Among the boutiques built along the Pont Alexandre III as part of the 1925 Exhibition, was one described as peerless — that housing the collaboration between Jacques Heim and Sonia Delaunay whose fabrics, known as *simultanés* were designed in accordance with the theories of cubism. Nothing more diametrically opposed to the decorative fantasies of the Art Déco fabrics of Dufy, Séguy or Bénedictus could be imagined than those of Madame Delaunay with their geometrical angular composition of squares, rectangles, triangles and stripes in bold, mainly primary colours.

Sonia and her husband Robert Delaunay had been among the pioneers of cubism and Madame Delaunay's interest in the theory of colour had led her to explore the relationships of colours to each other, the breaking up of a surface by the use of colour and the creation of spatial recessions by the juxtaposition of contrasting shades. Her first effort in putting her theories into practice was in 1911 when she made a coverlet for her small son's cradle in a patchwork of various red, black and ivory fabrics. After many experiments she was able fully to develop her theories of line and colour and by 1914 was producing dresses which were described as ' no longer pieces of material draped according to the current fashion but coherent compositions, living paintings or sculptures using living forms '.

The duration of the 1914-1918 war she spent in Spain, an enforced exile made more difficult by the revolution in her native Russia and the consequent loss of her nationality. She was, however, able to continue working, designing among other things the costumes for a revue in Madrid and in 1918 creating the décor and costumes for Diaghilev's ballet *Cléopâtre*. Her return to Paris in 1921 coincided with an interest in a number of younger designers in cubism or rather a form of geometrical decoration inspired by cubist paintings of the pre-war period. Sonia Delaunay's fabrics with their hard clear-cut designs in vibrant, almost primary, colours were in complete contrast to the current designs inspired by Chinese or Persian sources. To obtain the subtle gradations of colour she needed, Madame Delaunay found it necessary to establish her own printing factory, but before long printing alone was not sufficient adequately to express her ideas. Other forms of surface decoration, embroidery in woollen or metal thread were added to appliqué motifs of fabrics of contrasting textures. Working in conjunction with furriers she created cloaks and coats which had designs of differently coloured furs, ermine combined with mink or astrakhan complementing the design of the fabric of the dress. ' Her luxurious coats in the gradations of colour found in autumn or the delicate mists of morning are fit to be worn by empresses ' wrote a contemporary, ' and she works fur in an intensely personal manner, contrasting the subdued shades of the skins with an astonishing virtuosity; she mingles fur and embroidery, metal threads with wool or silk — but only metal threads of a dull tone — achieving the

95 Sonia Delaunay printed silk

effect of a rich and discreet elegance. She excels in all the accessories of the costume; hats, bags and belts reach an unsurpassable chic under her touch — nothing could be more elegant in their quiet richness than her handbags embroidered in gold with a perfection of finish comparable to that of jewelry. Everything she creates has the authentic touch of a true artist.'

The distribution of Madame Delaunay's fabrics was extremely wide and, owing to the number of film stars who were her clients, they were widely publicized. They proved very much to the taste of a generation surfeited with Art Déco ornament and veering toward the hard angular shapes associated with the machines which were fascinating artists as subject matter and which, through the works of these artists, were influencing the taste of the general public. Madame Delaunay actually painted a motor-car with the same *simultané* designs that she applied to fabrics. Raoul Dufy temporarily abandoned his use of floral motifs in favour of geometrical ones shortly before his break with the firm of Bianchini et Ferier, but these essays in the new style lacked the distinctive touch of his earlier work. Elise Djo-Bourgeois designed geometrical fabrics and carpets to complement the furniture created by her husband — these bore a close resemblance to Sonia Delaunay's designs. One noticeable tendency of these modernist fabrics and carpets was towards a uniformity of design, the limitations of the idiom imposing an anonymous quality which rendered Madame Delaunay's original work almost indistinguishable from that of a host of imitators. Combined with the equally limited range of design possible in the metal furniture with which these textiles were usually associated the result was a period of interior decoration when the work of various decorators shared an impersonal monotony.

Carpets

For obvious reasons very few of the large number of carpets made in the 'twenties have survived intact and the only records of this field of design are to be found in the photographs of interiors and, rarely, the reproduction of designs by a particular artist. The few examples in the Musée des Arts Décoratifs were acquired by the State from exhibitions for which they were specially made and are thus not particularly representative of the type of floor-covering available to the public. Problems of storage and the lack of available space for displaying carpets were factors against their being purchased by museums — any available funds or space being devoted to oriental carpets or important examples of earlier periods of European carpets.

The Studio felt that this state of affairs should be remedied, commenting in 1924 that 'The prominent place occupied by painters in the art world is, no doubt, in some measurement due to the energetic efforts of dealers whose concern it is by judicious publicity and the power of suggestion to keep alive the collector's instinct and, in particular, to encourage the speculative demands which are as considerable a factor in picture dealing as in the realms of commerce. The sale rooms, it is true, encourage competition for the craftsmanship of the past and public collections and acquire huge collections but modern work is almost entirely ignored... it appears to be no-one's concern to see that representative pieces of modern furniture, pottery and metal-work are acquired.'

The highly-polished parquet floors to be found in so many French houses were a source of pride, not to be covered over with large carpets but to be set off by small decorative rugs which enhanced the areas of gleaming wood. In the newer apartment houses being built after the Great War, parquet was less used owing to the world-wide shortage of timber and increasingly plain pile carpets or moquettes were used to cover the concrete or plank floors — small decorative rugs being used to break up the unadorned surface or to lessen wear in one particular spot. Technical advances in carpet weaving enabled designers to abandon the traditional square or rectangular shapes in favour of circles, polygons or ovals which were particularly in favour with Art Déco designers.

The older generation of artists, Maurice Dufrène, Paul Follot, Sue et Mare, Groult and Coudyser were faithful to the pre-war repertoire of Art Déco; baskets and garlands of conventionalized flowers, trellis work, arabesques and medallions, a repertoire echoing the motifs of the eighteenth century but combined with colours inspired by the Russian Ballet and Chinese and Persian art. Rugs from Poiret's Atelier Martine displayed a mass of brilliantly coloured flowers, real and imaginary, clustered with a naturalistic lack of symmetry on dark backgrounds. The Marseilles exhibition of 1922 inspired an interest among designers in the indigenous crafts of the French colonies and the traditional geometrical carpet patterns of Morocco and Algeria were adapted by Da Silva Bruhns in a series of rugs subdued in colouring which harmonized with the new furniture which was simpler in feeling. Bénedictus applied his talents for creating unusual repeat patterns on a small scale to designing moquettes intended for wall to wall carpeting.

The trend toward abstract geometrical designs, which superseded the decorative floral fantasies of Art Déco about 1925, brought new talents to the forefront. For Da Silva Bruhns it was short step from linear design based on North African originals to rugs decorated with bold interlocking shapes relieved by small, judiciously placed motifs. The influence of cubist paintings, and those of Picasso in particular, is evident in these handsome rugs with their deceptively simple but balanced patterns and they undoubtedly had a great influence on carpet design in France and at a later date in England. Rugs by Marion Dorn and McKnight Kauffer belong to the same school of design and one of Da Silva Bruhn's rugs was adapted into an undistinguished version by a British manufacturer at a slightly later date.

After 1926, when modernism had to all intents and purposes trimphed over Art Déco, a rug or carpet was often the only piece of positive decoration used by French designers. Increasingly the fabrics used for curtains and upholstery tended to be devoid of applied pattern or had woven designs in self colours; paintings if used at all were restricted to one example while ornaments were excluded, with the exception of possibly a piece of sculpture; the only note of decorative relief amid the austerity was to be found in the use of boldly patterned and brilliant coloured rugs from the studios of Eileen Gray, Evelyn Wild, Mlle Max Vibert or Jean Lurçat.

96 Da Silva Bruhns design for a carpet, *c.* 1926

97 Atelier Martine pile carpet, prior to 1925

Fashion

' The best men's tailors and shirtmakers may be in London but there is no woman who does not dream of being dressed in Paris. This supremacy in the field of fashion has brought to France not only financial profit but a far-reaching influence overseas. It is right that fashion should take a privileged place among the decorative arts displayed in the Grand Palais, for fashion is essentially an art. A carefully chosen toilette can enhance physical charms, can minimize imperfections, accentuate beauty or camouflage ugliness. Fashion, like all other arts, interprets beauty. An elegant woman in a beautiful dress constitutes a harmony and rhythm of line and colour.' This quotation from the official catalogue of the 1925 Paris Exhibition emphasizes the close relationship which had grown up during the previous decades between women's fashion and interior decoration.

In the previous century the leading dressmaker Worth had designed clothes of great style and beauty for his clients among whom were the Empress Eugénie, and at one time or another every elegant woman in Europe and Russia — from as far away as Madagascar, Queen Ranavalona sent to Worth for all her clothes. As far as fashion was concerned his word was law but at the end of the day's work, racked by migraine brought on by the heavy scents affected by his clients and the patchouli-sodden atmosphere of his showrooms, he would retire to his home — one that was notorious for its vulgarity in an age when exuberance in decoration was the general rule. Edmond de Goncourt, fascinated by its hideousness, hastened home and surrounded by exquisite eighteenth century furniture and pictures, recorded an account in his journal describing the glittering, tinkling nightmare of porcelain and glass, the walls covered with china dinner plates, 25,000 of them, the crystal drops and beads sewn or hung on every possible place, the chairs and settees fringed with rows of glass drops and fringes of crystal, the floors inlaid with mosaics of fragments of cut glass.

A generation later Jacques Doucet was a connoisseur and patron of the arts as well as one of the leaders of fashion from the last decades of the nineteenth century until his death in 1929, maintaining the same fastidious restraint and feeling for quality in his personal surroundings that were to be found in his designs for clothes. One of the first to appreciate the genius of Degas, he was one of the earliest collectors of Impressionist paintings and formed an outstanding collection of eighteenth century furniture, books and drawings; in the early years of the twentieth century he collected Picassos and Negro sculpture, developed an enthusiasm for cubism and decorated his apartment in the contemporary manner with furniture by Legrain and glass by Lalique, as a setting for his collection of modern paintings.

In 1898 a young man, Paul Poiret by name, brought some sketches for Doucet's inspection and was fortunate enough to be engaged as a very junior assistant designer in his dressmaking establishment. Poiret's admiration for Doucet was boundless: ' he was the man I wished to become,' he wrote in his autobiography, ' I did not want any other model in life save him... I would have liked to have been able to make myself in his image.' Poiret went even further than Doucet, for the latter's two identities as couturier and connoiseur were both imbued with the same refined and exquisite taste but they remained separate identities; Poiret, his devoted disciple, combined the two in his life. Interior decorator as well as dressmaker, he surrounded himself with painters, illustrators and designers, commissioning books, fabrics, designs for interiors and by so doing drew into the world of fashion talents which would otherwise have remained outside it. So too did another great couturier, Jeanne Lanvin, although not to the extent and range of Poiret.

The career of Paul Iribe, an extremely talented decorative artist, was furthered by his collaboration with Poiret on *Les Robes de Paul Poiret* a luxury volume publish-

98 Fashion plate, 1923
Dress left by **Paul Poiret**, dress right by **Molyneux**

99 Black velvet hat, 1919

ed in 1908 and intended partly as 'a tribute to all the great ladies of the world' partly as a collector's item of the future but mostly as a piece of indirect advertising. By 1912 Iribe was in such demand that *Comœdia Illustre* — a publication with a very small advertising section — had six drawings signed by Iribe, mostly reproduced in full colour and advertising such products as scent and lingerie, an indication of the new trend on the part of advertisers to employ the services of artists. A subsequent volume *Les Choses de Poiret* published in 1911 brought the attention of the public to the work of Georges Lepape, adding another name to the growing number of young and talented artists who were finding new opportunities in the worlds of fashion and interior decoration. The *Gazette du Bon Ton* founded by Lucien Vogel appeared from 1912 until 1925 with a break of some years during the war. Conceived on a lavish scale and printed on thick, expensive paper it was designed with taste and refinement. Seven couturiers, Redfern, Cheruit, Doeuillet, Lanvin, Worth, Poiret and Doucet were described in a note as the collaborators — which may have been an indication of financial support on their part — and each month one of their creations was featured in a colour plate from drawings by Benito, Pierre Brissaud, André Marty, Drian, Georges Lepape, Raoul Dufy or Boutet de Monval. Paul Iribe does not seem to have been invited to contribute but a disagreement with the irascible Paul Poiret (rumours had appeared in print that Poiret's models were really designed by Iribe and Marie Laurencin) probably prevented this. The *Gazette du Bon Ton* was exclusively devoted to fashion but an equally lavish portfolio magazine *Les Feuillets d'Art* appeared in May 1919 with articles of a more general artistic interest and again this offered opportunities to all those artists already mentioned. It may be said that the brilliant and imaginatively designed covers for *Vogue, House and Garden*, and *Harper's Bazaar*, which appeared until the late 'thirties (now, alas, replaced by repetitive and monotonous photographs of models) and the tradition of fashion drawing by artists had their origins in Poiret's two volumes.

The 1914-1918 war imperilled the position of Paris as the supreme arbiter of fashion throughout the world. Within a very few days of the declaration of war in August 1914 most of the big fashion houses had closed at least temporarily if not for the duration of the struggle, and their delivery vans were pressed into service as part of a private ambulance unit organized by Misia Sert, the wife of the Spanish painter. Poiret was among the first to be conscripted but before departing for the Front he found time to design a uniform for Jean Cocteau who was acting as Madame Sert's assistant. The appeals of the French Government to keep their businesses going as long as possible were useless as one couturier after another, faced with the conscription of most of their male staff and almost total disappearance of their clientele were forced to close their doors. Lady Duff Gordon who worked under the name 'Lucille' recounts in her memoirs the gloom of Paris in the early days of the war; how for the first time in a century the women of Paris, horrified by the enormous casualty lists of the first months, no longer cared what they wore; and how, deserted by her clients, her staff leaving to work in munition factories, she was forced to close the Paris branch of 'Lucille'.

By the middle of 1915 an optimistic reaction had set in. Part of France was still occupied by the German Forces but in spite of this the editor of the *Gazette du Bon Ton* affirmed that as France had escaped from the greatest peril and now certain victory lay ahead, an interest in more frivolous matters had awakened or as he lyrically expressed it 'feminine coquetry was giving the hint of a delicious smile'. The San Francisco Exhibition of 1915 gave several Parisian couturiers — mostly women or those too old to be conscripted into the armed forces — the opportunity

100 Worth chiffon tea-gown, 1919

101 Doeuillet velvet evening wrap, 1919

of reaffirming French eminence in fashion design. Beer, Callot, Cheruit, Doeuillet, Doucet, Jenny, Lanvin, Martial et Armand, Paquin, Premet and Worth exhibited some sixty creations as well as hats, bags, shoes, and other accessories — the dresses displayed on the wax figures designed by Pierre Imans. A special edition of the *Gazette du Bon Ton* recorded the importance of the occasion to French haute couture in drawings by Valentine Gross (later Valentine Hugo), Georges Lepape, Georges Barbier and Drian — drawings which show the radical changes in line which had occurred between the collections of 1913 and those of the following years.

The long clinging dresses for both day and evening wear, high-waisted and reminiscent of the Empire style mingled with the orient of the Russian Ballet, which had dominated the style in the pre-war years had been swept away to be replaced by others which, it was claimed, reflected the martial spirit of the times and the practical necessities of daily life in wartime. The waist descended abruptly from a line immediately under the breasts to its natural position while the floor-length

102 Benito cover for
Vogue, 1922

103 Paul Iribe paper fan from the
Château de Madrid, 1914

tight draped skirts rose to just above the ankles and became enormously full, resulting in a complete change of silhouette. These full skirts, reaching crinoline proportions in the more extreme cases, were, it was said, a practical solution to the problems involved in the virtual disappearance of automobiles and other means of transport and gave women the freedom to walk. The collars of dresses rose to ear-level, often completely concealing the neck to the chin. The emphasis on the full skirts was made complete by reducing the size of hats which were sometimes of a military nature or decorated with one upstanding tall feather or wing. Evening dresses, on the other hand, were rather conservative, as the occasions for their wear were few but these, too, were ankle length and the skirts were less voluminous than those decreed for day wear. Intended for exhibition purposes and designed to make an impact, this collection was more what couturiers wished women to wear than what was actually worn by more than a tiny proportion of women and was conceived in an optimism which was to be dissipated in the remaining years of the war which continued, as is the way with wars, far longer than the most pessimistic could imagine.

Returning to Paris in 1918 after a profitable sojourn in America where she had busily occupied herself beautifying the American woman both on and off the stage, Lucille found the city almost unrecognizably drab, shabby and dispirited in spite of the hectic gaiety which had reigned during war years when it was invaded by Allied soldiers desperately seeking forgetfulness from the horrors of the trenches. For the majority of people life was hard and penurious, prices rising and the franc falling to nearly half its pre-war value. In sharp contrast to the 'New Poor' — an expression which was to become only too familiar in the 'twenties — were the war profiteers whose displays of tasteless extravagance caused them to be hated by all except those tradesmen who found themselves dependant upon their patronage.

Faced with the demands for extravagant clothes from the wives of French, English and American war profiteers on the one hand and on the other an acute shortage of materials and labour, skilled and unskilled, such dressmakers as were able to reopen their houses were hard pressed to maintain their former creative activity. The textile industry upon which they depended entirely had almost closed down in war years either from damage to the factories in the north of France or due to the lack of orders from couturiers, while those that remained had been turned over to the manufacture of materials for uniforms or war supplies. Frantic efforts under Government sponsorship were made to reorganize an industry upon which so much of the country's financial security rested, but there was inevitably a hiatus during which little new material was available and the only fabrics available were rapidly dissipated hoards of pre-war luxury quality. Milliners, embroiderers, furriers, tailors, every kind of skilled worker were at a premium until new craftsmen could be trained and the cost in labour alone of the elaborate showy dresses in demand rose to exorbitant heights.

The end of the war found the fashion houses in a state of confusion where design was concerned. Some were pinning their hopes on a return to the styles of the pre-war years while others were beginning to face the unwelcome fact that life had changed for ever and that there was no going back to the leisurely years before the holocaust. The greater part of their old clientele had vanished to be replaced by those whose taste, as one writer delicately put it, needed educating. From necessity, women had learned to enjoy a certain freedom of movement and while they were anxious, perhaps as never before, to look as attractive as possible, they were not prepared to sacrifice any of their new liberty. The new conditions of post-war life made a new conception of fashion imperative. The elaborate and impractical fashions of the pre-war years were anachronistic in a world of harsher realities.

But this new conception had not been formulated in 1919 and it was to be several years before fashion settled down into some uniformity or resolved itself into a general style common to all couturiers. The oriental influence could still be seen in harem skirts — but for evening wear only — as well as skirts swathed and cut into panniers at the hips or skirts in two or three gathered tiers similiar to those on Minoan statuettes. Some houses showed skirts full enough to require hoops for support but the general hemline was raised to the mid-calf for day wear; many evening dresses were this length but in general they were longer and often touched the floor. The waistline was still in the normal place and the bodices of dresses were unfitted, with the bust flat as it was to remain for the rest of the decade. There was a curious paradox (noticeable in the illustrated catalogues of the Royal Academy and the Paris Salon) in that, in their portraits by Flora Lion, F. Cadogan Cowper, W. de Glenh, Richard Jack, Soloman J. Soloman, Jean Gabriel Doumergue and other fashionable portrait painters, women are invariably depicted as being flat-chested, while paintings and sculpture of nudes show them as having normal breasts.

Some fashion writers were extremely censorious about the general effect of nudity of the time. The fronts of evening dresses were cut down to the waist but filled in to the minimum with a ' modesty ' and the large armholes, narrow shoulder straps and backs also cut down to the waist provided grounds for their disapproval. Day dresses were cut with narrow shoulders and tight or batwing sleeves and had ' despite the Bolsheviks ' Russian collars or the Medici collars favoured by film vamps. Knitted woollen jumpers, shapeless and with V-necks fastened by two large woollen pom-poms on strings, were easy to make and extremely popular especially when accompanied by large woollen pancake berets. Tailor-mades, a pre-war innovation, were increasingly popular as an all-purpose daytime outfit, especially with some women who had grown used to wearing some kind of uniform during the war, and several couturiers tried to launch a fashion for copies of man's dinner jackets worn with a plain skirt. These were adopted by a small number of advanced ladies but were avoided by the majority of women whose only desire was to look as feminine as possible. Russian boots were worn with tailor-mades and these made several reappearances at times during the 'twenties.

An interesting feature of the advertising sections of the fashion magazines is that the advertisements for wigs, toupées and transformations far outnumber those for beauty preparations, the production of these being still in its infancy. Little beyond powder, toilet waters and scent was apparently available, with the exception of Helena Rubinstein's ' Crème Valaze ', but it was evident that other aids to beauty could be obtained discreetly, as mention of painted faces and rouged lips is common. The hair was still worn long by the great majority of women and the fashionable shape for the head was one resembling a Phrygian bonnet, a bun or knot of hair being fastened high at the back of the head leaving the nape exposed. The advertisements usually depict the hair as being elaborately waved but many women, to avoid the trouble and expense of permanent waving, wore their hair straight and drawn back from the forehead. Of necessity the hats had to have large crowns to accommodate all this hair and were drawn right down to the eyebrows, completely concealing the forehead. This practice continued until 1929 when the forehead was once more exposed; in some cases fashion drawings showed hats which completely concealed the eyes. As this combined with a brief fashion for coat-collars which concealed the chin and mouth, the recognition of female friends in the street must have been extremely difficult in 1929. Bandeaux were worn with evening dresses and these also were placed immediately above the eyebrows; these almost compulsory ornaments were made of the same material as the dress, or of lace, or artificial fuschia and

104 **Velvet** tea-gown, 1922   105 **Paul Poiret**
walking costume, 1923   106 **Drécoll** white woollen dress
trimmed with beaver, 1923

nasturtiums, with similar girdles and trailing ends. Belts of ancient coins or monkey-fur were considered particularly elegant.

Gradually some new materials were beginning to make their appearance as the textile industry was reorganized and production increased. Wool stockinette and charmeuse were two of these and both enjoyed a lasting popularity. The favourite fur — still a rarity — was mole, which was worked into elaborate designs '... Parisian furriers are making the life of the Scotch mole very hard these days '; second in favour being skunk which combined with black satin was considered particularly suitable for more youthful wearers.

An acknowledgement that life in peace time had its difficulties was a significant item in a fashion magazine making suggestions for dressing on a limited income. The realization was coming to the couturiers that however extravagant their new-rich clients might be there were not enough of them to offset the rising costs of wages and materials and in spite of the French Government's efforts to help by encouraging the bank to give extended overdrafts to the fashion industry many of the large houses were finding themselves in financial difficulties. The only hope lay in extending their markets by adventuring into lower income groups. Paul Poiret on his American lecture tour had been dismayed to find the amount of financial loss incurred to him and to other couturiers by the extensive pirating of designs by whole-

salers in the United States and, what was even worse, these mass-produced versions were sold under his name. The efforts to combat these dishonest practices had the effect of bringing the fashion houses into a mutual defensive alliance. 1920 saw little change in the general trend of fashion — skirts became a little shorter but the bust remained nonexistent and the waist normal; it was really a year when the milliners took the leading role.

Reboux, Lewis (a veteran who had designed hats for La Belle Otéro and Cléo de Mérode in the 'nineties), Evelyn Varon, Georgette, Alice and Maria Guy vied with each other in producing more and more versions of matador hats, harlequin hats, hats of aigrettes or glycerined ostrich plumes, all with very large crowns and covered with lace veils. Hair was being worn in coils over the ears but a number of women were daringly cutting off their hair, adding a false bun or chignon in the evening to hold the Spanish combs which were very popular.

A fashion which could be indulged in, however limited the income, was for long strings of beads which were worn in the normal way, hanging down the back, over one shoulder and even wound round the leg; beads in all materials from ivory and jade, real and artificial pearls to painted wood. An ivory bangle worn just above the elbow with a chiffon handkerchief was essential — not the massive barbaric African armlets fashionable a few years later, but narrow ones. Good quality gloves and shoes were still hard to come by and expensive but were elaborate. Moleskin remained the favourite fur but other skins were becoming available and broadtail ermine, sable, opossum, civet cat, musk-rat and Spanish goat were listed as suitable trimmings for the brocade evening cloaks being worn. The rich glowing colours so favoured by Bakst and Poiret, colours made familiar by the Ballets Russes before the war, were still predominant — canary yellow, bright blue, jade, cerise, cyclamen, henna and red. Much space was devoted in all the fashion periodicals in these years to describing and illustrating tea-gowns, a garment originally intended to be worn in the country between the hours when hunting kit was removed and the time to dress for a late dinner. Although women of means still changed their clothes several times a day to suit the occasion this habit was dying out even among those who had the leisure to do so, but the tea-gown remained as a becoming and useful garment which could be worn for informal dinners. Loose and comfortable, its function was to be decorative and it could be independent of the rules regarding the length of skirt, expressing the personality of its wearer in the choice of materials, chiffon, velvet, lamé, brocade and trimming, chinchilla borders, fringes, artificial flowers or embroidery. One firm in London, Dove, specialized in the designing of tea-gowns.

In 1921 articles began to appear in fashion periodicals with advice on dressing on a limited income — an acknowledgement that such things existed and had to be faced. The day of the paper pattern was at hand, not so much for the home dress-maker, for a great many of the patterns were extremely complicated, as for the ' little women round the corner' whose professional skill could interpret them for the benefit of the smart woman of limited means. Little change in the general line of fashion occurred during this year except that skirts lengthened and hats grew larger still. The longer skirts were circular in cut, the waist remained normal. Pearls suddenly were the only jewelry permissible. The growing participation of women in various sports was reflected in the articles on fashion, and bathing dresses of silk jersey were featured. The lack of any drastic change during this year was rather like a holding of breath before the rapid variations characteristic of the rest of the decade.

1922 saw the hemlines of day dresses dropping almost to the ankle while evening dresses touched the floor. The waist as suddenly moved down to the level of the hips. The emphasis was on vertical lines accentuated by the use of tunics of striped

107 Erté design for an evening dress, 1922

108 **Jeanne Lanvin** rose taffeta evening dress, 1920
109 **Martial et Armand** taffeta afternoon dress, 1921
110 Embroidered jersey bathing dress, 1921
111 **Paul Poiret** top coat in cloth and fur, 1923

fabric, the stripes being used vertically, or by vertical pleats and tucks, and this emphasis is reflected in the fashion drawings in which the models begin more and more to be depicted as improbably elongated. The bateau neckline, straight from one shoulder to the other, appeared on most models. The only alternative to this slim line was a full skirt gathered at the hips which appeared in taffeta dresses for day and evening — these full skirts were inspired by an exhibition of costume of the Second Empire held in Paris in June 1922. Hats with large brims were worn to balance the full skirts, but with narrower dresses hats were smaller and had tall crowns which accentuated the vertical feeling.

The craze for silver which swept the different aspects of interior decoration and was also applied to dress and accessories — a craze which was to last for several years — had its beginning in 1922. Inexplicable as most crazes are, this enthusiasm for silver in preference to gold was shown in the widespread use of silver patterned brocades, silver tissue, silver embroideries, silver lace, silver lamé, silver fringes — usually combined with backgrounds of black, coral or jade green. Silver, platinum or nickel jewelry was preferred to gold and necklaces of crystal, ivory or onyx were worn.

The vertical emphasis continued in 1923, the skirt length being still at ankle length even for day wear and the waistline around the hips — in some cases the waist was unmarked, a hint of the chemise dresses to come. Hats were still small with high crowns although by the end of the year the cloche was putting in a tentative appearance. Several houses tried to introduce new lines, mostly echoes of period styles but these were not well received. A return to the Empire line with a waistline immediately under the bust was no more successful than a nostalgic attempt to revive the bustle of the 1880s by placing large bows or draperies at the rear of the currently fashionable straight-up-and-down silhouette. More acceptable was the use of Egyptian motifs

112 **Cheruit** orange glacé taffeta evening dress, 1927
113 **Madeleine et Madeleine** black crêpe and diamanté evening dress, 1921
114 **Jenny** black and white evening dress, 1921
115 **Fortuny** pleated satin tea-gown, 1926

on printed silks, embroideries or jewelry which were inspired by the discovery in the previous year of the tomb of Tutankhamen, the richness of whose beautiful but decadent tomb furniture and ornaments had astonished the world.

French couturiers were beginning to realize the value of introducing sudden changes of line or length of skirt in their collections. The number of extremely rich women who could afford to dress in an individual and highly personal manner was rapidly diminishing and mass-production of comparatively inexpensive clothes was becoming highly organized, especially in America. Women in the United States and Europe were leading more active lives and, apart from a few, had less time and certainly less money to devote to elaborate fashions. The new American market, where unlike their European sisters women had no objection to wearing almost identical outfits, providing that they were according to the latest Paris fashions, was a factor which could not be ignored. Poiret, the arch-advocate of glamorous but rather impractical fashions, realized that his position as the leading designer in Paris was becoming precarious and set out on a long and arduous tour of the United States, where accompanied by mannequins displaying his latest creations, he lectured, flattered and insulted his female audiences at a fee of a thousand dollars a lecture.

The winter of 1923 witnessed the appearance, in all the collections, of the cloche hat, covering the head completely from the eyebrows to the nape of the neck and, unless the head was to appear disproportionately large, necessitating bobbed hair. The disarrangment of a carefully coiffed head of hair by the removal of the hat caused much anoyance in theatres and cinemas when requests were made by those seated behind a large hat, demanding its removal; requests which often led to angry scenes. There was, in addition, an etiquette to be followed regarding hats at the popular thé-dansants. An unattached male looking for a partner could ask a girl not wearing a hat for a dance without previously having been introduced as she would be a professional dancing partner — although he was warned not to offer a silver tip, nothing less than a note was considered proper. On the other hand, he could not speak to a girl wearing a hat without a formal introduction for she like himself would be a visitor to the hotel or ballroom and in this case, of course, a tip of any value would have been an insult.

Long hair dressed in a bun or 'ear-phones' distorted the shape of the new cloches and so women with one accord cut off their hair, the more prudent keeping a switch of their shorn locks for evening wear or in case the fashion suddenly changed. Almost overnight wigmakers faced ruin as more and more women discovered the convenience of short hair. After bobbing came the shingle — the hair cut as short as a man's at the back and involving much trouble with the shaving of short hairs — and finally the Eton crop, extremely becoming to those with well-shaped heads but its wearers taking the risk of suspicions of lesbianism. Long earrings of jade, onyx or crystal were worn with the new short hair and some went so far as to wear odd earrings, one large pearl stud, the other a long elaborate earring.

Make-up used during the day had achieved a degree of respectability, although some wearers tended to apply it with more enthusiasm than art. 'Your mouth can be painted', wrote the Hon. Mrs John Fortescue with some disapproval, 'in any shade from pink to magenta... you can gain the effect of all shades in the course of a meal and end with your natural pink lips. This will afford an interesting spectacle to onlookers, who can bet on the chances of painter's colic.' The use of lipstick was no longer considered fast or indicative of a life of sin. The 'cupid's bow' mouth made its appearance, and the examples of Mae Murray (an ex-Follies beauty who had had an undistinguished career in the films since 1916 before achieving world fame as the 'girl with the bee-stung mouth') of Colleen Moore, Clara Bow — the 'It' girl — and other film stars set women in Europe and America painting their mouths, regardless of their original shape, into exaggeratedly small heart shapes which would have been the envy of any Japanese geisha.

By this time, the French textile industry was fully recovered from the war and was producing endless varieties of new weaves — generally referred to in advertisements as 'novelty fabrics' — which went under such names as 'pompom marcollaine', 'piquellaflor' or 'djersatchine' to name only a few. These were, in the main, variations on already established favorite materials, Rodier was producing the beautiful woollens with motifs inspired by African and Near Eastern art while the still-popular silver was introduced into serge and other materials for day wear as well as into innumerable variations on metallic fabrics for evening wear.

The autumn collections of 1923 gave indications of the tendency to shorter skirts which followed in the next year; the hemline rising to mid-calf. The waistline had completely disappeared and most dresses consisted of a tube of material with a straight neckline, falling in an unbroken line from shoulder to hem, the bust being flattened and the hips being suppressed by corsets as much as possible. This silhouette was topped by the cloche which, according to fashion photographs and drawings, came so far down over the eyes as completely to conceal them. It is interesting to note that in spite of the growing tendency for fashions to be affected by Hollywood (much publicity being devoted to the wardrobes of such popular stars as Irene Rich, Pola Negri or Gloria Swanson) the cloche hat as worn in films showed more of the forehead than was the current fashion. The sudden changes of fashion were apt to take Hollywood by suprise and producers were disinclined to let their stars adopt any smart but dating craze as by the time the film was finally released the clothes of the star might be hopelessly démodé. The summer months of 1923 had seen many articles and illustrations concerning the correct wear for holidays

116 **Louiseboulanger** top coat in black velvet with fox border, 1926
117 **Yvonne** afternoon dress in red georgette, 1924
118 **Suzanne Talbot** gold and white evening dress, 1925

on the Riviera but at the same time there were indications that all the readers of *Vogue* were not of the leisured class in the growing number of articles intended for the 'nouvelles pauvres' — the rendering of the new poor into French presumably giving the unfortunate reader a feeling of chic. Advice was given as to the best method of arranging one's wardrobe to keep up appearances or as it was expressed more bluntly elsewhere 'to be poor and look poor is to be damned poor' — and to give the impression of having a larger selection of clothes than was actually the case, by having several matching or toning outfits of skirts, blouses and coats and ringing the changes by wearing different combinations of these. The paper-pattern industry was booming as more and more of the 'nouvelles pauvres', more from necessity than choice, were turning to home dressmaking. This was not always an easy feat, as the pattern-makers had not yet mastered the art of simplifying the patterns, and some were sold that would have taxed the skill of professional dressmakers and were more like jigsaw puzzles than dress patterns.

1925 saw skirts rising to unprecedented heights although they were not to reach their highest point until the following year. The starkly tubular fashions of the previous season were more varied although the waistless shift, with no indication of the presence of bust or hips, was still predominant. As well as being shorter, skirts tended to be fuller, either by means of pleats or a circular cut, the extra fullness appearing under a tunic effect which ended at the hips. Several couturiers showed dresses with skirts dipping at the back and in general the shorter skirts were worn by younger women with not always happy results as the shiny silk or artificial silk stockings of the time did little to help legs which were less than perfect. The cloche, like the dresses, ceased to be plain and was ornamented by

119 Black velvet hat with artificial rose, 1921
120 Black satin hat with feathered appliqué, 1923
121 **Marthe Regnier** hat designed for
Gloria Swanson, 1925
122 **Siégal**, display figure, Paris Exhibition, 1925

brooches of onyx, crystal or of coral or by decorations of pleats or tucks. Gloria Swanson's hats, made by Marthe Regnier for one of her trousseaux, received a great amount of attention in the press while the autumn collections featured hats covered in plumage and built up at the back with swathes of material.

The Paris Exhibition of 1925 gave considerable prominence to the creations of the leading dressmakers in two sections devoted to fashion — ' Le Pavillon d'Elégance ' and a large area of ' Le Grand Palais '. Jenny, Doeuillet, Jeanne Lanvin, Paquin, Adrienne Lemonnier, Worth, Callot Soeurs, Vionnet, Patou and Lelong were the main exhibitors in both sections and furs by Max Heim, Golstein, Sonia Delaunay, and Chanel were on display with gloves, stockings, shoes, hats and underwear.

A large section was devoted to underwear. Poiret also exhibited but his main display was elsewhere — on the three barges moored on the banks of the Seine and to which reference is made elsewhere. Unfortunately the total effect was found by a number of critics to be extremely disappointing. The various couturiers, anxious to outdo each other in novelty and ingenuity of design, produced dresses which admittedly were masterpieces of cut, workmanship and skill in elaborate embroidery — dresses which individually were beautiful — but which when grouped together gave an impression of eccentricity and even ugliness.

An unlooked for success, however, was the figures on which the dresses were displayed. For the first time in an exhibition of dresses, the conventional realistic dummies with carefully coiffed real hair, simpering smiles and glass eyes were replaced by stylized, semi-naturalistic figures with sculptured hair. Some of these were painted in flesh tones with eyes, mouths and hair indicated by colour but the majority were painted gold, silver, olive green and even black. Modelled by Vigneau-

123 Design for an advertisement, 1924

Siégal these new conceptions were highly praised after the first shock of suprise, although the black figure which displayed a black and white evening dress by Madeleine Vionnet was described as 'quelque peu troublant'. The stands in 'Le Pavillon d'Elégance' were decorated by Madame Lanvin with the collaboration of the sculptor Armand Rateau and Jean Dunand, both of whom worked on Madame Lanvin's own house, but Jean Dunand's beautiful lacquer screens and the elegant bronze furniture of Rateau surprisingly met with little appreciation, one writer dismissing Madame Lanvin's work with the comment 'One must thank her that it was no worse'

The impression seems to have grown up that skirts were knee-length and even shorter during the decade between 1920 and 1930 and the words 'the 'twenties' conjures up in most minds a vision of a girl in a bead-fringed, extremely short dress hectically dancing the Charleston and manipulating a long cigarette holder at the same time. It was, in fact, a fashion of comparatively brief duration and was not general to all collections. The extreme height, according to fashion periodicals, was just below the knee — a height unprecedented in European fashion but the impact of these short skirts was so great and the controversy in the press so intense that they have intended to overshadow, in retrospect, other fashions of the decade. Not all the couturiers showed skirts of this length. Some ignored the trend completely and designed skirts for day wear which were raised no higher than the mid-calf while others compromised with skirts dipping at the sides, back or front or with handkerchief skirts and the uneven hemlines (especially those of the handkerchief skirts) produced an odd and untidy look when worn with a knee-length coat or evening wrap — an effect which does not seem to have worried anyone at the

124 Vanity case c. 1925

time. The waist reappeared but had slipped down to the hips and a bloused bodice was caught in at tightly moulded hips. In general the trend was to a simplicity of line and cut and even the elaborately embroidered evening dresses were the exception. Hats, still drawn down to the eyebrows, were becoming softer and higher.

In spite of the economic stresses, the growing need for women to earn their living by taking jobs and a growing necessity for a more practical approach to life in general, the tea-gown (a relic of a more affluent and relaxed age) was still considered a necessary garment in any smart woman's wardrobe and fashion magazines gave up considerable space to examples of tea-gowns by Dove or Fortuny despite the fact that younger and more dashing women were taking to pyjamas (usually of satin with appliqués of Chinese embroidery) for evening as well as beach wear. Men's clothing was increasingly being adapted for women, as several writers commented with faint disapproval; navy blue blazers being worn with pleated skirts at the seaside, and shirts, complete with ties and cufflinks accompanying the tailor-mades which were cut on the lines of a man's suit — except of course for the trousers which were replaced by a plain skirt. Anny of Paris specialized in making dinner jackets for women which again were exact copies of those worn by men and these were simply ornamented by a feather carnation of deep Chanel red worn in the buttonhole.

The old-fashioned attitude that jewelry was only permissible — apart from grand occasions — if small and real and then for preference only in the evening was changing; under the influence of Chanel more and more women were taking to costume jewelry bold and heavy in design and frankly artificial — intended as decoration and not as imitations of real jewelry. Another fashion of the year was to wear one pearl on a thin gold chain which should be accompanied by at least twelve thin gold bracelets.

In the post-war years there were few dressmakers in London, apart from Lucille and Handley-Seymour, who were capable of comparison in style and originality of design with the French couturiers and any woman of means with aspirations to being considered well-dressed had to obtain her clothes either directly from Paris or from shops like Jay's, Marshall and Snelgrove or Debenham and Freebody where versions of original French models were on sale. Hence there was a potential market for original models, near to Paris, which offered possibilities for exploitation and by opening workrooms in London, French dressmakers could circumvent the heavy customs duties which bedevilled this and similiar luxury trades. One of the first to interest himself in these possibilities was Paul Poiret who had realized while on his combined lecture tour and sales-drive in the United States how many women were craving to buy his clothes. He had discovered too that unscrupulous wholesalers in the United States had attached his name to shoddy, badly designed models or were pirating his designs outright. A branch in London would have many advantages:

125 Drécoll afternoon dress in crêpe, 1926

the avoidance of customs duties, some measure of control over the dishonesties of wholesalers (although such practices were minimal in England compared to the United States) and, it was hoped, an increase in the number of English patrons. In 1924 advertisements were appearing in English fashion magazines announcing the opening of a London branch of Paul Poiret at No. 10 Albemarle Street, and simultaneously a branch, under the same roof, of his decorating business, L'Atelier Martine, for the sale of Poiret cushions, Poiret dolls and Poiret colour schemes. What was meant by 'colour schemes' was not explained but as unattributed photographs of wallpapers and textiles known from French sources to be products of Martine were illustrated in English periodicals around this time it was probably these that were referred to.

Paris in the 'twenties had a large population of Russian refugees from the Bolsheviks. Most of them were penniless but some who had managed to smuggle jewels or some sort of capital out of Russia were opening shops for the sale of Czarist relics and antiques. A number, usually en route for the United States and marriages with American heiresses, were becoming more titled and aristocratic the further east they travelled, but undeniably aristocratic and far from penniless were the Prince and Princess Youssoupoff who opened a dress shop in the rue Duphot. The Prince, whose part in the assassination of Rasputin is too well known to bear repetition, had always been interested in women's clothes and had, in fact, often worn them in public when younger in his native Russia and in Paris; with such success that it is recorded that he attracted the attention of Edward VII from whose overtures he had to beat a hasty retreat to avoid a scandal. This inclination he put to practical use under the name 'Irfé' and though it has not been possible to trace any of his designs, he enjoyed considerable success, opening a branch at Le Touquet and another in London in 1926 at 42 Berkeley Street, where 'robes, manteaux et frivolités' were on sale. In the same year Chanel extended her activities to London, selling the tailored casual outfits which were becoming identified with her name.

The extremely short skirts continued to be worn in 1927, although the autumn collection showed determined efforts to popularize the uneven hemlines which forecast the general dropping of the hemline. Day dresses, still belted around the hips, were simple or decorated at the most with details such as horizontal tucks, seaming or bias-cut panels and were often made of a combination of fabrics matching in colour, charmalaine and georgette for instance. Over these were worn coats with narrow sleeves and of the same colour and material as the dress. Dress, coat and accessories such as bag, gloves and hat were carefully matched in colour to give a monotone effect; if the dress was in one of the small geometrical prints currently fashionable, the 'rest of the ensemble would be in the darkest colour of the print. This alliance of a simple dress with either an oval or a V-neck worn with a cloche hat of more elaborate shape than those of previous seasons and a simply cut coat became a daytime uniform considered suitable for all occasions. Such an outfit was advertised by Woollands as 'Expressing good taste and refinement... favourable in price for Ascot, Hurlingham, Ranelagh, Goodwood and all social events attended by My Lady of Mayfair'. The bold and frankly false jewelry which Chanel had popularized was designed in sets consisting of clips for the hat and neckline, earrings, bracelets and for evening wear an important necklace. Evening dresses were in the same prints used for day dresses but one designer, Jane Regny, decorated evening dresses with large cubist flowers. An evening version of the day coat was worn with long and short dresses, Chanel edging her chiffon coats with bands of chrysanthemum petals of the same material. Extremely short hair was no longer fashionable.

126 Benito fashion drawing, 1928

1928 saw the determined effort on the part of Paris to abandon the boyish silhouette and the tubular dresses. Floating panels and bias-cut draperies from the hips had given the appearance of length to evening dresses but there was a resistance on the part of women to the lengthening of day dresses for they had become used to the freedom given by the short skirts and were loath to give it up. One way to give the appearance of length to the skirt was to push the waistline up nearer to its natural position, at the same time adding an extra inch to the length. The straight dresses became old-fashioned when compared with those shown in the collections, dresses intricately cut with swathed panels and intricate seaming. The bust was still

127 Bias-cut satin evening dress

flattened and the hips tightly corseted to accentuate the flaring lines of the skirt hems. Satin, and particularly white or ivory satin, was a favourite material for evening dresses, its soft texture lending itself ideally to the bias cut which was necessary for the draped effects. Similarly morocain or satin-backed crêpe was used for day dresses. Small geometrical prints and polka-dots were the alternatives to the plain textured fabrics and were produced in innumerable varieties. Hats with brims, often wired, were still worn to cover the forehead and during the summer small toques covered with artificial flowers were fashionable. Evening dresses were accompanied by gold and silver wigs and short jackets of the same material as the dress but covered in paillettes. Furs were flat in texture, caracul, breitschwantz, moiré lamb, astrakhan or Hudson seal... an exception being silver fox which was to be a favourite for some twenty years to come.

The lack of unanimity among the Paris houses as to the length of skirts resulted in what the press christened 'fever-chart hemlines'. In the main, the day length remained an inch or two below the knee, though many designers were making attempts to lower the hemline — or at least to give the appearance of doing so by means of detached panels at the sides or back and by dropping the hemline of afternoon dresses at the back — creating an effect known as the peacock skirt. For evening wear any length was permissible, including the Spanish-inspired ruffled dresses of Maggy Rouff. Poiret, as individual as ever but no longer the most influential designer, showed long skirts to the mid-calf for day wear and evening gowns that trailed on the floor, while at the same time Callot was designing short evening dresses. In spite of this marked lack of agreement as to the length, the indications were that skirts were becoming longer and that the waistline was returning to its natural position. The real innovation of the year was that hats, for the first time for many years, were lifted off the face to reveal the forehead. The brims introduced the previous year had become larger and were folded back over the head resulting in what was variously called the dustman's hat or the fisherman's hat. If brimless, the cloche had developed into an extended skull-cap of felt or velvet, folded or pleated into assymetrical shapes and often with a frill at the back resembling that on Victorian bonnets. To ease the shock of so many exposed foreheads, small eye-veils were worn. These small and head-hugging hats were necessary when worn with the huge collars of fur, silver, red or cross fox, which were featured in all the collections of the winter of 1929, collars which often continued as a border round the hem of the coat, which was invariably three-quarter length.

Poiret's mid-calf length skirts on day dresses in the winter collection of 1929 showed that the master had not lost his touch, for the following year all the other designers took the plunge and ended the period of indecision by dropping their hemlines with one accord to this level, while evening dresses touched the floor. They were also in agreement about the waistline which was once again in its natural position. The slim, elongated line which was the result, caused much anguish to fashion writers who complained that it could only be worn by those of their readers with perfect figures but these complaints were no deterrent either to the designers or to women in general. However, the flattened bustline still remained and the necklines of dresses were softened with bias-cut cowl collars or scarf necklines, which were common to both day and evening wear. Evening capes of ring velvet were much in evidence, short, tight and with cape sleeves, worn hugged round the hips, and in a colour setting off the flowered chiffon dresses over which they were worn. The dominant colours for the year were black and white combined with white fox. The cloche hat had disappeared in favour of the felt or fabric skull-caps with interest on one side and the forehead exposed.

Jewelry

Jewelry tends to fall into one of three categories, precious, decorative or costume. Precious jewelry, that is valuable ornaments of gold or platinum set with diamonds, sapphires or rubies (chemically the same stone but differing in colour) and emeralds, tends to be conservative in design, capable of being handed down from one generation to another without appearing old fashioned or, if it should appear démodé, is reset in a more acceptable pattern. It is worth doing this because the value of the stones is far greater than that of the workmanship involved and consequently, except in cases of historic jewelry, it is rare to find valuable jewelry in an extreme of fashion still in existence. Thus it is probable that extremely few pieces of jewelry designed in the 'twenties and incorporating valuable stones are still in existence, for the majority have long since been broken up and the gems reset in later fashions. Valuable jewelry is also more likely to be stolen and reduced to its component parts for disposal by the thieves.

Decorative jewelry of semi-precious stones set in silver or gold has a longer life as the metal and stones are of small value in themselves, the value lying usually in the workmanship and beauty of the design. Costume jewelry, frankly imitation in every respect, is made to satisfy a passing fashion, usually mass-produced and once broken is hardly worth the cost of repairing. The majority of jewelry of which a record was made or of which actual examples exist is of the decorative type, as might be expected, and the difference between the English and the French versions is marked. Englishwomen of the 'twenties had conservative tastes in jewelry and those who could afford such ornaments preferred something small but good — a string of pearls and possibly a regimental brooch in diamonds. The hard chic of French decorative jewelry was considered showy and even slightly 'fast'. Possibly because an apprenticeship in the making of jewelry was of long duration and the lessons in design absorbed in those formative years have a lingering influence, the craftworkers of the 'twenties in England showed strong influences of the Arts and Crafts School in their work.

The jewelry of Sybil Dunlop, Carrie Francis and others was strikingly similar to that of Kate Eadie, made before the war, and this in turn has affinities with the products of the Guild of Handicrafts. Echoes of Italian Renaissance ornaments can be seen and the use of elaborate floral settings and decorated chains in silver and the use of coloured semi-precious stones, chrysoprase, chalcedony, peridot, amethyst, moonstone or topaz, give the craft jewelry of the 1920s a close family resemblance. Much in favour with the artistically-minded rather than the conservative Englishwomen this jewelry is a world apart from the bold decorative work made in Paris, where the influence of Lalique could be still seen, although he had abdicated from his position as the leading jewelry designer some twenty years before.

The pre-war absorption with the oriental ballets of Diaghilev had brought about a fashion for jewelry made of onyx and crystal, coral and jade — and this fashion survived after the war, becoming still stronger. Black onyx and black enamel was used as a foil for Chinese motifs of carved coral and marcasite, not only for earrings, brooches and bracelets but for cigarette cases, vanity cases and even ashtrays.

128 Silver cigarette case with geometrical design in yellow and blue enamel; silver cigarette box with a panel of modernist design; silver cigarette box decorated in blue and black enamel; black enamel cigarette case: lapel watch; black enamel cigarette box; silver cigarette case with a Chinese design; yellow enamel cigarette case

129 Cigarette box of Chinese design; cigarette case in three shades of gold; silver cigarette box decorated with orange enamel and eggshell lacquer; cigarette case with modernist design; silver ashtray with Chinese motif; cigarette case of modernist design

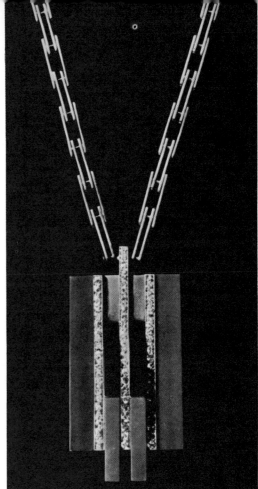

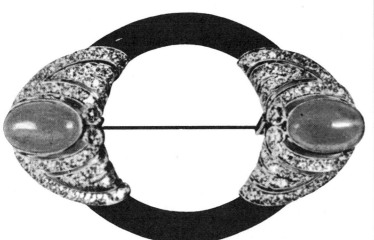

130 **Boucheron** brooch in onyx,
cabochon jade and diamonds

131 **Fouquet** pendant in semi-precious
stones and diamonds

Earrings were extremely long, to set off the hair tightly drawn to a large knot at
the back of the head and consisted of several links, round or square, of paste or
onyx from which depended large drops of jade or coral. Circular brooches of rings
of onyx had symmetrical motifs of jade or coral surrounded by brilliants. An ornament
which remained fashionable throughout the decade was the 'négligé' or pendant
hanging from a long thin chain. This could take the form of a tassel of seed pearls
surmounted by an onyx and diamond motif or alternatively a design of 'a brilliant
orange Mexican fire-opal suspended from a similar stone above and connected by
a pillar of black onyx with a green cornelian circle having dainty leaves embracing
it ' — a description of one designed by B.J.Tully in 1925 *

Ivory was popular, either in the form of painted and engraved pendants and earrings by Clément Mère, combined with onyx and jade or, during the mid-'twenties, in
the heavy and barbaric cylindrical African bracelets favoured by Nancy Cunard.

Georges Barbier, the current fashionable designer and illustrator, designed a collection of jewelry for Cartier in 1919 and, although no details are available, a drawing, *Laissez-moi-seule* by Barbier, published in a 1919 issue of *Feuillets d'Art* indicates
the probable tendencies of the collection; anklets of pearls linked to bracelets,
breastplates of pearls and a helmet, fastened under the chin and concealing the
hair, decorated with pearls and pheasant feathers. This extravagance of jewelry was
in line with the fantasy and elaboration of evening dress in the post-war years.

The motifs of Art Déco, baskets of conventionalized flowers, traceries of leaves,
octagonal panels, carved glass plaques of the type introduced originally by Lalique
can all be found in French jewelry in the years before 1925 when Art Déco was finally
vanquished by the angularities of modernism. The taste for Chinese motifs, however,
survived and so did that for black accents of onyx or enamel, enhancing coral and
brilliants or marcasite. Pairs of clips in geometrical designs — sometimes able to
be joined together to form a brooch, brooches in the form of arrows to decorate
the cloche hats which were almost a uniform, and wide flexible bracelets of dia-

* *The Studio* June 1925.

132 P. Turin bronze commemorative medal for the Paris Exhibition, 1925

monds or paste, worn from wrist to elbow, were innovations. The vocabulary of the diamond trade was enriched with new terms — 'batons', 'trapezes' and 'calibrés' — as new variations on the traditional forms of cutting were invented to add to the brilliance and lustre of gemstones. The settings became lighter, developing into frameworks resembling girders in miniature.

As the decade advanced women gradually led more active lives, partly from necessity, economic reasons forcing many to work for their living, and partly from choice, indulging in more strenuous forms of sport. The comparative simplicity of the chemise dresses worn during the day demanded some form of ornament and inexpensive costume jewelry was designed and made in increasing quantities. The pearl choker, a string of frankly artificial pearls worn at the base of the neck — an echo of a seventeenth century fashion — became almost as much of a uniform item as the cloche hat and not only were the fake pearls of improbable size but they were also made in improbable colours. A belt, if worn, had buckles which were often well designed although made of inexpensive materials and many of these have survived where rings, necklaces and earrings have disappeared. 'A new spirit has entered into the designing of jewelry. Whereas the craftsman used to seek only an effective setting for a precious stone as a thing in itself, he now adapts a jewel to a wearer's personality and costume, and since dress tends to become more and more practical so likewise does jewelry' wrote an anonymous correspondent in 1928 *, and mention is made in the same article of the importance of the dressmaker in the design of jewelry. Chanel is generally credited with having made artificial jewelry permissible for wear during the day. A new factor was the invention of artificial materials like rhodoid, galalithe and nacrolague, substances from which ornaments in a variety of colours could be mass-produced and sold at prices within the reach of all, and their lack of value ensured their popularity as fashionable adornments which could be discarded when the fashion died.

* *The Times Weekly Edition* 10 May 1928.

133 Paul Poiret sketch designs for costumes for the revue *Vogue* 1922

Paul Poiret

The name of Paul Poiret is almost synonymous with Art Déco. Versatility was a characteristic of many of the designers working in the Art Nouveau style and in the style of its successor, Art Déco, but Poiret extended his creative energies into more fields than any of his contemporaries. During the pre-war years and after the Armistice until the later 'twenties, Poiret was the most celebrated dressmaker in Paris; he launched a series of exotic scents under the name ' La Parfumerie Rosine ', called after one of his daughters; he founded a school of interior decoration named after another daughter, Martine, and this was later extended into a business firm; his costume balls, prior to the outbreak of war, were noted for their beauty and magnificence; his entertainments at L'Oasis from 1919 onwards featured the most celebrated stars of the theatre and music hall; he published books and periodicals and he was a generous, if somewhat tetchy, patron of many young artists including Erté.

The son of a cloth merchant of comfortable means, he was spoiled from an early age by his parents and three adoring elder sisters from whom he became estranged in later years. A love of the theatre led to an interest in theatrical décor and costumes, particularly the latter, and when he was old enough to be apprenticed to an umbrella-maker he made miniature dresses out of scraps of fabric left over from covering parasols. Madame Cheruit, the most elegant dressmaker in Paris, gave him practical encouragement by buying some of his early sketches, but the decisive influence in his life was Jacques Doucet, who employed him as a full-time designer. The ambition of the young Poiret was to model himself as much as possible upon Doucet and to follow in his footsteps as a famous couturier, a connoisseur of the arts and a polished and sophisticated man of the world. Doucet sent him to the best tailor in Paris; arranged for him to augment his earnings by a discreet relationship with a rich American soprano and pointed out to him the advantages to be gained by acquiring a young mistress who would economically maintain his small apartment and at the same time be a model for his creations. From Doucet he learned the grand manner and the confidence that would later enable him to outface the arrogance of the Comtesse de Greffuhle or subdue a Rothschild.

After his military service and a short period working at Worth, he opened his own establishment and was able to give full rein to his ideas of dressing women. For a beginning he declared war on the corset. For decades women had compressed and distorted their bodies with stays of iron, whalebone and elastic which enclosed them from armpits to knees. One actress was so intent on maintaining her fashionable shape that she had a special clause in all her contracts to the effect that she should never be required to sit during a performance as her tight corsets made it a physical impossibility to bend in any direction. Elegant women were at first loath to adopt the freedom he advocated but as the ' Poiret Look' became fashionable they changed their minds. But having freed women in one direction he proceeded to shackle them by decreeing the hobble skirt. It was, however, in adapting oriental fashions for Parisiennes, that he became celebrated.

It is generally assumed that the oriental splendours of Serge Diaghilev's ballet *She-herazade* with its fabulous décor by Léon Bakst were the inspiration for a wave of enthusiasm for exotic decorations which swept first Paris and later the whole of western Europe after the ballet was presented in 1908. In fact this nostalgia for a legendary Persia and Arabia had its beginnings around 1900 in Paris and was the result of the publication of Dr Mardrus' translations into French of *The Thousand and One Nights' Entertainments* — these appeared between 1896 and 1904. Edmund Dulac had in fact completed his illustrations for an English edition of *The Arabian*

Nights by 1906 and these were exhibited in London at the Leicester Galleries in 1907. *Sheherazade* was not so much the originator as the culmination of the oriental craze. Poiret himself, while rather grudgingly acknowledging the talents of Bakst, became extremely irritated if it was implied that he had been influenced by Bakst in the least degree. He maintained that from childhood he had always been fascinated by the beauty of Persian art and that while on a visit to London to supervise the making of the costumes he had designed for Alice Delysia in *Afgar* presented by Charles B. Cochran, he had been so impressed by a collection of Indian turbans in the Victoria and Albert Museum that he had sent to Paris for his head milliner who created versions of them for his next collection.

Poiret records in his autobiography that even as a child he had been entranced as much by scents as by colour and tells of his disappointment when the flowers he steeped in water failed to turn into scent but produced rather nasty smells. Later in life strong perfumes became a necessary adjunct to the oriental dresses which were his trade mark. He was probably the first couturier to develop the sale of scent, hitherto only sold by the manufacturers. Chemists worked under his close supervision to concoct the heady scents he demanded and in addition to the usual ingredients of musk, civet and ambergris, he claimed to have originated the use of balsam and geranium, the latter giving a distinctive character to his famous scent 'Borgia'. Exotic names suggesting forbidden sensations were given to his scents - 'L'Etrange Fleur', 'Le Fruit Défendu' and 'Nuit de Chine' - while one perfume even had a double name 'Antinéa ou Au Fond de la Mer'. An advertisement for this, consisting of a line-drawing by Mario Simon and featuring an extremely nude lady lying on the seabed, appeared in *Feuillets d'Art* for 1919. These Rosine scents were contained in flasks and boxes designed in the Atelier Martine, the glass bottles being blown in Murano under Poiret's supervision.

134 Atelier Martine *Eucalyptus* fabric

135 **Atelier Martine** bathroom

Paul Poiret's studied avoidance of mentioning any definite dates in his autobiography does not make the task of establishing the chronology of his creative activities particularly easy, but from cross-references it can be established that sometime in 1909 he paid a visit to Germany and Austria which made a great impression upon him. This was not his first visit to Germany, where it would appear he had been on several occasions to give lectures on fashion: each time he was struck by the intimate knowledge of Parisian life shown by his German hosts and could not help contrasting this with the complete ignorance of German art and developments in the German theatre displayed by his compatriots. On this occasion, however, he was introduced to the work of the Wiener Werkstatte in Vienna. This organization, founded in 1906 under the direction of Joseph Hoffmann and Koloman Moser, was an offshoot of the Vienna Secession — an anti-academic association of painters, sculptors and designers founded in 1897. Austria was in the throes of a renaissance of architecture, painting and the decorative arts and proved fertile soil for the ideas from foreign sources. Charles Rennie Mackintosh found that his highly individual style of architecture and ornament met with immediate recognition and praise in Vienna — in sharp contrast to the indifference with which it had been received elsewhere in Europe, outside Scotland. The work of English designers, Ashbee, Voysey and Baillie Scott, the paintings of the Glasgow School and those of Brangwyn (this prolific artist was represented in practically every exhibition of modern art in Europe around the turn of the century) combined to ferment a dissatisfaction in artistic circles in Vienna. In 1898 there had been a drastic reorganization of the Kunstgewebescholen — the Imperial Arts and Crafts School — which led to the resignation of its former directors and the appointment in May 1899 of Baron von Myrbach as director. Joseph Hoffmann, then twenty-nine, was in charge of the department of architecture and Professor Kolo Moser made the head of the decorative and applied arts section.

Ample financial support came from the Government, supplemented by allowances from local bodies and generous travelling scholarships donated by the Archduke Rainer and Baron Albert Rothschild. Exhibitions of the work of students, one-third of whom were women, were held every two years.

By 1909, when Poiret paid his visit to the school, a highly individual idiom of decoration had evolved. With nature as the sole source of inspiration, the naturalistic tendencies of the early days had become *Stylisierung* with the treatment of floral motifs derived from fuchsias, roses, pinks, forget-me-nots, chestnut leaves and blossoms and maple leaves in the manner of peasant art. Hoffmann's own work was

136 Atelier Martine
  silver lacquer chest,
  1923

137 Atelier Martine private dining room on the *Ile-de-France*, 1927

138 Atelier Martine bedroom, prior to 1925

distinguished by an extreme elegance of shape and a sophisticated placing of ornament showing affinities with the decorative work of Charles Rennie Mackintosh and, at the same time, anticipating the work of the modernist designers of twenty years later. Hoffmann's decorations for the Villa Stoclet impressed Poiret, although he disapproved of the submission of the owners to the designer in allowing him to impose his taste. Similarly he condemned the rigid disciplines imposed upon the students of art schools in Germany and Austria and in particular those of the Wiener Werkstatte where the pupils were made to dissect flowers and by a rearrangement of the petals create new geometrical floral forms.

Poiret's success as a couturier, his reputation as an organizer of *bals parés* and his work in the theatre were not enough to satisfy his creative urges and in consequence the examples of the schools he had visited in Germany and Austria gave him the idea of founding a School of Decorative Art where young children could be taught in an entirely new way with none of the rules or restrictions of official schools. In

139 Metal buckles

140 Atelier Martine paper fan

1912 the 'Atelier Martine' — named after one of his daughters — came into being. The pupils — all girls — were all about twelve years of age, had finished their schooling and were drawn from the working class. Setting apart a number of rooms in his house, Poiret set them to draw from nature and to express themselves in a free and spontaneous way unhampered by any academic preconceptions. Presumably his intention was to train children who, from their age and background, were least likely to have had any acquaintance with any form of artistic expression approved by society and could apply innocent minds to the creative act. Poiret declared himself more than satisfied with the results of his experiment for, after being taken on visits to zoos and conservatories, his pupils provided him with masses of drawings and designs which could be used as a basis for the collection of stuffs and tissues that influenced all fashion and the whole of the decorative art in the great days of the Maison Martine which was established a few months after.

Unfortunately Poiret, in his autobiography, gives no practical details of the Atelier Martine. Whether his pupils were paid, the attitude of their parents to the venture, how long they stayed or how new pupils were recruited — these questions are not touched upon and it is certain that on the transformation of the school into the Maison Martine some more professional talent or advice must have been enlisted to deal with the practical problems that would inevitably arise. Henri and Maurice Monnet are described as being associated with the designing side and, of course, Raoul Dufy's fabric designs were used in some of the decorative schemes.

How long the Maison Martine lasted as a commercial venture is difficult to discern. Poiret's career was dogged by financial crises attributable, according to his version, to the dishonesty of his series of accountants and book-keepers. He was still showing collections in 1929, a full description of his autumn collection was described in *Harper's Bazaar* for October of that year and a volume dealing with French decoration published in 1930 mentions the concern in the present tense, from which the conclusion must be drawn that it had somehow survived the bankruptcy to which Poiret refers in his autobiography. 'L'Atelier Martine produced interiors alive with brilliant contrasting colors. There is color everywhere, in the drapes, the rugs, the accessories and even the furniture itself is painted in contrasting shades or in gold or silver' wrote the American author Katherine Morrison Kahle in *Modern French Decoration* and continued with a comment which could not have pleased Poiret, 'This atelier seems more in sympathy with the modern German school than with the French'. A typical Martine interior was that exhibited in 1919 in the Salon d'Automne, the walls decorated in orange, gold and black, the furniture painted white, mattresses on the floor 'for smoking opium' and low tables in the Chinese manner. A characteristic touch was the use of silk tassels instead of the more conventional wood or metal handles for drawers of cupboards.

Poiret's wide acquaintance among the painters of the day led to his collaborating with some who later became well known. He was a patron of Tsugouharu Foujita; fourteen paintings, representing regattas, race courses, balls and casinos, painted by Dufy were incorporated in the decorations of one of Poiret's three barges moored on the Seine which formed part of the 1925 Paris Exhibition but much to Poiret's chagrin, Dufy's paintings were almost completely ignored by the public although his textile designs and woodcuts were widely praised: Fauconnet replaced Iribe and Lepape by designing the invitations to the 'Fêtes de Bacchus' given by Poiret in 1912 and later contributing painted panels for the Martine decorations for Jacques Doucet and for the apartment of Madame Spinelly, the music-hall artist. Still later, the fashion artist Mario Simon designed advertisements for Rosine scent, in 1919, and decorated some furniture for the Martine firm.

THE
DECORATIVE
ARTS
IN ENGLAND
AND AMERICA

Interior decoration

Shirley Wainwright, writing in *The Studio Year Book of Decorative Art* for 1923, commented 'In relation to the treatment of interiors the state of affairs in this country is less satisfactory. This in part is due no doubt to the system prevailing whereby the householder turns for advice and inspiration to the salesman in a furnishing establishment — too often, it is feared, to an individual without any real qualification to direct the aesthetic treatment of the home. This casual method of dealing with a highly technical and difficult subject is remarkable, but no alternative practice seems to be contemplated except in a few cases where an architect is commissioned to decorate or an expert called in to advise.'

It is perhaps difficult, in the 1960s when there are so many interior decorators of varying degrees of professionalism and talent, to realize that forty years ago the interior decorator, in the sense of an individual capitalizing on his or her personal taste and working in direct contact with a client, hardly existed at all. The owner of a new house or on a lesser scale, somebody wanting to redecorate one or two rooms, had no alternative but to patronize one of the big firms in London if they where not prepared to rely upon their own taste. These firms, some of whom are still in existence although shorn of most of their former influence and reputation, were equipped with drawing offices, building and decorating departments, cabinet-making factories and were equipped to carry out any kind of upholstery work. If more work was available than they were able to cope with themselves, and this was often the case, they could call upon other smaller firms to subcontract part of or even all of a job. In addition to work in private houses, they were capable of fulfilling large contracts for the redecoration of hotels, liners, embassies and often palaces in different parts of the world. Their showrooms usually contained a selection of antique furniture and a much larger section of reproduction furniture, made by skilled craftsmen and often indistinguishable from genuine antiques. This reproductive skill was necessary when, for instance, a client needed a number of dining chairs to add to an antique set, a copy of an existing antique commode or sidetable to balance a decorative scheme. In many cases these reproductions, made with great skill at a time when labour was still comparatively cheap, were indistinguishable from antique furniture. They were sold by some of the less scrupulous firms as genuine pieces and one firm, at least, made complete panelled rooms in pine or oak which were given false pedigrees and sold for what were high prices at that time. This practice had been current since the early years of the century and the number of 'antiques' in existence must have increased many times over, both in England and in France where the making of reproductions was carried out with even greater skill.

With a vested interest in period furniture, these firms had a very good reason for discouraging any tendencies on the part of their clients to favour modern trends. In fairness it must be said that the majority of designers and salesmen connected with the larger establishments believed genuinely that English furniture design stopped with Sheraton and Hepplewhite, while Victorian furniture and objects were not even considered.

The current interest in eighteenth century furniture was confined to that made before 1780 and very occasionally as late as 1800 — and it is interesting to note that even today, in the 'sixties, these are the limiting dates used in many books on glass, silver or porcelain. Anything later was considered unworthy of any interest — an attitude which took in anything of what is loosely called the Regency period. Regency furniture was regarded as decidedly inferior versions of designs by Sheraton and bordering on Victorian vulgarity — unsuitable for anything but domestic use.

When the contents of Deepdene were auctioned during the Great War, Edward Knoblock, the successful American author of *Kismet*, *My Lady's Dress* and many

141 Advertisement for Hamptons of Pall Mall, 1926

other plays, had been able to purchase the most important piece of furniture designed by Thomas Hope for practically nothing.

Plentiful and cheap, owing to the lack of any serious demand, Regency furniture was not considered worthwhile as an investment for the future for it was thought inconceivable that it could ever become valuable. At most it was sound furniture which would 'last another lifetime' and could be regarded as 'parlour furniture for the middle classes'. This opinion expressed in 1920 was unaffected by a series of articles three years later in *House and Garden* which attempted to awaken a keener interest in the Regency style, and another ten years or so were to pass before its cheapness made it attractive to those in search of something different — helped by the musical play *Conversation Piece* set in Regency Brighton. Photographs of interiors in the 'twenties occasionally show a piece of Regency furniture, usually chairs, but these were pieces with family associations rather than collectors' items. Although E. G. Halton had recorded, as early as 1911, that the Arts and Crafts movement 'which gave promise of such great things had almost ceased to exist' — the Arts and Crafts Society continued to exhibit until well into the 'twenties albeit to the profound indifference of critics and public alike. Nevertheless the medieval flavour of so much of the Arts and Crafts products had captured the imagination of the public even if their work failed to rouse any enthusiasm, and furniture and interior decoration in the years before and after the Great War was strongly influenced by the Tudor and Jacobean periods, a trend which continued through the 1920s. Contemporary periodicals show that the majority of houses, and certainly those built in rural areas, were of stone or half-timbering. The interiors were either completely panelled or with dados of oak panelling surmounted by plaster walls with Elizabethan style motifs, the plaster ceilings being versions of historic models. The furniture was of the same period and generally included, for comfort, a version of the Knole settee and armchairs in red jaspé velvet and panels of 'antique' Italian appliqué embroidery. In the more straitened economic times of the 1930s the elaborate oak panelling and plasterwork were less used but versions of Elizabethan furniture, adapted as three piece suites, dining room suites and cocktail cabinets, mass-produced and highly varnished, were popular until comparatively recently. Alternatives to the Tudor style were a bastard Queen Anne cum early Georgian and to a lesser extent a version of late eighteenth century, combining Hepplewhite, Sheraton and Adam.

142 Advertisement for Gill and Reigate, 1923

A conventional house of the period would have a drawing room panelled in pine stripped of paint and waxed. Originally painted, eighteenth century pine panelling, whether genuine or reproduction, was quite ruthlessly stripped of its paint to expose the wood, in spite of the fact that the grain of the wood was not particularly interesting and the reason for this may have been to demonstrate that the room was panelled throughout with real wood and that the same effect had not been obtained by applying mouldings to a plaster wall and that the carved decorations were of wood and not cast in plaster. This practice of stripping pine panelling became so generally accepted that the panelled rooms in museums were also deprived of their paintwork to conform to the prevailing fashion. The degree of elaboration was in proportion to the means of the owner, extreme prosperity being indicated by carved over-doors, window surrounds, swags of carved flowers on the chimney piece, semi-circular alcoves with carved shells for a display of Chelsea or Derby porcelain, while the panel mouldings and chair rails themselves were ornamented with carved egg and dart motifs and acanthus leaves. The chimney piece would enclose a painting, either a flower piece in the manner of van Huysum or an architectural view, often a Venetian scene which might have come from the studios of Canaletto or Marieschi. Persian rugs covered a parquet floor and mahogany furniture, Georgian and Chippendale, covered in damask, brocade or brocatelle, was placed symmetrically around the room. Invariable features would be a pair of wing chairs covered in real or imitation gros point, a Charles II cabinet in black or, for preference, red lacquer with an elaborate carved and gilded stand (this was often adapted as a cocktail cabinet) and a walnut cabriole card table which opened to reveal a top embroidered with a *trompe l'œil* design of playing cards. The illumination came from a chandelier and wall brackets of brass or gilt wood containing electric candles with brocade shades and table lamps of Chinese vases with silk lampshades elaborately painted with the motifs on the vase. The dining room would be panelled in oak from the floor to within a foot or so of the ceiling, the lower panels in linenfold with strapwork designs in relief on the horizontal panels running round the top of the walls. An intricate plaster frieze and ceiling completed the scheme while the fireplace was of stone in a flattened Tudor arch or featured delft tiles surrounding a more modern and functional grate. More Persian rugs on the polished floor, a long trestle table and chairs covered in leather or in red velvet to match the curtains masking the beaded panes of the windows. In a smaller house in the country the oak panelling would be simpler or replaced by beams interspersed between rough plaster panels, the fireplace would be of brick, the curtains of a chintz reproduction of Elizabethan embroidery while narrow shelves around the top of the walls would support plates of blue and white willow pattern china. These decorative schemes were interchangeable, of course, and the dining room could be Georgian and the drawing room Tudor. Bedrooms were hardly featured in periodicals; it was evidently regarded as being too great an intrusion into privacy to allow photographers to record such a personal part of the house.

Unless the designer was prepared to set up business on his own, and in the uncertain economic conditions prevailing during the immediate post-war period this
was not something lightly undertaken, he was only too glad to get a job in the studio
of a big firm even though it meant the stifling of any originality he might have and
that his tasks would be confined to doing sketches of furniture, elaborate detailed
watercolour drawings of proposals for interiors and making the full-size working
drawings of furniture and panelling. Without capital or a private income there were
few if any opportunities for the designer with originality even if he could find a
sufficiently large market for his work.

Few, if any, of the staffs of the drawing offices of English firms of decorators had
any formal training in design in general and, in spite of the current preoccupation
with period styles, even fewer had any knowledge of the decorative arts of other
European countries such as France or Italy. There were, in fact, no schools of interior
decoration as such and knowledge of furniture design was acquired by joining a
drawing office as a junior at a very low wage. These junior draughtsmen — whose
work was confined to making tracings of designs for future reference until they
became sufficiently skilled to be entrusted with less important original work, were
expected to attend evening classes in drawing or architecture at the Regent Street
Polytechnic or similiar institution. There was little encouragement for a draughtsman
to extend the range of his knowledge. The working hours of 9 am to 6 pm and 9 am to
1 pm on Saturdays, with an hour off for lunch, gave no opportunity for visiting
museums or the rare exhibition of current design: drawing offices usually had a small
reference library, the mainstay of which was *The Dictionary of English Furniture* by
McQuoid and Edwards, Strange's *English Furniture of the 18th Century* (the companion volume on French furniture was generally present but rarely used) and a
selection of books concerned with architectural details of panelling, fireplaces and
mouldings. As the average wage of a draughtsman was about seven pounds ten a week,
few could afford current periodicals on interior design — not that there were
many, for *House and Garden* only appeared irregularly during the 1920s and often
only as a supplement to *Vogue, The Architectural Review* only occasionally gave any
space to interior decorative schemes and *The Studio* was regarded as being something
only artists read. Thus the great majority of the decoration of hotels, ships and
private houses and the furniture which accompanied these decorative schemes was the
work of draughtsmen working in a narrow enclosed world, not only ignorant of but
indifferent to architecture, paintings and sculpture, not to mention the work of their
more enlightened contemporaries on the Continent. They could produce elaborate
drawings of interiors, technically accomplished and showing every last detail of the
period ornament, drawings which could take anything up to a fortnight to finish, they
could spend days refining by the thickness of a pencil line the curve on the full-size
drawing of a cabriole leg or the oval top for a dining table but they were, with few
exceptions, incapable of drawing a human figure. Should the client insist, in spite
of the persuasions of the salesman, on having a modern interior, then and then only
would an attempt be made to find photographs of contemporary work from which a
version of modernism would be concocted.

Concern about the lack of organized training in interior decoration was expressed
in a letter to *The Studio* from F. V. Villey in which he states that in a lecture which
he gave to the National Society of Art Masters, he mentioned the question of interior
decoration as a special subject and as far as he could ascertain it was not taught in
any schools of art — various branches of the decorative arts, furniture design, textile
design, mural painting being treated as separate subjects. 'We have, of course,
many decorating firms who are working on commercial lines and producing admir-

able work particularly, I think, in the great period styles ', he continued. ' I imagine that their designers and workers obtain their training in the business and not in art schools. Moreover, such commercial concerns are hardly in a position to undertake work of an experimental nature. Some of the exhibits of foreign countries at the recent Exhibition of Decorative Arts at Paris seemed to suggest that more research and experiment in decoration upon modern lines was taking place abroad than in this country. ' Similar opinions were expressed by George Sheringham: ' We now have a huge industry to support which is engaged in manufacturing brilliantly clever reproductions of " antiques " of all kinds which the public of course cannot distinguish from genuine old works of art... In France they think differently and their arts flourish because, for some reason, their governments... think, and have always thought the encouragement of art a matter of national importance. '

Simple Furnishing and Arrangement and *Simple Schemes for Decoration* by John Gloag, which were published in the early 1920s, both contain practical advice based on experience. ' It is the day of the amateur decorator and the exact, conventional and, too often, dull treatments provided by professionals will be replaced by individualism in decoration and in the houses of the future we shall see rooms that are extremely clever in the restraint and subtlety of their colouring ', wrote Mr Gloag, who spoke more prophetically than he could have realized. A great many of these amateur decorators, forced through lack of money to employ a professional firm, produced, as might be expected, interior decorations of considerable hideousness as a result of a lack of knowledge combined with an excess of enthusiasm. There were some, however, who achieved results sufficiently pleasing for their friends to ask them for help and advice. In spite of the witticism that a woman is either happily married or an interior decorator, it became accepted that a woman could become a professional interior decorator and by so doing add to her income without actually descending to becoming a tradesman — trade still being regarded as something to be lived down if it were in the family. Many of these would-be interior decorators whose assets consisted solely of that mythical attribute ' natural good taste ' or ' an eye for colour ', soon ended in the bankruptcy courts. But the more ruthless and determined, helped by society connections, a good accountant and, equally important, a talented draughtsman, survived into the 1930s and provided opportunities and, in many cases, a clientele, for another generation of interior decorators.

Elsie de Wolfe

The pioneer woman decorator, whose proud claim it also was to be the first woman director in America, was Elsie de Wolfe, later Lady Mendl. After a career of some years in the theatre — a career during which she played leading roles in spite of her complete lack of experience, and was more noted for her dresses than the range of her acting ability — she decided at the persuasion of her friends and in particular of Elizabeth Marbury, with whom she shared an apartment, to try her hand at interior decoration. Miss Marbury had a wide knowledge of French art and culture and was instrumental in guiding the taste in furniture and decoration of her young friend.

In 1904 Elsie de Wolfe rented a small office in New York, sent out printed cards and in a very short time was inundated with orders. In may seem inexplicable that a completely inexperienced young woman should be so much in demand but as Miss de Wolfe remarked in her autobiography ' friends have always been one of my great assets ' and this was no exaggeration for when she required financial backing offers of help came from such respected names as Vanderbilt, Kahn, Bache, and as she remarks, ' many others whose names, alas, I can no longer recall '. Her first test as a decorator on a large scale came in 1905 when her name was put forward to design the interiors of the new Colony Club, in itself an innovation as the first women's club in New York and founded by a committee of extremely rich women. This feminine stronghold, run on the lines of men's clubs, was designed by the architect Stanford White and it was he who defended the choice of Elsie de Wolfe as decorator when the members of the committee, with the exception of the redoubtable Miss Marbury and two other supporters, with one accord disapproved of the idea of giving such an important commission to an inexperienced woman. Halfway through the work she lost this ally in her battles with the members of the committee when Stanford White was murdered in public by a jealous husband. In spite of all her setbacks Elsie de Wolfe completed the job and the Colony Club was opened to its members.

The success of the decorations was instantaneous and from that moment her career as a decorator was assured. The use of chintz as loose covers for the chairs and settees throughout the building, an idea new to America and adopted from the the country houses in England and France which Elsie de Wolfe had visited in company with Miss Marbury, was an innovation acclaimed in spite of the misgivings of the committee and it earned for the decorator the sobriquet of ' The Chintz Lady '. The trellised room, based on the *treillage* garden architecture of France, was the first in America and was much praised, giving as it did an impression of coolness in the sweltering summer heat of New York in the days before air conditioning. The sensation made by the simplicity, clean colours and restraint of the Colony Club was all the greater at a time when interior decoration in America was a matter of over ornamentation and over furnishing. A subsequent commission, one of the many resulting from the success of the Colony Club, was a larger version of the by now famous trellis room, the walls white with green trellis designs based on eighteenth century French models, settees eight feet long covered with white velvet striped with designs of green leaves, a black and white marble floor and at each end of the settee a zinc lined jardinière holding flowering trees.

A commission from the millionaire Henry Frick to decorate and advise in the purchase of furniture for an entire floor of his mansion on Fifth Avenue, not only made Elsie de Wolfe a comparatively wealthy woman but gave her an insight into the dealings connected with the purchasing of the finest quality French furniture of the eighteenth century; an enlightening experience which led her to express the opinion that no more than a quarter of the eighteenth century French furniture in America was genuine.

Endowed with enormous vitality, Elsie de Wolfe established a position as the doyenne of interior decorators although faced with strong competition in later years from Lady Colefax, Syrie Maugham, Mrs Mann, the Marchesse Malacreda and in the United States, Rose Cumming, Marian Hall and Elsie Cobb Wilson. With clientele drawn from the rich, leisured classes, the work of these decorators of the 'twenties was rarely publicized to the extent that it is today when the photographers from an interior decorating magazine move in as the decorators move out. In the intermittent issues of *House and Garden* in the 1920s, for instance, it is extremely rare to find the name of the owner attached to photographs of interiors. Although all of these decorators no doubt prided themselves that their interiors carried the stamp of individual personality, there was, in fact, a common attitude which gave a family resemblance. The avoidance of the use of contemporary furniture for example; if a piece of furniture was required for which no antique prototype existed, such as a bedside table, then one with a 'period' flavour would be designed to harmonize with the rest of the room — a preference for decorative rather than 'good' furniture, the choice of painted French furniture over inlaid, ormulu encrusted pieces, and the use of light fresh colours, these were to be found in all their interior decorations.

Ronald Fleming

With minor variations, this school of decorating still exists today, carried on by the assistants who have themselves become established decorators. Ronald Fleming for instance, who later worked in association with Mrs Harrington Mann, designed the décor for an apartment in *Vogue* in 1927 which, based on the principles established by Elsie de Wolfe, carried these one step further by the inclusion of contemporary ideas — English eighteenth century armchairs in the Adam style covered in scarlet American cloth, a settee covered in natural holland piped with scarlet, the floor surrounding the *tête-de-nègre* carpet painted scarlet as a contrast to the white stippled distempered walls and the modern paintings 'of the Picasso school'. Combined with these touches of a more modern feeling were Empire side tables and red lacquer furniture, making an ensemble which would not be considered dated forty years later. Ronald Fleming's taste and discrimination combined with a sure sense of colour and an expert knowledge of period styles brought him recognition as one of England's leading decorators in the following decades.

Syrie Maugham

Le Touquet was much favoured by the rich in the 'twenties. One of the attractions was polo, some English players keeping a string of ponies permanently stabled there and going either by air or sea for long weekends. The 'Villa Eliza' owned by Syrie Maugham (wife of Somerset Maugham) was the scene of much entertainment and its decorations, the work of the hostess, were seen by many people and were thus influential in spreading interest in Mrs Maugham's personal style. Described in *House and Garden* in 1927, the drawing room was decorated solely in tones of beige relieved by the peach-coloured silk curtains. Devoid of mouldings, the walls matched the concrete floor, waxed to beige, the latter being almost concealed by beige sheepskins sewn together to make a large carpet. The coverings of the stripped and pickled furniture were also beige as was the material on the settees which were eight feet in length. The dining room was white: with white silk curtains ornamented with a modernist design in sapphire blue. The stripped oak chairs were covered with white leather. The dining table, also of oak, was set with the white porcelain-handled knives and forks, reproductions of early eighteenth century Meissen models, which became a Syrie Maugham trademark. Another innovation throughout the house was the lining of cupboards or wardrobes with hand-printed Italian book-end papers. Mrs Maugham's 'White House' in Chelsea was described at some length in periodicals in 1929. 'An unexpected house, a gay house and a light house' was the comment of a writer in *Harper's Bazaar* and the photographs accompanying the article show the treatment of the music room with its white walls and white satin curtains, white velvet lampshades, white chair covers with flower patterns and the two large decorative camellia bushes with porcelain flowers. Arrangements of white lilies stood on the black grand piano — no solution to the problem of making a piano less cumbrous had been found — and the furniture was a mixture of painted Louis XV bergères, wing chairs and an Italian bureau-bookcase in 'poor-man's lacquer' — 'a decoration of cut-out engravings stuck on a white painted ground and subsequently varnished'

The dining room panelling was pickled and waxed to a honey colour and contrasted with the white brocade curtains. White and gold painted chairs of an early eighteenth century pattern surrounded an oval table, which for the photographs was set with white porcelain on a fillet lace tablecloth. Four crystal candlesticks added to the light from the rock crystal appliqués on the panelling. A corridor was decorated with green and white painted wall hangings and panels of antiqued mirror, which reflected the porcelain birds hanging in rings on the windows, standing on the window ledges and grouped on the two Venetian lacquer commodes and a painted wrought-iron console table.

Colour in post-war rooms

The number of people who were able to afford the services of the big firms of decorators was comparatively small. Outnumbering them were those with considerably reduced incomes as a result of the war and for the guidance of these several books and periodicals dealing with the decoration of the home and domestic matters were published. For these New Poor redecoration was confined to the painting and repapering of those rooms which looked particularly shabby after the privations of the war — work which had to be done by small local builders and decorators. These firms shared the common problems of labour shortages and particularly the lack of skilled craftsmen; so that practical guidance for the amateur decorator was necessary. The idea of the householder doing his own decorating was inadvisable at a time when there were no quick-drying paints and the hanging of wallpaper by means of flour-paste was a hazardous business; the least trace of paste on the surface of the paper leaving an irremovable mark. In any case the shortage of paper was acute for some time after the end of the war and the usual recourse if redecorating had to be done was to paint or distemper.

As a reaction to the drabness of the war years, there was a tendency to the use of strong vivid colours when redecorating and advice about the use of colour was given in periodicals like *Our Homes and Gardens* a monthly magazine published in 1919 by Country Life. In the December issue for 1922 R.H.Wilson dealt with the question of colour in the home and the effect it could have on the occupants. A scarlet room 'would be very stimulating and exciting' but if blue or green cushions and objects were used the red would be augmented to straining point. An orange room 'would affect one as being forceful, aggressive and triumphant, sometimes bitter and sarcastic' while a yellow room, being clear, luminous, shrill and delightful, 'would be the room in which to romp with the children or to have light-hearted fun with your friends'. A green room, still, motionless and placid, would suggest peace and hope, but a yellowish green 'can become sickly and adolescent'. Blue, 'quiet and spiritual', violet 'suggesting old age and shadows', white 'unemotional intellectuality', grey 'neutral' and black which 'would draw you down to your lowest ebb till you feel you would choke if you attempted to utter a single syllable' were other colours considered. Also in 1922, *Simple Schemes for Decoration* by John Gloag gave hints on the use of colour (in less imaginative language than R.H.Wilson) as well as advice on panelling, doors, windows, fireplaces and the decoration of kitchens

143 F.C.Richter *Design for Interior* watercolour drawing, 1915

144 George Sheringham design for music room

145 W.J.Palmer Jones 'Chinese' room *c.* 1920

146 Aschermann Studio scheme for a dining room, prior to 1922

and nurseries. Gloag advocated a return to the decorative harmony of earlier periods for 'perhaps the war has been responsible for the tawdry and semi-barbaric ideals that have crept into decorative work: perhaps war has always exerted this deplorable influence, but whatever path serious decorating may be taking, the fact comes before us that many people are disregarding the professional decorator and doing work for themselves... and themselves instruct the unpretentious builder and house painter... it is the day of the amateur decorator'

Referring to colour, Gloag commented that the schemes of white, ivory and pale cream favoured by the Edwardians had been ousted in favour of more lively hues and his advice about the use of colour is practical and unsensational. Basil Ionides' *Colour and Interior Decoration* published four years later, in 1926, when the post-war shortages of materials had somewhat eased but the economic stresses had, if anything, increased, was illustrated with numerous reproductions of photographs and eight colour plates taken from paintings of interiors by W. Ranken R.I., himself a collector of lacquer furniture which he displayed against glossy black walls.

Basil Ionides was an interior decorator with a successful practice in the late 'twenties and during the subsequent decade, and his professional expertise is reflected in the detailed and exact instructions he gives, especially in the use of colour. In a white room, for instance, he advises the application of a first coat of scarlet paint which would give an almost imperceptible glow to the subsequent coats of thin white matt paint. 'It is in these details' he states, 'that true distinction lies and only by studying them will any real atmosphere be obtained'. Each chapter is devoted to the use of a single colour, brown, white, pink, blue, gold, green, grey, black, yellow, purple, red — and there is a chapter significantly entitled 'Turning one's failures into successes'. At the end of each chapter is a chart showing how the colour may be used in rooms of different kinds and what curtains, covers, cushions and ornaments are most suitable — throughout the book the rooms and furniture are in period styles, when not real antiques, and no contemporary pieces of any kind are shown.

Black rooms

The fashion for fabrics with black backgrounds, chintzes and damasks with printed or woven Chinoiserie designs was widespread around 1920 but more adventurous amateurs went to the point of having the walls and, in some cases, the ceilings, of living rooms painted or distempered black. 'Black ceilings should be rarer than they are. One might almost say they should be non-existent' wrote Basil Ionides. 'Black in decoration is a shade — not a colour — only to be used where occasion demands. It must not be used except where a scheme calls for it. This sometimes happens, though not as often as black appears.'

This would suggest that quite a number of people had made not too successful attempts to use black as a basis for a room. As black is not a good background for furniture of mahogany, walnut or satinwood, it was mainly used to set off lacquered or gilt furniture. Two such schemes were illustrated in *House and Garden* in 1922: a dining room in a house in Queen Anne's Gate where the black walls are a foil for the white mouldings of the late eighteenth century architecture and the white frames surrounding watercolour drawings of exotic birds, and the sitting room of W. Ranken the painter, with its furnishings in red lacquer.

147 F.G.R.Elwes dining room, prior to 1930

Silver rooms

The fashion for rooms with silver walls appears to have started in 1922 as a varian.
on the colours already popular. Probably the idea for this treatment came from the
speckled silver paper found as the lining of tea chests and the realization that this
would be an original and pleasant contrast to the brilliant colours fashionable and
a harmonious background for the Chinese lacquer furniture which was being used
so much. If the tea chest paper was difficult to obtain in sufficient quantities to paper
a room or ceiling, the same effect could be obtained by using silver leaf — a more
expensive medium and one requiring greater professional skill — or a cheaper paper,
obtainable in sheets, which had been coated with a paint containing metal resembling silver.

House and Garden in 1922 pointed out the pitfalls waiting for anyone wanting a
silver room — 'it is well to recognize at the outset that where silver predominates
the room will be more or less precious' in effect and therefore unsuited to the work-
aday sitting room. However, if the would-be decorator were willing to risk the label
'precious' there were still hurdles to be overcome. The aspect of the room had to
be taken into account and plenty of sunshine was important to counteract any effect
of coldness while the tone of the silver itself was important, for having 'a queer
oblique quality', it might, if too dull, produce a 'dim chilliness where the decorator
had looked for a recondite elegance'. If the room needed to be varnished to protect
the surface, it was important to use only the best quality varnish, as inferior brands
would turn yellow with the passage of time and instead of a silver room, the owner
would find it had turned into a dull gold. Basil Ionides considered that 'silver is

148 A. Godard porcelain candlestick; coloured bronze inkwell

pleasant but needs great care not to become morbid' and recommended silver paper for use in bathrooms as it could be hardwearing and inexpensive. *House and Garden* in 1923 featured a room with silver walls, curtains of jade green satin and red lacquer on the furniture and frames for Japanese prints.

This fashion spread to dress fabrics and most of the collections shown in Paris showed a predominance of silver lamé tissue or lace used for evening dresses and cloaks, while silver and platinum temporarily ousted gold as a setting for jewelry.

The Rowley Gallery produced furniture covered in silver leaf or silver lacquer in considerable quantities during the 'twenties and antique furniture was often stripped of its gold leaf which was replaced by an antiqued silver finish — particularly the carved wood stands for Chinese lacquer cabinets of the Charles II period, some of which were originally silver.

Wallpaper manufacturers faced this competition by producing papers to which silver leaf in squares had been applied as well as a variety of cheaper papers with silver finishes, jaspé or imitation canvas. The trend toward simpler rooms with modernistic decorations saw no lessening of the craze for silver and in the late 'twenties and early 'thirties silver oilcloth and silver satin — silver leaf applied on a dark blue background — were used as curtainings. Silver leaf walls and ceilings, tinted a pale pink or green, were used a great deal in hotels and restaurants about 1928, and were illuminated by chromium-plated chandeliers and wall brackets incorporating triangular panels of ground glass, similarly shaded in colour, which concealed the electric light bulbs.

The Egyptian taste

The discovery by Lord Carnarvon on 29 November 1922 of the tomb of Tutankhamen with its priceless treasures aroused an interest which was not confined to archeological circles. The sheer quantity of gold objects and in particular of gold coffins made an immediate appeal to the imagination of the general public while the furniture and personal belongings of the young king, which had escaped the plundering of tomb-robbers, spanned the centuries between and made him more real and understandable than the shrivelled and painted mummies of subsequent pharoahs which were all that the majority of people associated with Ancient Egypt. For a time the beautiful baroque objects, elegant to the point of decadence, were a source of inspiration to designers as photographs appeared in periodicals and newspapers of discoveries made in the course of clearing the tomb, and erroneous rumours, which were to grow in the following years, began to spread of curses placed on those who had disturbed the rest of the pharoah. For a while the predominently Chinese trend had a rival in Egyptian motifs which were applied to a variety of things ranging from wallpapers to cinemas — the Grange Cinema, Kilburn was one of a number redecorated throughout in a relentlessly Egyptian manner, and a nearby furniture store exhibited reproductions of all the furniture found in the tomb.

The Chinese taste

Throughout the 'twenties there was an interest in a romanticized Orient, not the mythical Persia and Arabia of the Russian Ballet, *Kismet, Hassan* and James Elroy Flecker's *Golden Road to Samarkand* but a more distant and equally unreal China. Lacquer furniture, real or fake, coromandel screens and Chinese porcelain vases adapted for electricity and crowned with silk shades painted to match the design of the vase, dwarf trees made of coral or turquoise matrix in cloisonné enamel bowls — these were for the well-to-do but those in straitened circumstances could assuage their oriental nostalgia less expensively.

At least two big stores in London, Liberty and Whiteley's Universal Stores, had large oriental departments. The former stocked artifacts of ivory, lacquer, bronze and jade of sufficiently high quality as to warrant the term 'works of art' and were competitors with other dealers in Far Eastern works such as Yamanaka, the Japanese-run shop in Bond Street closed very hurriedly at the outbreak of the Second World War. The oriental department at Whiteley's was more commercial, specializing in the hideous tortured ebony and ivory furniture made in Japan for the European market, embroidered red satin hangings 'from Chinese temples', decorative Chinese lanterns and the humbler delights of shells which when placed in a tumbler of water, slowly opened to reveal a brightly coloured flowering plant which gradually expanded in the water but which, after a few days, began to decompose.

Many a room was decorated with Elyse Lord's colour prints framed in gold passepartout — and these were so much in demand that *The Studio* published, in the series 'Masters of the Colour Print', a number of reproductions of her slight but attractive evocations of ancient China. According to an article in *Our Homes and Gardens* for 1919, the Yokohama Nursery Company were the chief suppliers of the dwarf trees which formed 'a piquant feature of the embellishment of a room' and these miniature maple, cedar, juniper and pine trees, carefully tended in Japan for anything up to a hundred years, perished through ignorance or neglect in hundreds of drawing rooms. More durable were the miniature gardens with lakes of mirror-glass, bridges, temples, and houses with inhabitants — all modelled in clay, which could be bought for five pounds or less while amateurs could make their own miniature gardens from a wide range of the toy houses etc (some Chinese and some Japanese in origin) costing a few pence at Woolworths — still proclaiming on the red and gold fascia that they sold 'Nothing Over Sixpence'.

Sticks and pastilles of incense were necessary to add to the oriental atmosphere and the lending libraries found that the novels of Louise Jordan Miln, set in China and usually concerned with a romance between an English or American girl and a noble, ivory-skinned Chinese aristocrat, ran a close second to those concerning the various adventures of 'The Sheik'. Sax Rohmer's lurid and highly enjoyable cha-

149 Lacquer standard lamp; gramophone cabinet decorated with lacquer;
chair decorated with lacquer, 1921

racter Dr Fu-Manchu represented a popular version of the current fears of 'The
Yellow Peril' while Thomas Burke's novels about Limehouse gave that rather un-
savoury district a false romantic reputation of masking behind innocent façades
a sinister world of opium dens and the white slave traffic.

Such a room in the Chinese taste Michael Arlen must have had in mind when,
in his novel *Young Men in Love*, set in the year 1924, he describes the room in
which one of his ill-fated and wanton women lies dying: 'The pieces of lacquer
had retreated into their own shadows. Everything in the room was soft and smud-
ged; it was as though an angel had passed by and had thoughtlessly put his thumb
on the room smudging it all, depriving each thing in the room of even any desire
to be itself, the red lacquer, the jade, the fat goldfish in their bowl, the green and
scarlet cushions with their tassels of gold and the golden cushions with their tassels
of crimson cord.' Cushions bought, one may hazard, from the London branch of
Atelier Martine who had recently, in that years of 1924, opened their branch at No. 10
Albemarle Street to sell 'Dolls by Poiret, Cushions by Poiret and Colour Schemes
by Poiret', illustrating the advertisement in *Vogue* with a photograph of a lady in
printed satin pyjamas posed against a screen painted with themes from a Persian
miniature.

Lacquer furniture

The Chinese craze and the consequent demand for lacquer furniture inevitably
led to the manufacture of imitations of late seventeenth and early eighteenth century
English lacquer furniture. This was mostly extremely unconvincing but there were
several Japanese working in London who were capable of producing imitations, not
of Chinese or Japanese lacquer, but of the lacquer made (often by lady amateurs)
around 1700 in England, imitations indistinguishable from the real thing. Their task
was made easier by the existence of pattern books for motifs in the oriental style
dating from the closing years of the seventeenth century and endless changes could
be rung on the disposition of these stock motifs executed in gold on red, black,
green and sometimes blue backgrounds.

150 Harold Nelson
advertisement, prior to 1926

151 Frank Brangwyn, advertisement, 1924

The demand for red lacquer cabinets on carved and silvered stands of the Charles II period far exceeded the supply — the drawers and shelves of these cabinets were ruthlessly scrapped and the interiors fitted out as cocktail cabinets — and innumerable versions were manufactured, complete with carved stands and the ornate brass hinges and locks which featured in all the trade catalogues of brass-founders. Both original and reproduction bureau-bookcases were covered in lacquer work by these skilled Japanese craftsmen, and many of these have come to be accepted as antiques in later years, the wear and tear of some fifty years plus some judicious restoration and renovation enabling them to pass muster as genuine.

Decorative accessories

A decorative accessory extremely popular in English homes during the 1920s was a ship model — usually a galleon of vaguely seventeenth century origin. This craze, for so it became, appears to have started in 1921 when articles about the decorative possibilities of model galleons began to appear in periodicals devoted to interior decoration, and before long they had become popular enough for instructions to be given for making them at home. It is not evident what started the fad for these dust-traps of ornaments but the enthusiasm with which countless numbers of model ships were disposed about Tudor style living rooms in England and to a lesser extent in America was boundless, though the fashion does not appear to have spread to France. *The Studio* published photographs of model galleons on a number of occasions and, in addition, published *Ship Models* by Keble Chatterton in a limited edition in 1923. 'The Armada Spectacle' at the British Empire Exhibition in 1924 increased interest in model galleons as ornaments, an interest increased also by the success of such movies as *The Sea Hawk* (1924), *Captain Blood* (1924) and *The Black Pirate* (1926) all of which had stirring spectacular battles at sea. Ship models which were more collectors' items than decorative accessories were much sought after and these were made by specialists with painstaking care for historical accuracy — a particularly fine example by Jeffrey Leighton was illustrated in *The Studio* in 1928.

Glass trees

The Tudor galleons had a rival in 1923 when glass trees appeared in Paris and were soon being copied in London and New York. Chinese trees and flowering plants of coral, turquoise or lapis-lazuli with leaves of jade or nephrite, the whole planted in a cloisonné enamel or carved red lacquer rectangular bowl, had been on sale for some years; some examples were antique but most were of modern manufacture. The occidental versions of these were completely made of glass of different colours. Leaf shapes of green or white glass and petals of various colours were wired together into the shape of small flowering plants, generally about fifteen inches high, the wire being covered in silk floss and the finished object mounted into an irregularly shaped base of white glass. As with model galleons the craze for these accessories became so intense that shops began to stock the component parts so that glass trees could be made at home at considerably less cost.

Cushions

Writing in 1921 Michel Dufet commented on the difficulty of defining a style of decoration in Paris for 'too many young designers consider that decoration consists of choosing cushions, placing low divans on the floor and arranging discreet lighting' — a description which could be taken to refer to a great many of the interiors designed by Paul Poiret's Atelier Martine. Suspecting that most of his clients had a hankering to be Sheherazade he usually gave the interiors he created for them an air of oriental voluptuousness by strewing large cushions of brocade and lamé, circular or square in shape with ruchings, braids and tassels of gold or silver, on the divans which were also an invariable feature. Some decorators in Paris, including Ruhlmann, followed the practice of placing large cushions on the floor, usually under a table or a desk. This habit spread to England and where an artistic 'Bohemian' effect was desired the cushion-spread divan would be accompanied by a standard lamp in imitation Chinese lacquer with an elaborate tasselled and fringed lampshade sometimes further decorated with bunches of taffeta grapes.

The importance of cushions and an indication of the serious thought that was given to their making and design is reflected in the fact that Basil Ionides in his book *Colour and Interior Decoration* published in 1926 devoted considerable space to advice concerning the best choice of material, edging and stuffing which should be for preference 'down or at least a feather stuffing. It is better to have no cushions than ones filled with a lumpy material'. Concerning the covering 'taffeta is one of the prettiest though it is a little slippery. Shantung, Japanese silk and such soft materials are also pleasant to the touch and one should remember that one is apt to lay one's head against the cushions and so materials like velvet, though they look lovely, will catch up stray hairs etc. Muslin over silk is cleanly and looks well in certain rooms. Linen is good but lasts clean a very short time. Cotton should not be used. Glazed chintz is nice but none too comfortable. Woollen materials are not very good as they are very stuffy. Alpaca is nice and so are many of the dress materials.' Uncut fringes were preferred and if cut fringes were used they should be very full and frills should never be used. Cushions should be twenty-seven inches square and all matching. Obviously the design of cushions had sobered since the immediate post-war days when a cushion was a 'creation' fit for an Arabian Night's palace and those recommended by Basil Ionides, square and simple, were very different from the complicated shapes covered in pleated fabrics, embellished with gold and silver lace or bunches of grapes made of cotton wool covered in violet taffeta, or that described in *Vogue* in 1920 which consisted of a large bunch of artificial pink roses covered with a gold lace veil.

152 Cushions by Harvey, Nichols and Co., 1919

Black American cloth

The enthusiasm in the later 'twenties for shiny-surfaced materials, chromium plate, glass or lacquer for instance, led to a revival of humble American cloth, hitherto regarded, in its patterned version, as only being suitable for covering kitchen tables or shelves where its smooth surface made it easy to clean with a damp cloth. When, however, it was made in plain, unadorned black, it closely resembled patent leather and was extremely popular for use as curtains, for not only did it look modernistic but it had the added advantage of being extremely inexpensive and its complete opaqueness made lining unnecessary. The New Poor found it extremely useful in giving the modern look to their homes.

The design and industries associations

Some attempts had been made to solve the problem of bringing about a closer rapprochement between art and industry and the founding, in 1915, of the Design and Industries Association with Lord Melchett as President, would, it was hoped, 'combat the unpractical influences in British design and industry'. The founders, it was pointed out, were not 'dreamers in Jaeger sweaters with blue eyes fixed on supramundane peaks' but had 'the larger vision which perceives that the disease of modern design and industry was due not to machinery but to the imperfect comprehension of its limitations and possibilities'.

Armed with the creed 'Fitness for purpose' its members endeavoured by means of exhibitions of the best current examples of commercial products, by the formation of trade groups of manufacturers, designers and distributors, by publishing literature and by endeavouring to bring education throughout the country into closer relationship with industry, to bring about a better standard of industrial design.

During the war years the DIA (as it became known) was, of course, forced to confine its activities to theorizing, for there was hardly any output of objects to which their activities could be directed. On the cessation of hostilities, however, one of the first concerns of the organization was to study the design of lettering. 'From shop signs and window tickets to notepaper headings the amazing perversion of the function of lettering was examined... with honourable exceptions it was disastrously evident that the prevalent treatment of lettering was factitious or grotesque' and 'legibility sacrificed to the ambition to be funny or conspicuous... at the end of this road negroid chaos and jazz lie in wait'.

The clear legible lettering used on the Tube railways was held up as an example to be followed and travelling exhibitions were circulated to demonstrate the advantages of 'straightforward, carrying lettering'. It was perhaps in this field that the DIA had the greatest influence and the high standard of lettering on the signposts and exhibition stands at the Wembley exhibition in 1924 can be attributed to them. How much influence the DIA was able to exercise in other fields of design is problematical and it is noticeable that in the Association's year books no specific claims of achievement are stated. The aims of the DIA were almost identical with those of the British Institute of Industrial Art, founded in 1920 under the joint auspices of the Board of Trade and the Board of Education — the purpose of the

153 Charles A. Richter dining table, 1928

154 Gordon Russell
cherrywood
writing cabinet

latter society being 'to secure that intimate co-operation of the Arts in Industry which is essential to quality productions'. Exhibitions of contemporary work by the Rowley Gallery, Messrs Heal, the silversmiths Omar Ramsden, Henry Wilson and Garrard and Co., enamels by Mr and Mrs Stabler, medals by Gilbert Bayes and Richard Garbe, ceramics by Wedgwood, Doulton, Pilkington and the Poole Potteries, glass by Powell and Sons as well as examples of printing and textiles, were held at premises in Knightsbridge and later at the Victoria and Albert Museum.

In 1922 the DIA and the British Institute of Industrial Art joined forces while keeping their separate identities, though little can be discovered of their joint activities during the remaining years, until 1934 when the British Institute of Industrial Art was closed down and its collection — mainly of textiles — was donated to the Victoria and Albert Museum.

The Arts and Crafts Society and the works of its members and associates had become, by the 1920s, so petrified that little critical notice was taken of their exhibitions. In 1926, thirty-eight years after the foundation of the society, a critic wrote in *The Studio* 'The decorative arts of this country are not really in such a bad way as the recent show of the Arts and Crafts Society Exhibition at Burlington House might lead one to suppose. The prevailing dullness was, it is true, redeemed by a fairly liberal sprinkling of good work by able and sincere artists but the general atmosphere was of sentimental loyalty to ideas and methods which provide no inspiration to the younger generation... the galleries seemed peopled with ghosts of the past.'

The original ideals of the Arts and Crafts Society were admirable but the legacy of those ideals in the post-war years was disastrous for the decorative arts. Social fac-

tors such as the shortage of eligible males as the result of the senseless carnage
of the war and economic factors such as the increases in taxation and the reduced
purchasing powers of fixed or inherited incomes, had the effect of forcing numbers
of 'gentlewomen' into some form of remunerative work. Deprived for the most part
of opportunities of marriage and by their upbringing unequipped for the increasingly
competitive life of the business world, their only means of eking out their dwindl-
ing incomes lay in some 'ladylike' occupation. Some opened Tudor 'tea-shoppes' or
flower shops but many ventured into the field of handicrafts and before long the
terms 'arts and crafts' had degenerated into 'arty-crafty'. Rents still being
very low by present standards, numbers of little shops opened, particularly in
the neighbourhood of Church Street Kensington and the Kings Road Chelsea, where
gentlewomen sold objects made by themselves or their friends. Handwoven fabrics,
silver jewelry set with colourful but semi-precious stones (the best of this was made
by Sibyl Dunlop whose work, influenced by C.R.Ashbee, displayed considerable craftsmanship and an individual taste in combining coloured stones) fabrics printed with
lino-blocks, painted furniture, lampshades of pleated parchment and powder bowls
with lids decorated with barbola flowers. Pottery, described as 'hand-thrown' was
produced in large quantities and most of these art shops carried a large stock of
only slightly misshapen vases, bowls and ashtrays — typical of the tendency to 'olde-
worldlinesse' of the period is the name of the Chelsea studio where lessons in pottery
were given — 'The Ymagynatyf Pottery'. It is easy to poke fun at the efforts of
these ladies who were actuated in many cases by a sincere belief in their own
artistic taste and ability as well as the need to earn a living, but the depressing fact
remains that they mainly represented the decorative arts in England as distinct from
the commercial manufacturers of pottery, porcelain, furniture and textiles.

Although their premises were in Church Street Kensington, the main centre at
the time of the 'handicraft' type of establishment, the Rowley Gallery could not
be classed in this category but neither at the same time could the work produced
there be said to have any affinity with the period-inspired furniture and decorations
emanating from the large commercial firms. Founded in 1898 the firm, under the
supervision of A.J.Rowley, undertook anything from a frame for an etching to a
complete scheme of decoration and during the 'twenties were foremost in advocating the use of silver leaf as a decorative texture. One of their specialities was the
making of decorative panels in an interior of coloured woods from designs by W. A.
Chase and Frank Brangwyn, panels which were used in screens or over mirrors.
Reminiscent of the inlaid panels in coloured woods used by Emile Gallé and Majorelle
(which may have been the source of their inspiration) they are simpler in design than
their Continental prototypes, the earlier examples being of artificially stained veneers
set into backgrounds coloured either cobalt or indigo blue, the later examples being
of the natural colours of the various woods used. Rowley furniture was generally
simple in design with, inevitably, a Chinese influence and was usually finished in
silver leaf — although gold leaf was occasionally used — on a gesso ground which
was slightly textured with incised lines before the leaf was applied. Picture frames
from the Rowley Gallery were simple, elegant and with their antiqued silver finish
were much in favour with painters whose work was not enhanced by the mock-
Spanish or imitation eighteenth century French versions which were the only alternative offered by the more conventional frame makers. Frank Brangwyn designed
a decorative fascia for the Rowley premises in Church Street, a decorative frieze of
carved and pierced wood carved in low relief, depicting the craftsman engaged in the
various activities in which the firm specialized. These carvings escaped the incen-
diary bombs which gutted the premises in World War II.

British exhibitions

The British Empire Exhibition 1924

The British Empire Exhibition at Wembley in 1924, of which the Wembley Stadium is a permanent relic, was not memorable for any great attention being paid to displays of decorative arts, although a number of firms participated in preference to the Paris Exhibition of the following year — a choice dictated more by economic reasons than an excess of chauvinism. The Wembley exhibition was intended primarily as a gesture of faith in the solidarity of the British Empire and an affirmation of its unity in a rapidly changing world. There was, however, an unexpected benefit for, among all the Empire fruits in glass vases, replicas of historic diamonds and examples of native handicrafts, there was a display of exotic woods from different colonies and the interest shown in these from furniture manufacturers encouraged the Stationery Office to issue a leaflet listing some seventy varieties of decoratively grained timbers which were available for use. The long ascendency of oak, walnut and mahogany ended and in the following years when veneers were increasingly used in conjunction with laminated woods, varieties of coloured woods in unusual grains were utilized for decorative purposes.

The British Pavilion at the 1925 Exhibition

The British Pavilion, designed by the architects Easton and Robertson and decorated by Henry Wilson, failed to make a favourable impression. A French critic described it as ' posing questions and provoking astonishment. Why the motley-coloured plaster, the glass steeple with the galleon perched on it like a weathercock? Is this all that old Albion can bring us? A fantasy created in an opium den by a retired colonel? I put these questions to the Secretary-General of the British Section. " As our pavilion ", he replied, " is sited on the bank of the Seine we have given it the stylized form of a boat to emphasize our naval power and our decorative additions have been inspired by our traditions of heraldry. Our architects have complied with the regulations of the Exhibition with something new and original. " Such a disarming reply obliges one to tolerate the British Pavilion as one does a highly coloured Christmas card.'

It cannot be denied that there was some justice in the French criticisms and the British effort was, to say the least, half-hearted. In justification it must be said that no great importance seems to have been attached to the Paris Exhibition by either the British government or manufacturers and our participation seems to have been gesture of politeness rather than an enthusiastic collaboration. Although the decorative arts had played a very minor role in the British Empire Exhibition at Wembley in the previous year, the manufacturers followed the lead of the government in making only a token showing in Paris and, although it was not actually put into words, the impression was given that it would have been preferable to all concerned to have ignored the exhibition as they had done on previous occasions. Financial factors played their part, for the official expenditure on the Wembley Exhibition had been lavish considering the general economic depression, while manufacturers saw little prospect of increasing trade with France, always a poor market for British goods and one which showed no signs of improvement. As exhibition space outside the official exhibit was expensive, few firms saw any advantage in renting separate areas and in consequence British goods had a poor showing.

149

155 Paul Frankl bookcase, prior to 1928

Decoration in America

An American critic, writing in 1930 and discussing the 'practical use of modern furniture in the American house', gives a rather surprising sidelight on the state of contemporary decorative art in the United States during the 'twenties. 'The time has come', she comments 'when the public no longer giggles and snickers at a display of Modern Decorative Art but rather seeks out such exhibitions and views them with an intelligent interest and a desire to understand. Indeed, many people are interested in the possibilities of introducing modern furniture into their homes... There are few examples of modern American decoration to choose from... our problem should be one of creation or adaptation, not of imitation'. Confirmation of her opinion comes from another source of two years earlier. 'The interiors of libraries, museums and railroad stations have developed a severe and impersonal artistic character. The last stronghold is now wakening and the modern home is bound to follow.' The 'dingy hangings and scroll-work chandeliers as well as the knick-knack cabinets and the gilt furnishings of past generations' were, the writer affirms, being relegated to the rubbish heap in favour of 'newer, happier and simpler designs in colour and form'. Elsewhere this author writes 'The modern decorative arts are a good way behind developments in other fields and it is a debatable question whether these arts will ever catch up' and lays the blame for the low level of craftsmanship

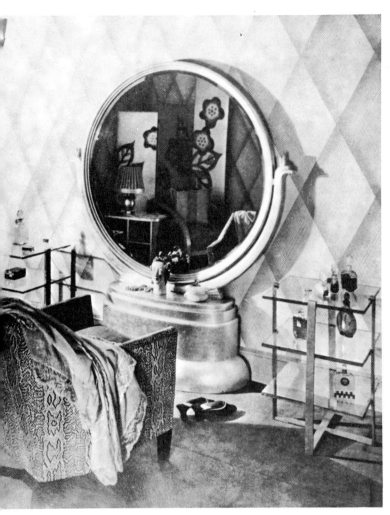 

156 Paul Frankl dressing table, prior to 1928   **157 Mellor, Meigs and Howe**, bedroom *c.* 1923

upon the manufacturers of inexpensive furniture who were only concerned with profits and avoiding payment for original creative furniture designs. 'We today, in America, need leaders in the field of the decorative arts to show the same vision and the same spirit of pioneering which has made this country the most modern in the world', he concludes, after regretting that the attempt by Joseph Urban to open a branch of the Wiener Werkstatte in New York some time previously had failed.

These opinions, expressed by writers of authority — one a lecturer in Interior Decoration at the University of California, the other designer for a firm in New York — are confirmed by articles and illustrations in various periodicals, and it is clear that decoration in America had the same strong bias toward 'period' influences as that in England. Paul Frankl's skyscraper furniture with its vertical arrangements of bookshelves and cupboards executed in California redwood has, as its name implies, a characteristic not found in contemporary European furniture but other furniture made by the same designer shows that he had made a close study of modern French examples and his interior decoration shares with French designers a taste for silver leaf, mirrors hung on ropes with large tassels, paintings by Marie Laurencin and fabrics by Rodier. Eugene Schoen's. furniture is somewhat reminiscent of that of Ruhlmann, monumental and unadorned except for the grain of the veneers.

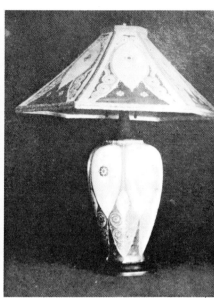

158 **Aschermann Studio** lamps with shades of batik silk, prior to 1922

The noticeable absence of any exhibits from the United States in the 1925 Paris Exhibition was explained by the American decorator Paul Frankl: 'The only reason why America was not represented at the Exhibition of decorative industrial art held in Paris in 1925 was because we found we had no decorative art. Not only was there a sad lack of any achievement that could be exhibited, but we discovered that there was not even a serious movement in this direction and that the general public was quite unconscious of the fact that modern art had been extended into the field of business and industry. On the other hand we had our skyscrapers and at that very date they had been developed to such an extent that, if it had been possible to have sent an entire building abroad, it would have been a more vital contribution in the field of modern art than all the things done in Europe added together.'

In the years following the 1925 Paris Exhibition the interest in contemporary idioms of decoration began to arouse as much attention in the United States as it did in England. Prior to that the focus had been fixed almost entirely upon antique furniture or on reproductions of such period styles as American Colonial, Italian and Spanish Renaissance, Tudor or the eighteenth century periods of England and France. Edward Stratton Holloway, the author of *The Practical Book of Furnishing the Small House and Apartment* published in 1922 lists only two American designers working in 'modern, non-period' styles, adding that there were 'many private individuals [who] have adapted this method in furnishing their own homes without professional aid'. Of these two Pieter Meyer, 'sometime of Holland and Java' worked in Greenwich Village and, understandably in view of his past background, most of his designs for furniture were strongly influenced by Chinese prototypes and reflect the current fashion for Chinoiserie in England. The other designer named, Edward Aschermann of the Aschermann Studio in New York was, as Mr Holloway pointed out, more influenced by the Vienna Secession and the undated illustrations of interiors designed by him could well have been done before the war and are strongly reminiscent of the schemes suggested by Shirley Wainwright in the year books of *The Studio*. The section devoted to modern decoration occupies only a comparatively small section of Mr Holloway's book and the majority of the illustrations of furniture which he advises and recommends for the guidance of his readers are of reproductions of Colonial furniture by the Charak Furniture Co., Boston, versions of painted Italian furniture by the William French Furniture Co. of Minneapolis, Chamberlayne Inc., New York and other manufacturers too numerous to mention.

159 Aschermann Studio bachelor's living room, prior to 1922

160 Aschermann Studio dining room, prior to 1922

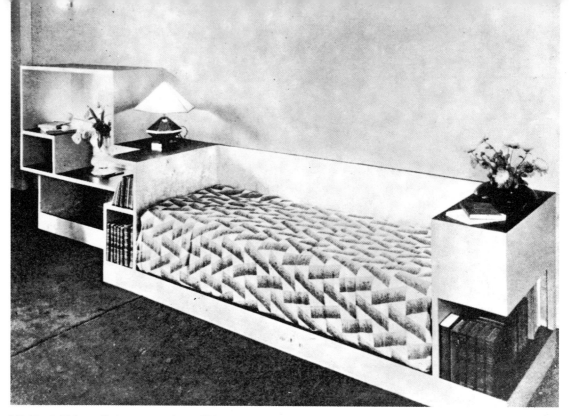

161 Paul Nelson living room in a Chicago apartment

The cause of contemporary design was taken up by the Metropolitan Museum of New York by their purchase of a table by Emile Ruhlmann from his exhibit in the 1925 Paris Exhibition. In the following year the Museum held an exhibition of works by Ruhlmann, Armand Rateau, Jean Dunand, Edgar Brandt and other master craftsmen and designers whose creations had been such a feature of the Paris Exhibition. This display gave rise to great interest and the *American Magazine of Art* records that Walter Kantack was the first designer in New York to be influenced by the French styles.

In January 1927 the Metropolitan Museum brought to the attention of American designers and manufacturers yet another aspect of contemporary European design by staging an important show of Swedish Decorative Arts. This exhibition moved to Detroit after a successful stay in New York.

There can be little doubt that the success of these two exhibitions and the considerable interest they aroused led to the 'Living Room Furniture Design Competition' organized by the Art Alliance in 1927. The winning designs were to be awarded prizes totalling five thousand dollars offered by S. Karpen Brothers who planned to make up the schemes and send them on a tour of the United States. The organizers followed the requirements laid down by the committee of the 1925 Paris Exhibition in stipulating that the designs submitted should have no period influences of any kind and that they should 'embody beauty, utility and suitability for the American Home'. Over four hundred designs were entered and the first prize was divided between J.W.Peters of Los Angeles (a former pupil of Peter Behrens and currently the Art Director of the Famous-Players-Lasky film studios in Hollywood) and a New York designer Richard Havilland Smythe. Among the winners of smaller prizes were Kem Webber, another Hollywood designer, and Paul Frankl of New York, a firm advocate of the new modernism. The jury noted an absence of 'the freakish or bizarre' in the entries which, for the most part, featured straight lines and unornamented surfaces. As a writer in the *American Magazine of Art* commented, this competition was 'the first concrete and constructive step towards interesting American designers to express themselves in furniture design, a field heretofore neglected by creative designers due to the fact that the period motif held sway'. This competition did much to eradicate the cause for complaint expressed by Edward Stratton Holloway five years before to the effect that 'in America the modern move-

162 Kem Webber bedroom, prior to 1929

ment is even yet not at all organized or greatly to the fore. There are but few men and women working in this direction and they are doing so individually'.

By 1928 the new design had gained sufficient ground to become a matter for controversy and articles putting forward arguments either in favour or expressing disapproval were appearing in various periodicals devoted to the arts — one such entitled ' Where to Modernism? ' appearing in the *American Magazine of Art*. The new trends were particularly welcomed by those who had deplored the conservatism of artworkers in the United States. Since the founding of the Society of Arts and Crafts at Boston in 1897 — there were no schools for training in the arts and crafts at that time — the number of craftworkers had increased until was estimated that in 1927 there were thirteen hundred craftsmen earning a livelihood from pottery, bookbinding, making jewelry or weaving. With few exceptions their work was conservative and based on period models.

A similar preoccupation with the past had been a characteristic of the exhibits submitted to the annual exhibition of American Industrial Art held at the Metropolitan Museum. This could be attributed to the fact that objects in the Museum (the great majority of which were the products of civilizations of the past) formed the sources of inspiration. Museums, not necessarily those newly founded and with curators anxious to build up collections of precious work from the past but also those, in Europe as well as in the United States, with established collections, were paying little if any attention to contemporary work. Reference has been made to the acquisition by the Metropolitan Museum of a modern table by Ruhlmann but this was an exceptional occurrence.

However on the occasion of the eleventh exhibition a new policy, under the aegis of the Director, Edward Robinson, decreed that in future the exhibition should demonstrate more clearly the co-operation between the designer and the producer and that work submitted should be of American design and manufacture throughout — a policy endorsed by the committee, which included the Detroit architect Elie Saarinen, Joseph Urban, Eugene Schoen and Leon Solon, a ceramic artist of many years experience in France and England at that time working at the Robertson Art Tile Co., Trenton. In spite of the insistence that the exhibition should be a reflection of the contemporary scene, considerable influence from Europe and in particular from France could be seen in the specimen rooms on view.

163 Joseph Urban project for a conservatory, 11th Exhibition of American Industrial Art, 1929
164 Raymond Hood office, 11th Exhibition of American Industrial Art, 1929

Inevitably the exhibition encountered hostile criticism from conservative sources and Thomas Craven, writing in *Forum* for August 1929 denounced ' these modernist rooms, the most impersonal or dehumanized that have ever been contrived... shall we throw out of our living quarters those things which reflect and charm and relax the many-sided personality of man and for the sake of a shallow theory of beauty, substitute the slippery, sterilized commodities manufactured by indigent Frenchmen? No doubt this eccentric trash will appeal to the fiendish and excitable Americans who maintain homes but do not inhabit them and who rush hither and thither avid of vicious amusements and shocking adventures...'.

However the American public, whether fiendish and excitable or not, was more favourably inclined to the new modernism — a fact shrewdly exploited by the department stores. Lord and Taylor, a firm maintaining an enlightened attitude towards the latest trends in interior decoration in the late 1920s and the following decades, held an exhibition early in 1928 of Modern French Decorative Art consisting of furniture, textiles, lacquer, ceramics and glass by Ruhlmann, Sue et Mare and the more avant-garde designers such as Pierre Chareau and DIM. At the same time a number of rooms by American designers were on show, each interpreting the twentieth century style as applied to American life. Later in the same year Macys commissioned Lee Simonson, the theatrical designer, to create a setting for a large collection — some five thousand in number — of artifacts from France, Germany, Sweden, Italy and Austria as well as some home-designed products. Significantly, no mention was made of anything from England being included in the show.

The growing interest on the part of the public was stressed at a conference of sales representatives of the furniture trades at Grand Rapids, Michigan. Emphasis was made in speeches by a number of delegates that there was a new awareness on the part of customers — an awareness fostered by the increasing number of articles on interior decoration in magazines, by lectures to women's clubs and by newly founded courses in the decorative arts in schools and colleges. The public and in particular the younger generation was no longer content to live in rooms reflecting the life of their parents or even their grandparents but was desirous of surroundings which reflected the rapidly changing social scene.

165 Eugene Schoen living room, prior to 1928   **166 Joseph Urban** a man's den, 1929

167 John Wellborn Root woman's bedroom, 11th Exhibition of American Industrial Art, 1929

168 D.S.O'Meara dining table, prior to 1928

169 Ralph T.Walker man's study, 11th Exhibition of American Industrial Art, 1929

Decorative painting

There has been no tradition of decorative painting in England as there was on the Continent and in France in particular. Such mural paintings or decorative work as there has been was the work of foreign artists, Verrio Laguerre, Kaufmann or, greatest of all, Rubens. The only notable exception was James Thornhill, creator of the paintings at Greenwich Hospital.

The 1920s were no more favourable for mural paintings in England. The housing shortages, the heavy taxation and recurring financial crises which accompanied the reckoning of the cost of the war, crises which forced more and more people to seek smaller houses or flats as they found their incomes shrinking — these were factors enough to discourage any patronage of decorative artists in this field. The uncertainty of life as a factor which had to be taken into consideration was pointed out by a contemporary. ' Town life has become so nomadic that one often hesitates to have beautiful decorations done which cannot be taken away in a pantechnicon when one moves. Who knows if next year a nicer house may not be possible or a smaller one inevitable. ' *

In addition the preoccupation of the public with ' period ' interiors and furnishing, and in particular with the Tudor period, gave little opportunity for including large mural paintings into schemes of decoration, and the large firms of interior decorators were more intent on inducing any rich clients to cover their walls with expensive panelling, genuine or reproduction, than with bringing in outside artists from whose efforts they would make considerably less profit. Private patronage being, to all intents and purposes, non-existent, any aspiring mural painter would be forced to look to municipal bodies or the church for commissions only to find that such painters as Frank Brangwyn or Anning Bell were more than capable of supplying whatever small demand there might be.

Brangwyn could be described as the English equivalent of José-Maria Sert (he was Belgian by birth in fact, but had made his home in England) and his designs for triumphal arches and street decorations for ceremonial occasions, the coronation of George V, the celebrations of peace, have considerable affinities with Sert's work, especially in the use of massive pylons and obelisks, supporting great swags of laurel, triumphal arches surmounted by massive allegorical sculptures, picturesque processions which included elephants and fantastic barges on the Thames — projects which, unfortunately, never became more than designs. Brangwyn's colourful compositions, crowded with heroic figures of muscular workmen, shipworkers and carpenters, picturesquely draped in clothes of no particular period — he managed to impart a vaguely medieval air to private soldiers of the First World War — and with every available corner crammed with decorative still-lives of foliage, fruit and flowers, were to be found in municipal buildings in England, America, Canada and Japan.

When Gordon Selfridge was planning the gigantic store in Oxford Street which was to replace the muddle of small shops which formerly occupied the site, the original conception of a neo-classical block was to have a soaring tower, designed by Sir John Burnet, a tower which should have been a landmark. Frank Brangwyn was the obvious choice to decorate the vast dome of the interior of the tower, the imposing dimensions of which — a diameter of seventy feet with the crown of the dome one hundred and thirty feet above the ground — gave him ample opportunities for working on a grand scale. Conceived originally as decorative paintings, the composition was to have been carried out in a smooth-faced mosaic reproducing the paintings.

* *The New Interior Decoration* by Dorothy Todd and Raymond Mortimer, Batsford, 1929.

159

Whether the building regulations forbade, at that time, the erection of a tower of this height or Gordon Selfridge's fortune was not sufficient is uncertain, but the project was not carried out.

Brangwyn's work was usually on a large scale but he also painted a number of panels of smaller dimensions which could be used as decorations over mantelpieces, as did George Sheringham (working in a modernized form of Chinoiserie) and Philip Connard, whose paintings of decorative birds and vases of flowers were an invariable feature of the annual exhibition at the Royal Academy.

Rex Whistler's mural paintings for the restaurant at the Tate Gallery appeared at a time (1927-8) when they could receive the greatest appreciation and signalled the emergence of a decorative artist who was to play an important and influential rôle for nearly twenty years until his lamented and early death, at the height of his creative ability, in the Second World War. Although his best work in mural decoration and in the theatre was to be done in the 'thirties and 'forties, the Tate Gallery murals (for some reason never finished) and his superb illustrations to the Cresset Press limited edition of *Gulliver's Travels*, were accomplished before 1930. A magnificent draughtsman, he had an encyclopaedic knowledge of Palladian architecture which he interpreted with wit and fantasy, and, although summarily dismissed too often as a pasticheur, his lively imagination allied to his technical skill placed him far ahead of the host of imitators who followed later in his wake.

The comment of an eminent critic that Duncan Grant's pictures are the best work that the English school has produced since the death of Constable in the opinion of many good judges is open to doubt and the inclusion of thirty-nine examples of decorative work by Grant and Vanessa Bell in a volume by that critic published in 1920 had led a modern Italian writer to state that these artists, together with Douglas Davidson, were 'the fashionable decorators of the day'. In fact the work they did was confined to the houses of a small circle of friends connected with the Bloomsbury Group and was a continuation of that of the Omega Workshops. Roger Fry's brave but misguided attempts at educating popular taste had closed in 1919, having foundered in financial difficulties. In spite of the various talents associated with this venture — Gaudier-Brzeska, Wyndham Lewis, William Roberts in addition to Duncan Grant and Vanessa Bell — the results were too often amateurish in execution, particularly where the painted furniture and screens were concerned, and the collection of work from the Omega Workshops (now in the Bethnal Green Museum) presents a sad and depressing spectacle.

The tragic premature death of Claude Lovat Fraser in 1921 robbed the theatre of one of its best designers — his décor and costumes for *The Beggar's Opera* made this production a notable theatrical event — and deprived the decorative arts of one of the most promising exponents. Both he and George Sheringham were fascinated by the eighteenth century which they interpreted in a fashion flavoured by a contemporary use of colour. Sheringham continued to work in the theatre and to design textiles through the 'twenties but it was not until 1927 that a new exponent of the eighteenth century pastiche appeared in the person of Rex Whistler, whose reputation was to eclipse them both.

170 Coloured plaster figurine of Sylvia Nelis as Polly Peachum in *The Beggar's Opera*, after the original design by **Claude Lovat Fraser**

Furniture

The Tudor revival had run its course and through endless repetition was begin-ning to sink into a certain disrepute. Ribbon developments of mock-Tudor semi-detached villas, old-oak teashops and the absurd and pretentious building erected by Liberty's (apparently this monstrosity had originally been planned for Regent Street but as it did not fit in with the neo-Georgian aspect of the rebuilding of that thoroughfare the scheme was adapted for Great Marlborough Street); probably more than anything, the cheap 'reproductions' in the Tudor style sold by the hire purchase firms, had led to even the few genuine antique pieces of furniture being eyed askance by those with pretensions to taste, though the mock-Tudor furniture still continued to be made and sold for another twenty years or more. The modern-ist furniture which began to appear about 1927 or 1928 was found by many to be too stark and advanced for their tastes and in consequence the styles of the eigh-teenth century, which had never completely gone out of fashion although temporarily eclipsed during the nineteenth century, began to find even greater favour and not only English work of that period but also that of Italy, due to the appearance in 1924 of Sacheverell Sitwell's *Southern Baroque Art.*

In spite of this renewed interest, a set of late eighteenth century painted panels representing West Indian scenes, which had been removed from the Camperini Palace in Venice, languished unsold on the walls of a staircase of a West End firm of deco-rators for over ten years from about 1923 when, failing to find a purchaser, they were consigned to the furnace of the firm's heating system. The only French furniture which could be sold in London about this period was the ornate inlaid, ormulu-encrusted type much in favour with nouveaux riches and a few firms in the West End specialized in antique (but more often reproduction) examples of this kind. The simpler painted or unadorned wood furniture of the Louis XV or Louis XVI periods was, on the whole, regarded as being an inferior version of Adam, Hepple-white or Sheraton and similarly Empire furniture was classified in the same category — as was English Regency with which it was usually confused.

It must be emphasized that forty years ago the choice of furnishing offered to prospective clients was limited, that taste was conservative and that antique shops and interior decorators did not proliferate as they do now. There were adventurous individuals who were prepared to be labelled as eccentric or arty by experimenting with Victoriana or some other style but for the more conventional the choice was virtually limited to Tudor, Georgian or modernistic and of these three Georgian or neo-Georgian had the lead — one it was to keep for the greater part of the 'twenties.

Maurice Adams

Mention has been made elsewhere of the English attitude to contemporary French work and the remarks made by Maurice Adams in the introduction to a book on his work as a decorator and furniture designer are typical: 'The Continent has during recent years embodied novel ideas in furniture. This type of thing is at the back of all the 'modern' furniture that English house furnishers are vainly endeavouring to popularize. Unusual forms carried out in highly decorative materials may at first sight appear up-to-date and so attractive. Very little of it is beautiful. Mostly it is definitely ugly: being devoid of any relationship with art in any form. It is the product of impudent incompetence. As an essay or passing fad, some of this work is not devoid of interest. The bare idea is insufferable — to live for any length of time in the restless and semi-exotic atmosphere produced by such exotic furniture.'

171 Maurice Adams
the 'Alexandra' dressing
table *c.* 1928

Adams' diatribe is nearly equal in spleen to those from academic circles which
greated the appearance of the Donaldson bequest of French modern furniture by
Gallé, Majorelle and others at the South Kensington Museum in 1901 and the same
tone of smug superiority can be discerned. The above quotation is taken from *Modern
Decorative Art*, a book written by Adams and published in 1930, and though the title
gives expectations of a survey of contemporary work it is in fact a catalogue of
furniture, mirrors and electric light fittings designed, or rather brought into being,
by Adams who, in the text, refers to himself by name whenever possible or by the
regal suffix ' we '. Designer of to my mind some of the most unattractive furniture of
the 'twenties, he would not warrant any attention were it not for the fact
that his furniture was only too typical of much that was produced by the manufacturers in the latter half of the decade.

Adams had spent twenty-five years in the furniture trade, from apprenticeship, and
had architectural training before opening a business as an architect and decorator
in the West End. Experience in neither cabinet making nor architecture, no matter
how long that experience may be, can be a guarantee of artistic judgement and skill
— gifts with which Adams considered himself liberally endowed. The case is known
of a cabinet maker in the 1920s who, after fifty years' experience of making reproductions of antique furniture was quite incapable of distinguishing one period from
another — a failing shared by many of the salesmen attached to the larger firms --
while architects at this period were only concerned with the exteriors of the
houses, and had little regard for the interiors. Often the decorator would find he
had to deal with windows which were pushed into the corner of the room with
no space allowed for curtains; fireplaces or chimney breasts not centred on the wall
or similar aberrations caused by the architect's preoccupation with the symmetry
of the external façade. Clients beguiled by architectural drawings of the outside of

172 DIM interior of a Farman aeroplane, furniture and textiles, prior to 1925

173 Serge Chermayeff sideboard, 1928

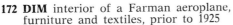

the proposed Georgian-style house would find with dismay that the architect had presented them with a series of lop-sided rooms and it was the task of the decorator to bring some order into them.

Maurice Adams claimed to have been the first to make low dressing tables in England, showing the 'King George' model at the Palace of Arts, Wembley in 1924 and a subsequent model the 'Queen Mary' at Olympia the following year. Similar dressing tables had been made on the Continent so Adams' professed scorn for French furniture did not prevent his borrowing ideas on occasion. There followed during the next five years a number of series, 'Coronet', 'Connaught', 'Alexandra', 'Grosvenor', 'Marlborough', each based on a single design which was adapted into suites of drawing room or bedroom furniture; they were the originals of the cheap, highly varnished and mass-produced versions sold by hire purchase firms in the late 'twenties and through the 'thirties.

The designs originated by Adams, loosely based on Queen Anne originals and executed in 'the richest and most gloriously figured walnut procurable' were an alternative choice to the 'Tudor' with its heavily carved bulbous supports and lavish application of stamped 'period' ornament. In either style the showy surface decoration and French-polished surface concealed workmanship applied to cheap timber, and in some cases the window dressers of hire purchase firms were hard put

174 Serge Chermayeff bedroom, 1928

to conceal from the public the backs of the furniture on display, going to the lengths of pinning fabric on the back of any piece which could not be placed against the wall of the shop windows.

Waring and Gillow 1929

' It has been said ' ran the text of an advertisement in 1925 ' that what Ruskin did for Art in Painting, Waring's have done for Art in Furnishing '; a somewhat ambiguous claim which was hardly justified by the unadventurous interior depicted in the majority of advertisements of that firm. In 1929, however, Waring's took the decisive step of reorganizing their decoration department, at the same time making a tacit acknowledgement that modernistic decoration was more than a passing fashion. For some time, as it has been indicated elsewhere, the big firms had been feeling the effects of the economic strains which followed the post-war boom and the growing numbers of independent interior decorators were beginning to deprive them of some of their best clients. Some new attraction had to be found, either to bring back old clients or to interest new ones.

In the previous year the decorating firm of Shoolbred's had held an exhibition of work by the French association DIM. and the furniture and decorative accessories

175 Paul Follot dining room designed for Waring and Gillow, 1928

by Joubert and Petit had met with a sufficiently appreciative reception for Waring's to experiment on the same lines. Curtis Moffat subsequently took over the English agency for DIM in the early 1930s. Paul Follot, one of the original exhibitors at La Maison Moderne in 1895 was entrusted with the design, in collaboration with Serge Chermayeff, the latter, however, taking full charge after the opening — Follot's name not being mentioned in subsequent advertising. Follot who had started his career as a designer in the Art Nouveau manner, was not a complete stranger to the field of design in England for he had been invited to design for the Wedgwood factory in 1914 by Cecil Wedgwood but the death of the latter in 1916 and the cessation of production of decorative porcelain during the war years had delayed until 1919 the realization of his designs (none of which has it been possible to trace). By 1929 Follot had adapted his style from Art Déco to the new angular modernistic manner. No less than sixty rooms, the joint work of Follot and Chermayeff, were completely decorated and furnished for this display of continental design to the English public and it was hoped that 'Lord Waring's belief in the new movement should have important reactions on the furnishing industries in the future' — a hope that was not realized to the extent that had been expected.

English manufacturers showed 'a curious detachment in outlook and astonishing ignorance of the modern movement and the sane and rational principles which have inspired it'. Partly from an ingrained prejudice against 'Continental' ideas and partly from a disinclination to invest large capital sums in the production of carpets, light-fittings, glass or china in a style which might not after all catch on with the general public, the majority of manufacturers chose to play safe and to continue to use the designs which in some cases dated back to pre-war or even earlier years. Consequently as the editors of *The Studio* complained, quantities of French and other continental productions were imported to the detriment of British labour. Two factors, however, brought to English manufacturers the sharp realization that a drastic change of approach had to be faced; the economic depression following the Wall Street Crash and the exhibition of Swedish Decorative Art in 1931. The sparse, elegant simplicity of much of the furniture and decorative objects in this exhibition had a more telling effect than the luxurious displays at Waring's and it was soon realized that similar furniture and objects could be manufactured at a much lower cost and

176 R.W.Symonds and **Robert Lutyens** chest of drawers from a bedroom suite

sold at correspondingly lower prices — a consideration of the utmost importance during the worst financial depression since the Armistice. A contemporary comment that the 'taste for bare rooms is without doubt partly due to an unconscious feeling that they are healthier' could have been amplified by mentioning that bare rooms are also cheaper.

The new trend — 'the fashionable modernist style' as the newspapers described it — was not so widely accepted as it would appear from a study of *The Studio Year Book of Decorative Art*, probably its most enthusiastic supporter, and even in the following decade most new decoration was predominantly period in taste. Drawing a contrast between the adventurous spirit of wealthy patrons on the Continent and the conservatism of their English counterparts, Raymond Mortimer commented in *The New Interior Decoration* that 'in England the rich are content to devote their fortunes to grouse moors and racing stables: if they buy a picture, it is by an artist who is safely dead: if they require a house, they either purchase an old one or order one that will look old from an architect with a talent for pastiche... the absence of buildings in the contemporary style such as have spread over the Continent has caused interior decoration in England to develop on peculiar lines. Most professional decorators are content with pastiches, more or less intelligent, of Georgian styles. And even the best are much less revolutionary than their rivals in France. It does not follow that they are less gfted or less intelligent. The problem they are dealing with is different. It will be a long while, after all, before more than a small minority will be living in houses designed on the new system. Most of us are obliged to live in Georgian, Victorian or Edwardian houses. Very often these houses have been divided into flats, and while some of us are living in a few very large rooms (formerly the reception rooms of the house) others are living in the small low-ceilinged rooms at the top (originally the servants' bedrooms). In ninety-nine cases out of a hundred, the decorator has to make something of an old room, not merely to furnish a new one'. Few clients could afford, even if their landlords had been willing, to alter the physical characteristics of a room by removing period mouldings, fireplaces or ceilings in spite of advice given by a writer in *Vogue* magazine that a complete transformation of a room could be effected at an outlay of fifty pounds.

The use of plywood

The new simplicity in the design of interiors — a simplicity which became, in many cases, an angular starkness with the furniture reduced to the minimum — was made possible by technological discoveries in the treatment of wood and the bonding of wood and metal.

The tendency of natural wood to warp, twist or crack had, until the twentieth century, been a limiting factor in the design of large pieces of furniture and architectural woodwork. Continental cabinet-makers during the nineteenth century had overcome this problem by a laborious method of building a wardrobe door, for instance, of a core of strips of wood glued together and facing these on each side with thin sheets of wood with the grain running in the opposite direction, thus by a series of opposing stresses, ensuring that the door remained fairly true in differing atmospheric conditions. For commercial purposes this process was developed into what is now known as plywood — three sheets of veneer, the grain of the centre layer at right angles to that of the two outer layers — but it was not until around 1890 when the Russian invention of water resistant glues became known that three, five or seven ply was made in large quantities in the Baltic countries Finland (where the first factory was opened in 1912) Latvia and Estonia. Improvements in the techniques of cutting veneers and especially the American developments in the rotary cutting machine — a French invention of the 1870s — by means of which a rotating log was peeled off a long continuous strip of veneer by a thin knife, brought about a more economical use of wood. 'Laminboards' or 'ibus' was a similar improvement on the old method, thin slats of wood joined under pressure and faced with two rotary-cut sheets of veneer — these were more suitable for architectural use or for table tops. Natural wood could, under certain circumstances, shrink as much as eight per cent. The new plywood, however, resisted this tendency: in addition it was tougher, more resilient that natural wood. If three ply it could be curved and could be obtained in practically any size. With no tendency to crack it was ideal for drawer bottoms, mirror backings and the backs of furniture. It was obtainable faced in birch, alder, gaboon mahogany from West Africa (generally used in a painted scheme) pine, oak, ash, while cheaper varieties, less proof against warping, were made from beech, poplar and cottonwood.

The use of plywood in furniture was condemned by the more traditional decorating firms although the use of laminated boards was permitted for practical reasons in the construction of large fitted cupboards. However, the manufacturers of the shoddy furniture sold by hire purchase firms realized its possibilities during the 'twenties and 'thirties, and most of their products were made of the cheapest plywood covered with elaborately figured and highly varnished veneers. In many cases the furniture was falling to pieces before the last instalment had been paid and this helped to bring plywood into a certain disrepute regardless of the fact that, properly used, it had great advantages and gave a greater freedom to designers.

177 Design for a dining room using plywood and ibus as wall covering, prior to 1926

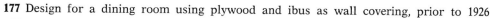

178 J. Murray Easton and **Howard Robertson** sitting room of a London flat

Metal furniture

The same prejudices which had greeted metal furniture in France were shown when it was introduced into England shortly afterwards, in the late 'twenties. After a struggle with English conservatism *The Studio* took up the cause of metal furniture as being suitable for those of its readers with modernist leanings. Thonet opened a branch in London about 1930, their first installation of metal furniture on a large scale being at the Capital Cinema Epsom. Tubular furniture had been in production for a year or more previously and Cox and Co. were advertising their models in tubular steel and the Bath Cabinet Makers were also announcing their examples designed by H.J.W.Hyde. Sponsored by several newly established decorating firms, Green and Abbott advertised a modern dining table with a chromium-plated frame and a top of polished birch, suitable for six people. Its comparatively low cost of nine guineas should have made it attractive to the public at the beginning of the 'thirties when money was scarcer than at any time during the previous decade and the 1929 Wall Street crash was having disastrous reverberations in Europe. Little if anything was produced in England to compare with the luxury models of France of the pre-1929 era. The simple mass-produced chairs and tables were used in great numbers in canteens and other commercial concerns but failed to find favour in the home. The middle classes were too addicted to fumed oak Tudor reproductions which could be bought on the instalment system while those with little money but more discrimination were discovering the more decorative charms of Regency and Victorian furniture.

Post-1927 furniture

Toward the end of the 'twenties, approximately from 1927 onwards, a noticeable change can be observed in the function of furniture, quite apart from any consideration of decorative styles. Two items of bedroom furniture in particular were affected by changing conditions and the advances in technology. The wardrobe, an essential and cumbrous feature of bedroom suites, was largely abandoned in favour of the built-in cupboards which were incorporated into the design of bedrooms in new blocks of flats. These cupboards, painted to match the walls of the room, were made possible by the use of the new laminated woods which were becoming plentiful and had the advantage of enabling a builder to make larger doors than had hitherto been possible without the danger of warping or shrinking. Built-in cupboards might occupy as much space as a conventional wardrobe but appeared to occupy less, an important factor when smaller flats became a necessary evil to a great many people.

Another piece of furniture which virtually disappeared in upper class households was the washstand, formerly a necessity when hot water was brought to the bedroom for toilet use and a toilet set of basin, water jug, slop pail and soap dishes in decorated china was a necessary adjunct to any bedroom. The increased use of central heating in the bathrooms of newly built flats or houses and improvements in plumbing brought about the social change of putting all the washing facilities, bath and basin into the bathroom, with the consequent disuse of a washstand in the bedroom. Its disappearance seems to have been slower than the partial disappearance of the wardrobe and was mainly confined to newer houses and the younger generation, older people clinging to its use.

The divan was another piece of furniture which rather altered its function during the 'twenties. In the Russian Ballet phase of the pre-war years it had been a regular feature of ' studios ', disguised under Spanish shawls or panels of Chinese embroidery and piled high with colourful cushions. In the post-war years it had been a necessity in bed-sitting rooms, serving the purposes of a couch by day and a bed by night. The increasing taste for built-in furniture in the late 'twenties made the divan, surrounded by low bookshelves, into a respectable decorative part of a scheme. The settee, however, maintained its popularity as the central feature of many new schemes and with the addition of two completely upholstered easy chairs became the three piece suite considered a necessity in many middle and working class homes in the 1930s. These easy chairs were often of monumental proportions — one designed by

179 R.W.Symonds and **Robert Lutyens**
writing desk, 1928

180 Pel chromium-plated tubular
metal chair, 1929

181 Bookbinding in black American cloth for
My 30 Years' War by Margaret Anderson, 1930

Arundell Clarke about 1930 was advertised as being able to accommodate seven people, one in the conventional seat, two seated on the back and two on each arm — and those turned out in thousands by the 'Curtain Road' cheap furniture manufacturers reached heights of unparalleled hideousness.

The growing social custom of the cocktail party in the post-war years necessitated some receptacle where the bottles, glasses and ice could be kept and this problem was solved in rooms with period decorations by adapting a convenient antique piece of furniture, often a lacquer cabinet with the original interior ruthlessly scrapped and replaced by glass shelves. In a modernistic décor the cocktail cabinet became a piece of furniture in its own right with lead-lined containers for ice, a mirrored interior (often lighting up when the cabinet was opened) and compartments for bottles and glasses.

In 1928 there were signs of a desire for novelty for its own sake and a searching for fantasy as a reaction against both the conventionality of traditional styles and the stark functionalism of the modernistic school. Curtains covered in gold sequins, curtains of cream damask edged with white monkey fur, and foreign newspapers, varnished, used as a substitute for wallpaper in a dining room, were forerunners of more theatrical schemes in the 'thirties when Italian baroque and Austrian rococo furniture, carved and painted Venetian blackamoors, were combined with Victorian bead embroidery and papier mâché inlaid with mother-of-pearl.

182 F.G.R.Elwes bedroom, prior to 1930

183 Machine printed wallpaper
by Sanderson and Sons

184 W. Turner wallpaper designed for
Jeffrey and Co., prior to 1926

Wallpapers

The main tendencies of English decoration in the post-war years being strongly influenced by the Tudor and Georgian periods, there was little scope for designers to produce any wallpapers with contemporary patterns and, in fact, there was no evidence of any contemporary or original style they could follow. A mock-Tudor décor demanded distempered walls in cream or white; those in Georgian style were either painted in plain colours or had a wallpaper with Chinoiserie designs adapted from antique Chinese floral wallpapers. These were similar in design to the many chintzes and cretonnes used for soft furnishing and curtains and probably designed by the same artists — a constantly recurring motif being one of pheasants or some other exotic bird flying or perching among boughs of peonies. Other Chinoiserie designs were of landscapes with figures, either copied or adapted from lacquer screens, placed against black grounds.

Suggestions for the use of these Chinese-inspired wallpapers were made by John Gloag. 'A thin gold bead may be employed... and this is particularly attractive when panels of Chinese wallpaper designs are found in a room inspired by Chinese designs. Many patterns of Chinese paper are manufactured, and in some cases the paper may be treated with colour when hung and varnished afterwards. Arranged in panels, with a shade of green, for instance, stippled on lightly so that the pattern is not obliterated, varnished with an eggshell glaze and edged by gilt beading, Chinese paper can produce a background full of interest and colour suitable for lacquer and Chinese Chippendale furniture', and as extra touches, 'there are possibilities for carrying out details of decoration and helping out colour schemes with the aid of door furniture, for instance in a room that aims at a Chinese style which is furnished with Chinese Chippendale creations and lacquer old and new, the finger plates and door handle can be painted black and decorated with designs in gold that will be in keeping with the general scheme of decoration.'

Wallpapers are rarely illustrated in periodicals of the time but it seems that versions of William Morris papers as well as the originals were sold — the William Morris premises in George Street, Hanover Square were still active — and two papers of this kind were among those shown in the British exhibit at the 1925 Paris Exhibition.

Manufacturers appear to have had difficulty in finding new designs as Sanderson's were advertising for new and original work throughout the 'twenties — Léon Bakst is reported to have designed a paper for this firm in 1924 — but the low fees offered for designs were no encouragement for artists or for the teaching of

185 Paul Véra *Les Baigneuses* wallpaper printed from woodcuts, prior to 1925

wallpaper design in art schools. In addition very few papers were sold for more than half a crown a roll and most were only a few pence a roll, and in consequence the poorest quality paper was used, paper which deteriorates rapidly if kept in a roll for long — a fact which explains why samples of papers of this period have failed to survive. Although a successful design may be in production for a number of years, few manufacturers kept patterns when no longer needed.

Even the cheapest paper needs a reasonably skilled paperhanger to apply it to the walls successfully and the shortage of skilled labour after the war made the use of coloured distemper popular — a trend which became more prevalent as time went on and technical improvements in this medium made its application easier still. Floral designs, however, maintained their popularity and later, geometrical patterns inspired by continental designs. English taste in wallpaper was essentially conservative with a preference for pale colours and inconspicuous patterns. French taste, on the other hand, inclined toward bolder and more original designs and a

186 Henri Stéphany wallpaper, 1928   **187 Henri Stéphany** wallpaper, *c.* 1926

use of colour which at times became garish.

Wallpaper had always been used more in France. In 1851 France produced more than England and the United States combined and, although not so advanced technically in the field of mechanical printing, the cost of printing by hand was low enough to offset the extra time taken. Hand printing by means of the *pochoir* method (a variation on screen printing), or, more rarely, by blocks, enabled more experimental work to be done and a wider variety of design obtained than was permissible by machine printing, when a design had to be commercially safe and consequently conservative, so that it could be sold in sufficient quantities to show a profit on the considerable initial outlay. Consequently the French firms of artist-decorators could produce papers printed in a small workshop to their own design and in harmony with the design of their furniture. The same artists responsible for the textiles created patterns of wallpapers; Stéphany, the Atelier Martine, Bénedictus, Séguy, Georges Barbier, Marie Laurencin, Laboureur and Jean Lurçat.

Ceramics and glass

The British contribution to the commercial pottery section in the 1925 Paris Exhibition was described as having ' a real lack of the spirit of adventure on the artistic side ' — as being lifeless ' a little more virility in the treatment of the day by our distinguished potters would have added savour to the whole British contribution '. This evaluation of the British section of commercial pottery and porcelain, even taking into account the fact that many British firms did not trouble to exhibit as France was a poor market for British pottery, indicated once again the depressing lack of interest on the part of commercial firms in the rôle of the designer and these words of Gordon Forsyth, himself a teacher of pottery, are echoed four years later by H.W.Maxwell, curator of the Stoke-on-Trent Museum, when writing in *The Studio* he comments that ' the forward movement in design is perhaps somewhat impeded by the comparative isolation of North Staffordshire. The kaleidoscopic exhibitions of modern art in London and Paris have comparatively small effect and it is only within quite recent years that exhibitions of modern art have been held at closer quarters and then somewhat limited in scope and there has been little attempt at anything on the lines of research work on modern design. ' At the same time he praises the work of Gordon Forsyth and his efforts to bring a closer relationship between industry and the art schools, which he used as research departments for training young designers for the pottery trade.

The older firms found their largest market in repetitions of old designs executed in painting or transfers on white or cream bodies of bone china or fine earthenware and there was a constant demand for their dinner services (popular wedding presents) or for replacements of parts of services. Wedgwood, Copeland (a descendant of the Spode factory) Minton's and the Royal Worcester factories were foremost in this field and relied heavily on traditional patterns especially the less expensive handpainted or transfer patterns.

New designs were, on the whole, undistinguished and usually applied to traditional forms, although with the advent of modernistic idioms about 1927, square teapots, cups and saucers were introduced but failed to find general approval. Wedgwood produced some pleasant designs in cream-coloured ware, decorated by Alfred Powell in silver lustre designs of abstract foliage, finely drawn in a manner reminiscent of Duncan Grant and a strikingly similar design by Susie Cooper was utilized by A.E.Gray and Co., also executed in silver or copper ' Gloria ' lustre on a cream ground. Alfred Powell and his wife Louise worked in association with the Wedgwood factory which made bowls and pots to their design and after they had applied their painted designs in a style which harked back to William Morris, the glazing and firing was done in the factory. The Poole Pottery — John Adams, Truda Adams, Harold Stabler, J. Radley-Young and Erna Manners was an amalgamation of a tile-making firm, Messrs Carter of Poole, and a studio of artists making hand made pottery for domestic and architectural use. The output from the Poole Pottery was considerable and the cream or ivory vessels, covered in a dull glaze and decorated with linear floral designs in pastel shades, are still to be found in large numbers. An interesting, if temporary, addition to the Poole Pottery studio was Minnie McLeish, for a long time one of the most talented and original textile designers working in England. Another firm which started making tiles for flooring was that of Messrs Pilkington, founded about 1900. A small department started soon after for the making of pottery, particularly that with lustre glazes, prospered under the direction of Joseph Burton (an enthusiast for Chinese pottery) with the assistance of the designer Gwladys Rogers who followed in the footsteps of Walter Crane and Louis F. Day, the firm's earliest artistic advisers. The influence of the Arts and Crafts Movement which they bequeathed can still be seen in the work produced in

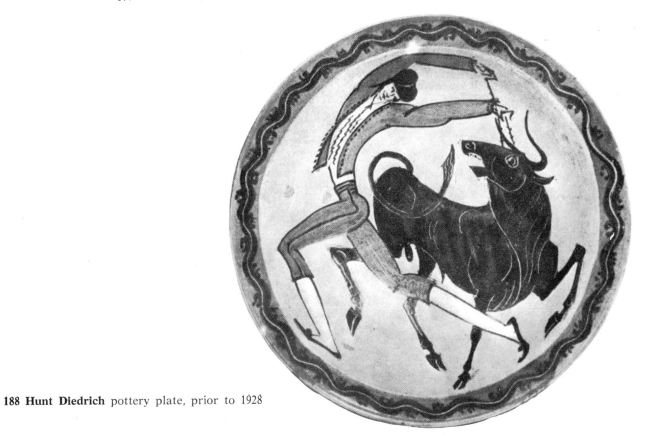

188 Hunt Diedrich pottery plate, prior to 1928

189 Cylindrical vase, Royal Worcester porcelain, 1919   **190 Frank Brangwyn** pottery vase, Royal Doulton, probably *c.* 1926

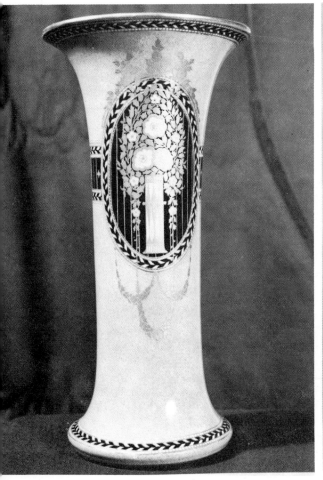

191 Charles Vyse *The Tulip Girl* porcelain figure, prior to 1920

192 Emile Lenoble group of pottery

193 Bernard Leach glazed pottery vase, prior to 1923

the 'twenties. The Royal Lancastrian Ware and the individually designed and painted vases with lustre glazes received much contemporary praise and were favourably compared with the finest productions of Persia and of Gubbio. Mention should be made of the high temperature 'flambé' vases from the Ruskin pottery, under the direction of M. Howson Taylor. By means of leadless glazes fired at a high temperature effects closely resembling those of the later Chinese potters were obtained, each vase or bowl being an individual and an unrepeatable item. So close was the imitation of Chinese idioms that in some cases the carved hardwood stands of the originals were incorporated into the vase and reproduced in the same material as the vase. The Ashstead Potters in Sussex were founded with the intention of giving work to disabled ex-servicemen, generous assistance being given to the venture by manufacturers. The fourteen potters employed at the beginning grew by 1925 to thirty and as their skills increased the simple white-glazed earthenware acquired painted decoration of linear patterns, landscapes and eventually figures which were modelled by Percy Metcalfe.

The most original work in pottery was, however, done by the 'studio' potters, although much of this too was uninspiring and derivative — the British studio pottery exhibit at the 1925 Exhibition was also criticized as 'lacking in virility... inclined to be affected and to err on the pretty-pretty side'. The influence of Chinese pottery of the Sung, Tang and Han periods (pottery from the last-named dynasty had only recently been brought to the attention of the western world through excavations), of Korean celadon and the sophisticated vessels used in the Japanese tea ceremonies was paramount and too many craftsmen were 'worshippers at the shrine of the old Chinese potters' — a description applied to W. Staite Murray whose work, admirable as it was, could have been mistaken for that of Chinese potters of the Sung or Tang dynasties. It seemed as if potters were resolute in reproducing oriental effects of glaze or texture and were incapable of learning and applying that knowledge to the creation of something entirely original, a failing shared by most of their French contemporaries.

The doyen of the English studio potters during the 'twenties was Bernard Leach

194 English porcelain cigarette box, Crown Devon; porcelain decanter by **Robj**; tin biscuit box

who had returned to England to found a studio at St Ives after a period of years spent in Japan studying the potter's craft under the tutelage of Kenzan, the sixth of a line of potters highly esteemed as artists. As a result of this apprenticeship spent in Japan, Leach had a closer acquaintance with historic Japanese pottery and, in addition, with that of the greatest periods of Chinese art, examples of which were collected by Japanese connoisseurs. In Japan, he became aware of specimens in the Tokyo Museum of the Dutch delft which had been brought by traders in the seventeenth century and these and the English slipware of the same period by Ralph Toft played their part in influencing him when he began work at St Ives. Until the late 1920s, Leach's work consisted mostly of individual pieces of considerable cost intended for connoisseurs. Around 1929, however, he was joined by Michael Cardew and less expensive work, suitable for a larger market, was produced.

The amount of work turned out by the small studios or by individual potters was considerable, though little was produced of any distinction and in the main these works were derivative and strongly influenced by Leach and Staite Murray, the two acknowledged masters of the period. The painted and glazed figurines by Phoebe and Harold Stabler, Stella Crofts, Gwendolen Parnell, Harry Parr and others have decorative qualities while figurines by Charles Vyse, *The Balloon Women*, *The Tulip Girl* and *The Lavender Seller*, all dating from about 1920 and modelled from real costers and gypsies, had a robust quality which ensured their popularity.

In contrast with the prodigal display of talent allied to imagination displayed by glass workers in France, Sweden, Austria, Hungary and Germany during the 'twenties, the record of England's achievements in the same period is a melancholy one. 'Very little glass with any claim to distinction can be placed to the credit of this country', wrote a contributor to the *Studio Year Book of Decorative Art* in 1925 and the subsequent years did little if anything to improve the situation. Any demand there may have been for decorative glass seems to have been satisfied by elaborately faceted cut glass and few homes were considered complete without at least one rosebowl, flower vase or fruit bowl of invariably poor design, in spite of technical excellence. Unrestricted importation of cheap table glass — Woolworths sold simple and often elegant wine glasses made in Poland or Czechoslovakia for sixpence — gave manufacturers no inducement to make innovations and very little effort was made to train the young in this field, some art schools under government sponsorship having no equipment for practical work — a sharp contrast to the practice in Sweden or Czechoslovakia where every encouragement was given to young students. James Powell and Sons produced some glass which was not without merit but the popular 'Monart' glass made by Moncreiff of Perth is not comparable with Continental work.

Textiles

English textiles

A common complaint in the immediate post-war years was that while there was a wide range of inexpensive plain fabrics of different weaves and good colours such as Liberty's 'Baghdad' casement cloth obtainable 'in the brilliant colours of the Orient', the patterned materials available, cretonnes, chintzes and printed linens, were 'as a rule commonplace and uninteresting'. Various new and adventurous designs had been shunned by the trade buyers and 'the type of design favoured by the suburban draper once again reigns supreme'. Innovations in the design of textiles were legitimate, it was felt, on the Continent but in England more conservative tastes prevailed for the reason that 'most people have antique furniture' and designs based on traditional themes provide a more harmonious background. Salesmen in the furnishing fabric departments of the big firms found that their customers, unwilling to make too drastic a change in their surroundings, tended to replace a fabric that had worn out with another of similar design and colour.

The prevailing trend to period furnishing, either Tudor, eighteenth century or Chinese, influenced the choice of fabrics made available. Stock designs or new variations (almost indistinguishable) in both woven and printed fabrics tended to fall into categories of those based on Elizabethan or Italian Renaissance sources, versions of the bird and tree patterns from Chinese painted wallpapers and innumerable variations of floral designs, the last being semi-naturalistic with easily recognizable flowers, roses, hollyhocks, delphiniums, poppies or marigolds. Black backgrounds were extremely popular in 1920 and maintained their appeal for some years to come — a favourite covering for three piece suites in imitation Chinese lacquer frames, was a black fabric woven with designs of grotesque Chinese figures and temples in gold-coloured threads. Most chintzes were produced with black backgrounds as an alternative to the more conventional blue, tango, bronze, yellow, fawn, grey, taupe or cream. Long acquaintance with these designs, for many of them are still to be found, has, perhaps, dulled appreciation of their virtues of good drawing in the design and an undoubted technical excellence. Owing to the policy of anonymity favoured by most textile manufacturers, the designers' names have been lost but one firm, W. Foxton Ltd, was exceptional in marketing new and original printed fabrics and publicizing the names of the designers — Claude Lovat Fraser, whose designs for the Nigel Playfair production of *The Beggar's Opera* made theatrical history, Charles Rennie Mackintosh, Constance Irving, Gladys Barraclough, Dorothy Hutton and Minnie McLeish. The last-named produced numerous designs featuring conventionalized floral motifs which were strongly reminiscent of examples of textiles from the Weiner Werkstatte (work emanating from that organization had been illustrated in *The Studio* before the 1914 war) and, none the worse for that, her textiles were well drawn, imaginative and would bear revival.

George Sheringham, a decorative artist fascinated by the decorative aspects of Hogarthian England (he succeeded Lovat Fraser as designer of costumes and scenery for Nigel Playfair's revivals of eighteenth century classics after Lovat Fraser's tragic early death) was commissioned by Sefton and Co. to design textiles — an indication of the fact that in spite of the indifference of the public, one or two more enlightened firms were willing to gamble on the chance of finding even a small responsive number of clients for original work. There had been, since the war, a number of individual textile printers whose work, hand printed from wood or lino blocks, had been attracting attention. Working for private people, Phyllis Barron, Dorothy Larcher, Enid Marx and Francis Wollard had considerable prestige — Phyllis Barron's materials were used on the Duke of Westminster's yacht — but until the

195 Phyllis Barron hand block-printed fabric

opening of the firm 'Footprints' in Beauchamp Place, London, their fabrics were little known to the general public. Neither traditional nor aggressively modernist, their designs were based on small abstract geometrical repeats, the scale of which was governed by the size of the blocks used, and, being subdued in colour, they were found to harmonize with antique or modern decorative schemes. Characterized by a strong family resemblance it is not easy to distinguish between a print by Phyllis Barron and one by Enid Marx for instance, but they all have the same quality of unobtrusiveness — a contemporary comment was that 'the genuine originality and modernity of their outlook escapes the notice of those who only recognize novelty when it becomes eccentricity'. Footprints were also agents for work by Paul Nash, Eric Kennington, Norman Wilkinson and Marion Dorn who, with her husband McKnight Kauffer, was in the forefront of modernist designers in England. From her first exhibition of carpets and rugs with bold geometrical motifs, similar to those of Da Silva Bruhns in Paris, her work was constantly featured in periodicals. Marion Dorn's work was not confined to carpets, though it was for these that she was generally known: she also designed and executed 'by means of a special process' (details of which are unfortunately not forthcoming) large and striking curtains which, when drawn, formed a decorative panel. By this process she interpreted designs of negroes by Matisse for the Gargoyle club in Soho, a well known rendezvous for the Bright Young Things of the 'twenties.

The hand block-printed silks by Crysede Ltd at St Ives, Cornwall were colourful fabrics with more than a superficial resemblance to materials by Raoul Dufy. They were, in fact, the work of Alec Walker, a painter who was brought up in the silk industry, studied painting in Paris and used his own paintings of Cornish scenes as starting-off points for abstract designs for fabrics.

The heavier woven fabrics were, if it were possible, more traditional in feeling than printed ones. Less easily worn out and consequently having a longer life they were usually chosen for either richness of texture, cut velvets and brocades woven with metal threads, or for anonymity of design — the less striking the design the less likely to become a source of irritation. Experimental design was confined to flimsier and cheaper fabrics. Ecclesiastical fabrics, those used for church furnishings and vestments, were even less likely to need constant renewal and the silk tissues exhibited by Warner and Son in the 1925 Exhibition have a strong flavour of the 1890s.

The St Edmondsbury Weaving Works made a speciality of hand-woven silks with gold and silver thread designs, mostly intended for ecclesiastical use and notable for the attempt to break with traditional concepts and to bring a more modern feeling into church vestments and altar cloths. The vegetable-dyed backgrounds of their fabrics were in rich jewel-colours and provided contrasts to the well drawn decorative motifs in metal threads. There were a considerable number of small studios devoted to hand-weaving; the Artificers' Guild of Cambridge, the Kensington Weavers, the Knotty Ash Weavers (Marion Best and Marjorie Shaw), the Escote Weavers, the London School of Weaving, to name only a few, and in addition there were individual weavers whose output was necessarily limited. Their fabrics were usually sold in the numerous arts-and-crafts shops which sprang up in the late 'twenties. Kensington Church Street was a centre for these shops which sold pottery, art jewellery, hand-blocked textiles and book-end papers and other artifacts for which there was a small but steady market.

The simplicity which became a characteristic of interiors and furniture at the end of the decade was reflected in the use of plain materials and cotton or artificial silk or satins; tweeds and heavy slub materials were used in conjunction with metal furniture. Such patterns as were introduced were geometrical in feeling and show influences of those fabrics made by Rodier in France. The main manufacturer of this type was the ' Old Glamis Fabrics '.

England had its exponents of the Javanese batik dyeing which was having a successful revival in Paris under the aegis of Madame Pangon. A silk dress by Alice Pashley with a reserve design on a cerise background was purchased in 1924 by the Victoria and Albert Museum while Jessie M. King, an illustrator in water colours since the 1890s and later a designer of textiles, experimented in the field of batik during the early 'twenties, one of her dresses being illustrated in *The Studio* for 1923. .She also wrote a book dealing with the techniques of batik dyeing, called *How Cinderella got to the Ball.*

American textiles

An attempt to assert the individuality of American design ' for modern American women by modern American artists reflecting the modern American scene and temper just as vitally as Oberkampf's Toiles de Jouy told the story of eighteenth century France ' was inaugurated by the Stehli Silk Corporation in 1925. Ralph Barton, Clayton Knight, Katherine Sturges, Charles Falls, Neysa McMain, Rene Clarke and the eminent photographer Steichen were invited to collaborate in the venture and were given a free hand in creating designs which would achieve the aims stated and in addition break the monopoly of flower prints and polka dot patterns of which there was a surfeit in the American stores. Without preconceived ideas these artists produced fabrics which betrayed their technical ignorance but with some acquired knowledge of the processes of fabric printing and of dress design, some original and inventive designs were produced. Steichen's contributions were photographs of small everyday objects, such as matches and matchboxes, carefully lit to give a dramatic quality and arranged in unusual and interesting patterns. *Metropolis* by F. V. Carpenter had an abstract design suggesting the crowded streets of Manhattan, Dwight Taylor's *Thrill* was inspired by the switchbacks at Coney Island, Clayton Knight's *April* had an amusing allover pattern of open umbrellas, slating rain and an occasional rainbow — an allusion, perhaps, to the popular song *April Showers*. Ruzzie Green's *It*, a typographical design in blue and green, was again a reference to the name given by Elinor Glyn to sex appeal — Clara Bow, a vital star of silent movies was publicized as the 'It Girl'.

196 André Marty *La Vie au Grand Air* printed on cotton,
Paris Exhibition, 1925 (See chapter on French textiles, p. 84)

Posters

English posters

In 1902 there were three advertising and commercial artists listed in the London Post Office Directory: by 1925 the number had risen to one hundred and three. Neither figure, of course, included those designers who worked part time or on the occasional commission from an agency, but the increase in numbers is indicative of the growing importance of advertising and the recognition of the necessity of using the talents of artists specializing in this particular genre — artists with the ability to create designs with an immediate appeal to the eye and a working knowledge of the technical processes involved in the reproduction of their original work. There was, however, no affiliation in England of the various branches of poster or commercial art similar to that in France where artists, publishers, printers and the agents responsible for the siting of posters were allied together in the 'Union de l'Affiche Française'.

During the war years the main production of posters was to boost the morale of the public or to help in recruiting, and few of these patriotic posters have more than a historic interest. In the troubled years after the armistice, advertising acquired a new significance as a means of selling goods or services and the difference in approach in England and in France is marked. In England the main patrons of poster designers proved to be the London Underground and the railways. The message which the Underground wished to convey to the public was one to the effect that travel by this means was clean, comfortable and speedy, and here it should be mentioned that the Underground was in direct competition with the trams and bus services, who in turn had the rivalry of the 'pirate' buses. The upper decks of these vehicles being uncovered (leather flaps, attached to the back of the seats, could be fastened in bad weather to afford a little protection to the passengers) suffered the disadvantage of being extremely uncomfortable in wet weather. Underground advertising therefore concentrated on the message that beauty spots in the Green Belt around London could be reached in comfort as easily as the various places of historic interest in the capital. Incidentally the Underground trains themselves rarely if ever figured in the advertisements.

F.C.Herrick (his was the only poster submitted to the jury of the 1925 Paris Exhibition) was consistently commissioned by the Underground in the early 'twenties and occasional designs by George Sheringham, Frank Brangwyn, Aubrey Hammond, Lionel Edwards, Dorothy Hutton, Rex Whistler and McKnight Kauffer were used at various times — all of an extremely high standard and combined with the excellent legible lettering used in all the Underground advertising. E. McKnight Kauffer, an American resident in England and married to Marion Dorn, the carpet designer, brought a new idiom of expression to commercial art in England, an idiom inspired by cubism which after a hostile reception — his 1919 poster for the Arts League of Service had to be withdrawn because of the adverse criticism it inspired — gradually won acceptance and widespread imitation. McKnight Kauffer finally achieved respectability, being commissioned to redesign the cover for *The Studio*.

At this time, only a very few people thought of spending their annual holiday abroad, and it was thus in the interests of both seaside resorts and the various railways — Southern, Great Western, London and North Eastern and the London Midland and Scottish, to advertise the attractions of resorts and beauty spots in England and Scotland. Consequently some of the best and most striking posters were commissioned by the railways. One of the earliest was the 'Skegness is so Bracing' poster by John Hassall which became a classic of humorous advertising, but the majority of posters advertising seaside resorts and inland towns inclined to

197 E. McKnight Kauffer *The Studio* cover design

stress the historic importance or natural beauty of the countryside by means of bold, simplified views carried out in flat colours with an elimination of unnecessary details. Tom Purvis, Norman Wilkinson, Fred Taylor and Tom Grainger were particularly adept in this type of design and successfully broke down the traditional attitude that the ideal poster was an oil painting reproduced in chromo-lithography of the kind represented by Millais, *Bubbles*. From 1927 onwards the Empire Marketing Board showed itself alive to the need for commissioning artists to help in the growing export trade, inviting leading artists to design posters.

198 Simon Bussy poster for the London and North Eastern Railway

The opportunities offered by posters advertising films seem to have been ignored — probably because the custom of changing the programme in cinemas twice a week would have entailed a considerable expenditure in fees for artists of any standing to supply designs for so many feature films — and almost without exception this type of poster was lurid, badly designed and poorly printed. Beyond announcing the names of the film and the leading players, films hardly needed any publicity outside London as apart from repertory theatres, the films had no competition during the 'twenties — an evening at the cinema could comprise two films, newsreels, serials, orchestral interludes and often two or more live variety acts, a programme unaffected as yet by that offered by the wireless.

The explosion of talent in painting and sculpture in Paris during the 1920s had little or no effect on posters, contrary to what might have been expected. To quote John Harrison, writing in 1927: ' The larger French public is in reality very conservative and the French advertiser is exceedingly loath to offend his public or to go against his own inclinations in giving to the world the audacities of young artists '. This may seem a drastic change in public opinion from that of the 1890s when a new and exciting poster by Jules Chéret, Alphonse Mucha or Toulouse-Lautrec was an event and the streets of Paris were described as the picture gallery of the man in the street. But these posters were displayed in only a limited area and that one where their artistic qualities would be appreciated, and thirty years later sites for posters had sprung up in provincial towns and even the countryside as competition in commerce became more intense. The travel poster, so much a feature of English life, was to be seen to a far less degree in France, although some good posters were produced to advertise resorts like Deauville or Trouville and A.M.Cassandre's railway posters were among the best produced anywhere. In comparison with English

199 E. McKnight Kauffer
Royal Wilton carpet, 1928

200 Ruzzie Green
It printed silk, 1928

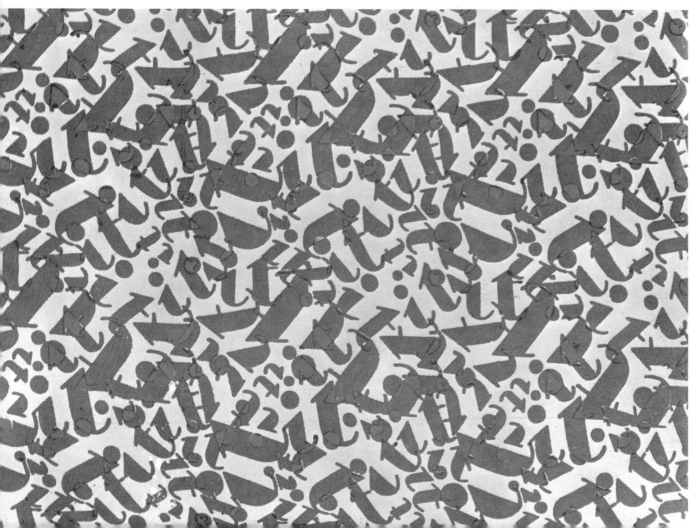

201 Tom Purvis poster for Austin Reed

posters, deplored by critics as resembling Punch cartoons with captions underneath, their French counterparts had the virtue of conveying a quick message easily assimilated from a moving vehicle, although on the whole the lettering was inferior to that of English posters. Jean d'Ylen continued the tradition set by Chéret and his boldly designed dancing figures caught in mid-air in arrested movement were a colourful part of the French scene. Cassandre, working in a cubist idiom, was, like McKnight Kauffer in England, an innovator of the formalized designs of the 1930s with realism banished in favour of geometrical representations of the products.

202 Jean d'Ylen poster for Sandeman's

203 Aubrey Hammond poster for the Folkestone Theatre, 1927

French posters

The real style and distinction in France was to be found in posters advertising performances by such public favourites as Maurice Chevalier, Marguerite Templey, Arletty (van Dongen drew an arresting portrait of her for a poster) and in those for the luxury trades where the talents of Jean Dupas, for example, were given full rein. Directed toward a more sophisticated market, designers had more freedom to indulge in imaginative flights with no fear of antagonizing a potential market and the best of French commercial art is to be found in the pamphlets and trade cards of the couturiers, decorators and others in the luxury trades.

204 Delis poster for Clotilde and Alexandre Sakharoff, 1923

205 Pico poster for the Folies Bergères, prior to 1928

206 Jean Dupas poster for Arnold Constable, *c.* 1926

207 Michel Bouchaud *Monte Carlo* poster, 1929

208 Poster for the Paris dressmakers' ball

Advances in methods of reproduction of photographs enlarged the range of techniques in the latter part of the decade. Sparingly used in the post-war years, photographs had only been used as an inset to illustrate a vase, a piece of furniture, a piece of jewelry, usually surrounded by text. About 1927, however, a new trend is discernible — one attributed by a contemporary writer to the influence of the films, and Russian films in particular. The unusual camera angles and cross-cutting employed by the Russians to convey their message in the silent propaganda films of the 'twenties made a great impact in spite of their limited exhibition in this country and the advertising agencies and commercial artists were quick to adapt the vivid imagery in terms of posters and press advertisements, incorporating photographs, drawings and text into their work.

209 Press advertisement for Worth scent, 1928

Envoi

The 'twenties ended, to all intents, on Thursday October 24, 1929 when the New York Stock Exchange closed its doors. Thousands of speculators, large and small, were ruined overnight — it was estimated that savings approximating ten thousand million dollars were lost — and the concept of the United States as a modern Eldorado was shattered. Following on a financial crash of a lesser scale in the previous September when the failure of the Hatry Group had sent prices on the London Stock Exchange plummeting to rock bottom this greater disaster closed the decade on a sombre note which was to reverberate in the form of slumps and depression for some years afterwards. There had been financial crises during the 1920s but to a certain extent the optimism of the post-war years had carried people through what were regarded as the teething troubles of a New Age. By the end of the 1920s, however, a deep feeling of disillusion was beginning to make itself felt — a feeling intensified by the major financial crises of 1929. People stopped spending, some because they no longer had any to spend while the more fortunate became determined to hold on to what they had in case things became worse. Inevitably the luxury trades and the decorative arts suffered and the 'thirties began in an atmosphere of strain and uncertainty. The 'twenties had been an exciting period, with an atmosphere all its own. It was a time of reassessment and discovery. There were at the beginning many traces of the pre-war style, luxury and elegance — it was after all possible to be young in Edwardian days and middle-aged in the 'twenties and even in straitened circumstances old habits die hard. But social change was in the air and the younger generation was impatient with the patterns of life of their elders and wanted to experiment with new ideas and new sensations whether in sex, music or drugs. This new outlook was reflected in the way people dressed, the way they decorated their homes and in the choice of objects with which they surrounded themselves. Sometimes these objects shared the gaiety, the rather endearing silliness which was a particular attribute of the period before the soul-chilling horrors which came into being in the following decade; sometimes they had a quality and distinction which could enable them to rank with the best of previous ages. But frivolous or serious, the artifacts of the decorative 'twenties form a link in the chain of design. Whether this link is strong or weak is a verdict which lies in the future.

210 Carlègle housemark for Léon Pichon, prior to 1924

Notes on the illustrations

In a survey of a period of only ten years and one where a considerable change in style can be observed, the question of citing the dates of the objects illustrated has to be rather more exact than if a longer period were under examination. In many cases the exact date can be given but in other cases the date has to be given as prior to the earliest appearance of the object in a magazine or book. The temptation to assign an exact date to anything illustrated in the *Studio Year Book of Decorative Art* — in all other respects a mine of valuable information — and to assume that anything illustrated in the 1927 volume, for instance, was made in 1926 (allowing approximately a year for the preparation of the volume) has to be avoided as cross reference to other periodicals can reveal that a prior date of anything up to five years is more accurate and each volume cannot be regarded as a summary of the previous year's work.

1 Barbara Greg. Woodcut. Book illustration.

2 M. Dufet. Advertisement for the decorating firm Chez Fernande Cabanel. 1922.

3 F.C. Bayliss, architect. Smith's Tea Room, 248 Rue de Rivoli, Paris. Plasterwork, mural heraldry and leaded lights by F.E. Osborne, woodwork by Sledmere of Paris. An interior conforming to the tradition of representing England abroad as a country still living in the sixteenth century.

4 *La Soie.* Pottery figure after a model by Marcel Renard. Signed. French. Exhibited in the 1925 Paris Exhibition.
Oval bowl covered with a crackled turquoise glaze and decorated with panels of incised ornament covered with dark blue glaze. Inscribed 'Atelier Primavera Longwy'. Circular box with lid in pottery glazed in dark blue, aubergine, green and yellow with a crackled finish. Decorated with a nude female figure on the lid. Inscribed ' Primavera Longwy France' with a coat of arms. The Atelier Primavera, a department of the Parisian store Au Printemps, was founded in September 1912 for the sale of furniture and decorative accessories. By the mid-'twenties there were no fewer than 13,750 different models of ceramics obtainable, emanating from a factory at Sainte-Radegonde near Tours. As these pieces are both marked 'Longwy' it would appear that another factory was operating. Cabinet making, and the production of bronzes, sculpture, ironwork and lacquer was at Montreuil-sous-Bois. Stylistically these pieces date from about 1920.
Vase with a mottled glaze in tones of greenish-blue and iron-red. Signed 'Simmen'. Henri Simmen was a well-known potter active in the 'twenties and his work was regularly shown in exhibitions of decorative art.

5 *Le Café.* C. Saupique. Decorative panel modelled in relief and coloured for the Café du Dôme. 1924. The Café du Dôme and the neighbouring La Coupole were the meeting places for the bohemians of Paris in the 'twenties.

6 P. Turin. Bronze commemorative metal for the Paris Exhibition, 1925.

7 Ormulu electric table lamp with shaded opaque glass shade. Signed ' C. Ranc'.

8 Renouvin. Music stool. Prior to 1925. Mahogany with the motifs on the supports and the carved panels lacquered beige. The upholstered centre portion lifts up to reveal a compartment for music. Modern embroidery.

9 Anonymous. Gilt single chair, part of a suite of drawing room furniture. c. 1923. Modern covering.

10 Maurice Dufrène. Interior designed for La Maîtrise. 1928. The angular modernistic lines of this interior show how Dufrène had changed from the designs of the Art Nouveau period when he had begun his career.

11 Maurice Dufrène. Boudoir. 1914. Furniture in maplewood ornamented with lacquer and gilded carvings. A typical Art Déco interior with oval mirrors, rounded forms in the furniture and elaborate cushions — note the characteristic placing of a large cushion on the floor.

12 Motor-car body decorated by Maurice Dufrène for La Carosserie Nouvelle (H. Lévy). Exhibited at the Paris Exhibition, 1925. Madame Sonia Delaunay similarly decorated an automobile with *simultané* designs.

13 *Printemps.* Large silvered metal version of medal designed by P. Turin for the 1925 Exhibition. Signed ' P. Turin '.

14 Woodcut decoration from an advertisement. Anonymous. 1925.

15 Sue et Mare. Oval mirror with gilded bronze frame. 1923.

16 Coffee set in Limoges porcelain decorated with floral motifs in brown, orange and gold. *c.* 1923.

17 Boxes for confectionery and writing paper. Prior to 1925. French.

18 Advertisement for Bergue, one of the many firms producing decorative ironwork in Paris. 1925.

19 Daum. Glass vase with typical Art Déco motifs of conventionalized flowers and spirals.

20 A. Piguet. Wrought-iron door, with panel of lacquered metal by Claudius Linossier, a pupil of Jean Dunand and like him influenced by the discoveries of jewelry and metalwork at Mycenae.

21 J. Leleu. Armchair. Exhibited at the 1925 Exhibition.

22 Jean Puiforcat. Silver and lapis-lazuli dish and cover. Exhibited at the 1925 Exhibition.

23 Pierre Patout. Entrance from the Place de la Concorde to the 1925 Exhibition. Statue by De Jean, bas-reliefs by Jan and Jöel Martel.

24 Pierre Laprade. Pavilion for Studium Louvre at the 1925 Exhibition.

25 ' Le Pavillon d'un Collectionneur '. Pierre Patout, architect. Paris Exhibition 1925. Sculpture and bas-reliefs by Bernard.

26 Jacques Ruhlmann. Study in ' Le Pavillon d'un Ambassadeur' in the 1925 Exhibition. See plate 28 for details of the table in the far corner of the room.

27 Jacques Ruhlmann. Cabinet. Prior to 1925. One of the pieces of furniture bearing Ruhlmann's signature which justified the claim by his admirers that his work rivalled that of the great *ébénistes* of the eighteenth century. The elaborate inlay of circles of ivory, the use of a sculptured bronze plaque and the massive proportions are in the tradition of Boulle.

28 Jacques Ruhlmann. Ebony and burr-walnut table. 1925. The octagonal top veneered with burr-walnut and inlaid with a circular motif of ivory circles, the edge of the top inlaid with sections of ivory. Ebony undershelf and tapering legs of square section with ivory feet. Signed 'Ruhlmann'.

29 Jacques Ruhlmann. Single chair and small table. Prior to 1925. The chair is based on the *gondole* form popular at the end of the eighteenth and the beginning of the nineteenth centuries, while the table shows the characteristic Ruhlmann touches in the tapering reeded legs, the ivory feet and handles.

30 The salon of 'Le Pavillon d'un Collectionneur' designed by Ruhlmann for the 1925 Exhibition. The brocade wall covering in violet and grey was designed by Henri Stéphany.

31 André Groult. Interior with mural panels by Charles Martin. 1921. The armchairs have traditional forms but the back is decorated with the Art Déco motif of a basket of conventionalized flowers, executed in carved and painted wood. A similar set of chairs, probably based on Groult's model, appeared as set dressing for a number of Hollywood movies including *The Affairs of Anatol*, 1921 and *Enter Madame*, 1922.

32 *La Danse.* Painted panel by Charles Martin (see plate 31).

33 *Les Cigognes d'Alsace.* Edgar Brandt. Wrought-iron and bronze decorative panels. *c.* 1923. Replicas of these panels were installed in the interiors of the lifts at Selfridges in Oxford Street, London.

34 Edgar Brandt. Advertisement. 1925.

35 *L'Oasis.* Five-fold screen by Edgar Brandt after a design by his collaborator Henri Favier. Exhibited at the 1925 Exhibition.

36 Raymond Subes. Radiator case in wrought iron and brass.

37 Jean Dunand. Lacquer furniture and screens. Prior to 1928.

38 Jean Dunand. Two vases of hammered metal inlaid with silver.

39 Jean Dunand. Four metal vases and a covered box. Prior to 1925.

40 Anonymous. Motif of baskets of flowers. From *Die Kunst*, 1906.

41 Anonymous. Motif of a basket of flowers in an oval panel. From *Die Kunst*, 1906.

42 Eileen Gray. Lacquer screen. Commissioned by Jacques Doucet.

43 Armand Rateau. Bathroom for the Duchess of Alba, Madrid. 1925. Several pieces of the bronze furniture in this room were identical with those in the bathrooms designed by Rateau for Madame Jeanne Lanvin in Paris and Mrs Blumenthal in New York.

44 *Les Perruches*. Jean Dupas. Decorative panel over the fireplace of the salon in 'Le Pavillon d'un Collectionneur' designed by Ruhlmann for the 1925 Paris Exhibition (see plate 30).

45 Djo-Bourgeois. Interior. *c.* 1927. An innovation is the treatment of the divan as a piece of boxed-in furniture.

46 Robert Mallet-Stevens. Modernist interior. Carpet by Fernand Léger, fabrics by Hélène Henry, glass by Jan and Jöel Martel. 1927.

47 Jean Michel Frank. Interior. Prior to 1929.

48 Madame Lipska and Henri Martin. Office in the glass house of Antoine.

49 Wrought-iron guéridon, base of walnut with beige marble top. *c.* 1923.
Christofle. One of a pair of vases in metal, one lacquered black with silver geometrical design, the other lacquered tango. *c.* 1923.

50a DIM. Tubular metal chair with laced leather seat and back. Prior to 1929.

50b DIM. Tubular metal chair with velvet upholstery. Prior to 1929.

51 J. Adnet. Table with marble top on nickelled metal support. Prior to 1929.

52a J. Adnet. Metal armchair with leather upholstery. Prior to 1929.

52b J. Adnet. A tubular metal chair with leather upholstered seat. Prior to 1929.

53 Eugène Printz. Table with walnut top on metal supports. Prior to 1929.

54 Lucie Renaudot. Design for a smoking room. *c.* 1926. This room was actually built for exhibition purposes and indications of the reaction against Art Déco can be seen in the lack of applied ornament, the reliance upon the grain of the wood, the textures of the plain fabrics used for effect, and the use of the metal support to the table.

55 Georges Champion. Interior designed for Studios Gué. *c.* 1926. Influenced by the Dutch De Stijl movement of which Theo van Doesburg was the leading exponent in the 'twenties, contributing a long article to *The Little Review* in 1925. Doesburg maintained that the new architecture (which included interior decoration) should do away with symmetry and monotonous repetition, proposing in its place the balanced relationship of unequal parts.

56 DIM. Dressing table in plate glass and metal. Prior to 1930.

57 Pierre Legrain. Glass piano.

58 René Lalique. Clock in coloured glass. The clock movement is set in a circle of thick glass upon which is a figure of a female nude in relief on the back of the glass and a similar male figure in intaglio. The simple bronze base in which the plaque is fixed contains an electric light fitting which illuminated the two figures.
Motor-car mascot in the form of a fish in opalescent glass by René Lalique.
Vase in dark grey glass with vertical bands of formalized floral ornament. Signed 'Sabino'.

59 René Lalique. Vase of opalescent glass with a design of lovebirds in relief. Prior to 1925 when this model was exhibited in the Paris Exhibition.
René Lalique. Vase with a design of leaves on the interior. Opalescent glass. *c.* 1925.

60 *Suzanne*. René Lalique. Figure of a semi-nude girl with arms extended holding draperies. 1922. This model of opalescent glass is sometimes found with a bronze base which conceals an electric light fitting.

René Lalique. Bottle with panels of nude female figures in low relief, lightly coloured blue. The stopper has a figure of a crouching female nude. A similar bottle was used as a set dressing in the film *The Affairs of Anatol* starring Gloria Swanson and Wallace Reid, made in 1921.

René Lalique. Packaging for facepowder designed for Coty. This is one of the earliest and most successful of the designs commissioned from Lalique by the famous firm of scent makers.

61 Group of scent bottles and scent sprays dating from 1920 to 1930. The bottle for Guerlain's 'Mitsouko' dates from 1921 when that scent was first introduced.

62 René Lalique. Decorative lamp. Exhibited at the 1925 Exhibition.

63 René Lalique. Glass lamp. A fan-shaped slab of clear glass engraved on the back with a mythological bird-woman perched on a bough; supported on a square hollow bronze base with a decoration of incised butterflies; an electric light bulb is concealed in the base and the light shines upwards to illuminate the figure. Lalique exhibited a number of similar lamps in the 1925 Exhibition and these models were advertised in English periodicals as being on sale at the Brèves Galeries in London.

64 René Lalique. Dining room designed for 'Le Pavillon de la Manufacture Nationale de Sèvres'. Paris Exhibition 1925.

65 Circular dish of pressed glass in a geometrical design. c. 1927. Signed 'A. Hunebelle France'.

66 Maurice Marinot. Glass bottle.

67 Vase of mottled orange glass with flecks of gold leaf enclosed in a wrought-iron framework. 1920. The glass by Daum, the ironwork by Majorelle. Signed 'Daum Nancy' and 'L. Majorelle'.

68 Marcel Goupy. Enamelled glass vase. Compare the decorative use of similar motifs on this vase with those on the Daum vase (plate 67).

69 Large vase of white glass overlaid with orange (tango) opaque glass cut away in a design of triangles. Signed 'Degne'. Tapering cylindrical vase of mottled beige glass overlaid with glass of an aubergine colour mottled with blue, cut away to reveal the ground in a bold geometrical design. Signed 'Charder'. The technique and glass is similar to those found in glass signed 'Le Verre de France' (see plate 71).

Large vase of mottled brown glass acid etched with a band of design in relief incorporating geometrical elements and formalized flowers. Signed 'Legras'.

Vase of mottled amber coloured glass acid engraved with a design of geometrical leaves and berries. Signed 'Daum Nancy France'. This vase corresponds in description with a group of vases exhibited by the Daum factory in the 1925 Exhibition.

70 Vase of clear glass with air bubbles, enamelled with a design of conventionalized sunflowers in yellow, orange and dark grey enamels joined by lines of spots on gold and dark grey. Signed in gold on the base 'Delvaux 18 Rue Royale Paris'.

Vase of clear glass decorated with a design of geometric roses and leaves in black, white, grey and terracotta opaque enamel. Part of the body of the vase has been treated to give a pitted surface which forms a background for the design. Signed 'H. Laroyer France'.

Bowl of straw-coloured opaque glass enamelled with a floral design in black and cream enamels. Supported on a wrought-iron base. Signed 'Quénvit'.

71 Large vase (one of a pair) of pale blue mottled glass overlaid with a layer of bright blue glass which is cut away in a design of circular motifs enclosing formalized flowers. The stepped design on the base is found on other vases from this factory. Inscribed 'Le Verre de France'.

Clear glass bottle with stopper enamelled with circular bunches of rosebuds, leaves and ribbons in white, gold, black, and deep blue opaque enamels. Inscribed in gold 'Delvaux 18 Rue Royale Paris'.

Clear glass bottle enamelled in two shades of blue and gold. By Nelia Casella, who, with her sister, lived and worked in Brighton exhibiting examples of enamelled glass and decorated leatherwork in group shows in Brighton and London.

Small covered bowl of clear glass enamelled with flowers in blue, white and black. Inscribed in gold 'Delvaux 18 Rue Royale Paris'.

Flower vase of tapering shape of mottled opaque blue glass decorated with relief designs of birds. Signed 'Legras'.

72 *La Carpe.* Wood engraving by Raoul Dufy. An illustration for *Le Bestiaire ou Cortège d'Orphée* by Guillaume Apollinaire. 1911.

73 Foujita. Illustration for *Amal et la Lettre du Roi* by Rabindranath Ṭagore translated by André Gide. 1922.

74 Picart Le Doux. Illustration for *L'Illustre Magicien* by Count Arthur Gobineau. 1920. Wood engraving.

75 Maxime Dethomas. Illustration for *Les Folies Françaises* by François Couperin. 1920. Pen drawing rendered as a wood engraving by Léon Pichon. Published by Léon Pichon.

76 Pierre Legrain. Bookbinding in leather for *Les Plus Beaux Contes de Rudyard Kipling.* A number of works by Rudyard Kipling appear among the éditions de luxe published in France during the 'twenties.

77 *Lettre.* Illustration by Georges Barbier to *Fêtes Galantes* by Paul Verlaine. Published by H. Piazza, 1928. Barbier's illustrations for Verlaine's poems were done between the years 1921 and 1922, though not published until six years later when a subsequent drawing for the cover of the volume was added. The reproduction of the drawings is of the finest quality and constitutes a technical tour-de-force.

78 Bookbinding in coloured leather with gold and blind tooling by Pierre Legrain. For *Paul et Virginie* by Bernardin de St Pierre. Prior to 1925. The treatment of the tropical leaves can be compared with similar motifs in the wrought-iron screen *L'Oasis* by Edgar Brandt (plate 35).

79 Sylvain Sauvage. Illustration for *Contes Antiques* by Pierre Loüys. Published by Editions du Bois Sacré. Copper engravings in colour.

80 Edouard Bénedictus. Moquette carpet. Compare with the Stéphany design, plate 187.

81 Séguy. Fabric designs. *c.* 1925. Reproduced by the *pochoir* process. One of a number of loose plates (undated but probably from an album), all of which reproduce designs based on butterflies, dragonflies and other insects.

82 André Mare. Printed fabric border. Mare was a partner with Louis Sue in La Compagnie des Arts Français founded in 1919; the partnership was dissolved in 1930 after Mare's decision to devote himself to painting but his first show received bad notices from the critics.

83 Two designs for fabrics or wallpaper borders. Anonymous.

84 Jacques Ruhlmann. Printed silk. Prior to 1925.

85 Foujita. Printed silk designed for Lesur. The Japanese painter Tsugouharu Foujita was considered to be one of the most promising artists of the 'twenties and his work was collected by Paul Poiret.

86 *La Jungle.* Brocade in three colours designed by Raoul Dufy for Bianchini et Ferier. 1923.

87 Raoul Dufy. Printed fabric designed for Bianchini et Ferier.

88 *La Pêche.* Printed fabric designed by Raoul Dufy for Bianchini et Ferier.

89 *Les Moissonneurs.* Printed fabric designed by Raoul Dufy for Bianchini et Ferier.

90 *Journée Orageuse.* Printed cotton by Robert Mahias.

91 *Mon Chapeau s'envole.* Printed cotton by Robert Mahias. In designing these fabrics Robert Mahias followed the tradition of the eighteenth century *toiles de Jouy* in incorporating figures dressed in contemporary costume, in this case that of 1922. A similar treatment of furniture can be seen in the chest of drawers by Mario Simon, plate 136.

92 *Sauvagesses.* Printed fabric designed for DIM by Drésa.

93 *Les Divinités Champêtres.* Printed fabric by Paul Véra. 1922.

94 Rodier. Woven fabric, showing the influence of Sonia Delaunay.

95 Sonia Delaunay. Printed silk (*simultané*) in brown. beige, cream and grey. Although flowers had been treated in a geometrical fashion by designers in the Art Déco manner, Madame Delaunay was one of the first to banish all naturalistic elements from her designs and to use geometrical elements only, thus, by the popularity of her work, helping to bring about the decline of Art Déco in favour of modernism.

96 Da Silva Bruhns. Design for a carpet. *c.* 1926. The carpets of Da Silva Bruhns were at first influenced by the traditional patterns by the carpet-weavers of North Africa and later by the cubist paintings of Pablo Picasso. This design was inspired by Picasso's painting *Man leaning on a Table*, dating from 1915. In turn Da Silva Bruhns influenced Marion Dorn and McKnight Kauffer (plate 199) and an inferior version of this design was produced in an Axminster carpet from John Crossley and Sons, Halifax, in the early 'thirties.

97 Atelier Martine. Pile carpet. Prior to 1925.

98 Fashion plate. Anonymous. November 1923. The dress on the left, 'Albion' by Paul Poiret, is described as 'a sweet harmony in "Pétale" crêpe and orange velvet ornamented with black and gold embroidery' while that on the right by Molyneux is in gold and silver lamé with embroidery in several colours.
  The gilt and painted furniture was designed by Mercier Frères.

99 Black velvet hat. 1919.

100 Worth. A tea-gown in chiffon and pearls. 1919.

101 Doeuillet. Evening wrap in velvet with multicoloured embroidery. 1919.

102 Benito. Cover for *Vogue*. October 1922. Benito's career as a fashion artist started in the 'twenties and in this drawing he reflects the current craze for silver fabrics and the low-waisted frocks then in fashion. The oval mirror, the red lacquered sofa and the pattern on the upholstery are typical of the French taste in the post-war years.

103 Paper fan from the Château de Madrid, reproduced from an original design by Paul Iribe and dated 1914. '...the magically white faces of women, the lights in the night making love to the black shadows in their hair, their lips red as lobsters, their armpits clean as ivory, the men talking with facile gestures, the whole tapestry of the Château de Madrid like a painted fan against a summer night...'. *The Green Hat* by Michael Arlen. W. Collins & Sons Ltd. 1924.

104 Tea-gown in velvet with mink edging. 1922.

105 Paul Poiret. Walking costume. 1923.

106 *St. Sebastién.* Drécoll. White woollen dress trimmed with beaver. 1923.

107 Erté (Romain de Tirtoff). Design for an evening dress in silver tissue with embroidered train for Mrs William Randolph Hearst. 1922. The cloak to accompany this dress was of fur (moleskin?) embroidered in silver in geometrical designs.

108 Jeanne Lanvin. Evening dress in rose taffeta with navy blue decoration. 1920.

109 Martial et Armand. Afternoon dress in taffeta. 1921. Hat by Lewis.

110 Embroidered jersey bathing dress. 1921.

111 *Persienne.* Paul Poiret. Top coat in cloth and fur. 1923.

112 Cheruit. Orange glacé taffeta evening dress. 1927.

113 Madeleine et Madeleine. Black crêpe and diamanté evening dress. 1921.

114 Jenny. Black and white evening dress. 1921.

115 Fortuny. Tea-gown in pleated satin. 1926.

116 Louiseboulanger. Top coat in black velvet with fox border. 1926.

117 Yvonne of Belgrave Square. Afternoon dress in tomato red georgette over black satin slip, embroidery of Chinese motifs. 1924.

118 *Aphrodite.* Suzanne Talbot. Gold and white evening dress. 1925.

119 Black velvet hat with artificial rose. 1921.

120 Black satin hat with feathered appliqué. 1923.

121 Marthe Regnier. Hat designed for Gloria Swanson. 1925.

122 Siégel. Display figure covered in mirror in a harlequin pattern and draped with a *simultané* fabric by Sonia Delaunay. From the 1925 Exhibition.

123 Anonymous design for an advertisement for the couturier Agnès. 1924.

124 Vanity case. *c.* 1925. Lined with pink silk and fitted with a mirror and compartments for lipstick and money. Made of one of the artificial materials — in this case in imitation of ivory — which were being produced about this time.

125 Drécoll. Afternoon dress in crêpe. 1926.

126 Benito. Fashion drawing. 1928.

127 Bias-cut satin evening dress.

128 Silver cigarette case with geometrical design in yellow and blue enamel.
   Silver cigarette box with a panel of modernist design in multi-coloured enamels on a black ground.
   Silver cigarette box decorated in blue and black enamel, the sliding fastening decorated with a cabochon moonstone surrounded by marcasites.
   Black enamel cigarette case with marcasite motif of Chinese design.
   Lapel watch in black, scarlet and green enamel.
   Black enamel cigarette box with carved coral motif set with marcasites.
   Silver cigarette case decorated with a Chinese design in apple green enamel. Inscribed 'No, No, Nanette. 11-3-1925 — 16-10-1926' and signed by Messrs Clayton and Waller, the producers of the show.
   Cigarette case of yellow enamel with an openwork panel of a bowl of flowers in multi-coloured enamels.

129 Cigarette box of Chinese design in orange and black lacquer on silver.
   Cigarette case in three shades of gold, decorated with black and orange lacquer.
   Silver cigarette box decorated with orange enamel and eggshell lacquer; clasp set with a cabochon sapphire.
   Cigarette case with modernist design in black, red and eggshell lacquer on silver. In the style of Raymond Templier.

Silver ashtray with Chinese motif in scarlet lacquer, the ground in black lacquer. Similar ashtrays were sold by the firm of Yamanaka in Bond Street.
   Cigarette case of modernist design in black, red and eggshell lacquer on silver.

130 Boucheron. Brooch in onyx, cabochon jade and diamonds.

131 Fouquet. Pendant in semi-precious stones and diamonds.

132 P. Turin. Bronze commemorative metal for the 1925 Exhibition.

133 Paul Poiret. Sketch designs for costumes for the revue *Vogue* presented at the Théâtre Michelet in February 1922.

134 *Eucalyptus.* Fabric designed by the pupils of the Atelier Martine.

135 Atelier Martine. Bathroom.

136 Atelier Martine. Silver lacquer chest with incised decorations in black from designs by Mario Simon. 1923. Handles of silk tassels. Compare plates 90 and 91 for the use of figures in contemporary costume.

137 Atelier Martine. Private dining room on the *Ile-de-France*. The *S.S. Ile-de-France*, launched in 1927, was a floating showcase of contemporary French decorative art and no expense was spared to demonstrate the work of the best French designers and artists of the time. The main staircase had wrought iron decorations by Raymond Subes, Ruhlmann designed a large *salon de thé*, the main dining room was the work of Patout with glass decorations by René Lalique and the main salon was designed by Sue et Mare. The dining room illustrated was in one of the private suites and had walls decorated with straw inlay in tones of blue, red and green with furniture designed after Chinese originals.

138 Atelier Martine. Bedroom. Pror to 1925. The large divan, the elaborate cushions and the low table in the Chinese manner are typical of the early décors from Paul Poiret's decorating studio.

139 Metal belt buckle enamelled in black and white.
   Metal buckle enamelled in white and two

shades of blue; inset with motifs in moulded glass.

Metal buckle with panels of pressed glass and blackened steel.

Similar buckles by Paul Piel et Fils were shown at the 1925 Exhibition.

140 Atelier Martine. Paper fan printed with a floral design. On the reverse is a list of the scents produced by the Parfumerie Rosine. Autographed by Paul Poiret.

141 Advertisement for Hampton's of Pall Mall. 1926.

142 Advertisement for Gill and Reigate, 1923. A design for a Tudor interior by one of the leading firms of antique dealers and interior decorators in London. Their premises extending from Soho Square to Oxford Street were conveniently near to Wardour Street, at that time a centre for antique dealers, and were later moved to George Street, Hanover Square.

143 *Design for Interior*. F.C. Richter. 1915. Watercolour drawing. An example of the simpler type of 'Georgian' scheme which remained in fashion with minor variations from the early 1900s until well into the 1930s.

144 George Sheringham. Design for the music room at Besant Cottage, Frognal, London.

145 W.J. Palmer Jones. A 'Chinese' room. *c.* 1920.

146 Aschermann Studio, New York. Scheme for a Long Island dining room. Prior to 1922.

147 F.G.R. Elwes. Dining room. Prior to 1930. Chairs and table of silver-finished wood, upholstery in faded cherry colour. This interior offers a striking contrast to that illustrated in plate 178. They are both in modern blocks of flats but here Elwes avoids the severity of modernism by the use of modern versions of antique furniture with what must have seemed at the time to be a slightly theatrical effect, especially in the exaggeratedly high backs to the dining chairs. The carved mirror frame placed over a marbleized bolection moulding surrounding the false fireplace would later become a cliché.

148 Porcelain candlestick with decoration in blue and gold. Signed 'A. Godard', marked 'Aladin, France'. Height 6 in.

Coloured bronze inkwell, the head lifting to reveal a porcelain inkwell. Height 4½ in. Width 7¾ in.

149 Lacquer standard lamp with a silk shade painted in the Chinese taste, gramophone cabinet decorated with 'Chinese' lacquer; single chair with lacquer decoration. 1921.

150 Harold Nelson. Advertisement for Dewar's Whisky. Prior to 1926.

151 Frank Brangwyn. Pen drawing advertisement for Stephenson's Floor Polish. 1924. A summing up of the ideal English home, complete with model galleon.

152 Cushions made by Harvey, Nichols and Co., 1919.

153 Charles A. Richter. Dining table in French walnut inlaid with sycamore; ebony inlaid lines and plinth. 1928. (Compare with plate 174).

154 Writing cabinet of cherrywood with ornamental handles of ebony and laburnum. The lowest drawer extended with the front let down forms a desk. Designed by Gordon Russell and executed by Russell and Sons, Broadway, Worcestershire. Gordon Russell combined traditional craftsmanship with simplicity of design and can be credited with the best-designed English furniture of the 'twenties.

155 Paul Frankl. Bookcase. Prior to 1928. Frankl, an American decorator, was one of the very few working in the modern idiom in the United States in the latter years of the decade and, in an attempt to break away from French influences and to give a nationalistic character to his interiors, he used the skyscraper — which he admired as a peculiarly American invention — as a motif in his designs for furniture, creating a range of pieces which he called 'skyscraper furniture'. His idea was that the furniture in the room should harmonize with the lines of the urban landscape seen through the windows.

156 Paul Frankl. Dressing table finished in silver leaf. Prior to 1928.

157 Mellor, Meigs and Howe, architects. Bedroom in a house at Laverock, Philadelphia, USA. *c.* 1923. Pseudo-Spanish Renaissance combined with Edwardian lace table runners.

158 Aschermann Studio, New York. Lamps with shades of batik silk. Prior to 1922.

159 Aschermann Studio, New York. Bachelor's living room. Prior to 1922.

160 Aschermann Studio. Dining room in 'modern style'. Prior to 1922.

161 Paul Nelson. Living room in an apartment in Chicago. The work of this American decorator shows strong influences of such contemporary French decorators as Djo-Bourgeois.

162 Kem Webber, Hollywood. Bedroom in silvered wood and black lacquer. Prior to 1929.

163 Joseph Urban. Project for a conservatory, with furniture in cadmium-plated steel. Exhibited in the 11th Exhibition of American Industrial Art at the Metropolitan Museum, New York, in 1929.

164 Raymond Hood. Office with aluminium furniture, the walls covered in 'fabrikoid'. 11th Exhibition of American Industrial Art, 1929.

165 Eugene Schoen. Living room with furniture in macassar ebony and rosewood. Prior to 1928.

166 Joseph Urban. A man's den. 1929.

167 John Wellborn Root. Woman's bedroom in tones of grey, the upholstery in blue, the dressing table and chair of pewter. 11th Exhibition of American Industrial Art. 1929.

168 D.S. O'Meara. Dining table. Prior to 1928.

169 Ralph T. Walker. Man's study. 11th Exhibition of American Industrial Art, 1929.

170 Miss Sylvia Nelis as Polly Peachum in *The Beggar's Opera*. Figurine in coloured plaster modelled after the original design by Claude Lovat Fraser. Nigel Playfair's revival of *The Beggar's Opera* at the Lyric Theatre, Hammersmith, in 1921 made the reputation of Lovat Fraser (a model of the permanent setting can be seen in the Victoria and Albert Museum, London) but the sudden death of the designer, as an indirect result of shell shock during the Great War, soon after the play's opening cut short a career which gave promise of a great future as a theatrical designer and graphic artist. His work, however, had considerable, influence on a number of designers in the 'twenties.

171 Maurice Adams. The 'Alexandra' dressing table. *c.* 1928.

172 Interior of a Farman aeroplane. Furniture and textiles designed by DIM (Robert Joubert and Philippe Petit). Prior to 1925.

173 Serge Chermayeff. Sideboard in walnut and macassar ebony. 1928.

174 Decoration and furnishing of a bedroom by Serge Chermayeff. Furniture veneered in macassar ebony and walnut. 1928. This room formed part of the exhibit at Waring and Gillow which had a decisive influence on English furniture design, the use of extravagantly figured veneers being widely copied in subsequent years. Although described as strictly contemporary the greater proportion of the exhibits were more in the spirit of Art Déco and were not typical of the latest trends in Paris.

175 Paul Follot. Dining room designed for Waring and Gillow. 1928.

176 R.W. Symonds and Robert Lutyens. Chest of drawers from a bedroom suite. Veneeered in plain and burr walnut with silk tassels in flame coloured silk. For the use of silk tassels as drawer handles compare the Atelier Martine example (plate 136) of some years earlier. The current fashion for frankly artificial flowers made of different materials can be seen in the bouquet of flowers made from oyster shells.

177 Anonymous design for a dining room using plywood and ibus as wall covering. Prior to 1926. At this date the preoccupation with Tudor motifs was so strong that even when using new materials they were thought of as being pressed into service to make inexpensive versions of Elizabethan panelling.

178 J. Murray Easton and Howard Robertson. Sitting room of a flat in Portman Square. Walls painted primrose with a skirting of stainless steel; frieze of mirror glass hiding electric lighting; black glass shelf continuing over fireplace, bookshelves and settee. Curtains of green oiled silk. An interior in extremely modernist style, the easy chair betraying a grim determination not to echo any style of the past.

179 R.W.Symonds and Robert Lutyens. Writing desk in walnut and ebony. 1928. An example of the new modernism with no period references which became popular at this time, the choice of woods being characteristic.

180 Pel. Chromium-plated tubular metal chair. 1929. Modern covering. One of the first chairs with a metal framework to be produced in England.

181 *My 30 Years' War* by Margaret Anderson. Bookbinding in black American cloth with vermilion impressed lettering. 1930. Margaret Anderson and Jane Heap were the editors of an avant-garde quarterly journal *The Little Review*, published in Greenwich Village, and claiming to be 'the only journal in the English language devoted entirely to the new movements in the arts'.

182 F.G.R. Elwes. Bedroom. Prior to 1930. A modified baroque interior of a style which was then considered a novelty and still has its adherents.

183 Machine printed wallpaper by Sanderson and Sons.

184 W. Turner. Wallpaper designed for Jeffrey and Co. Prior to 1926. This version of Elizabethan 'blackwork' embroidery was intended for use in the Tudor interiors which were popular in England at this date.

185 *Les Baigneuses*. Wallpaper printed in two colours from woodcuts by Paul Véra. Prior to 1925.

186 Henri Stéphany. Wallpaper. 1928.

187 Henri Stéphany. Wallpaper. c. 1926. The use of a chequered background with a superimposed design can be compared with a similar treatment in the moquette designed by Edouard Bénedictus (plate 80).

188 Hunt Diedrich. Pottery plate decorated with a design of a toreador and a bull. American. Prior to 1928.

189 Cylindrical vase with concave sides, of porcelain. The mottled orange ground has a design of two panels enclosing a basket of flowers in black and white outlined in gold connected by bands of ornament in the same colours. Royal Worcester porcelain. 1919.

190 Frank Brangwyn. Pottery vase ornamented with incised and painted grapes and lea-ves. Date uncertain, probably c. 1926. Height 8 in. Marked 'Brangwynware Royal Doulton'.

191 *The Tulip Girl*. Porcelain figure by Charles Vyse. Prior to 1920.

192 Emile Lenoble. Group of pottery. Lenoble, like most of the studio potters in both France and England was strongly influenced by the work of the Chinese and Japanese potters; the large dish reproduces the techniques of the Sung Dynasty while the small rust-coloured bowl is reminiscent of the vessels used in the Japanese tea ceremony.

193 Bernard Leach. Glazed pottery vase. Prior to 1923.

194 English porcelain cigarette box with geometrical design in orange and black decorated with gold flowers. Marked 'Crown Devon Fieldings England'.
Porcelain decanter with stopper. Signed 'Robj'. P. Deleyrac in an article entitled 'L'Humeur dans le Bibelot' (*L'Amour de l'Art*, 1929) prophesied that the porcelain bottles, cream-pots, cigarette boxes, cocktail shakers and ramekins bearing the signature 'Robj' would be as eagerly collected by future generations as the Staffordshire figures of Queen Victoria or the Prince Consort. The problem of finding useful and ornamental objects which would not be out of place in an interior by Ruhlmann or Fernand Nathan was, in the opinion of M. Deleyrac, solved by 'these smiling household gods'.
Biscuit box of tin with transfer decoration in green, orange and grey on a black ground. A contributor to *Our Homes and Gardens*, 1920, praised the design, delightful colours and surface quality of these and similar boxes, comparing them with those 'masquerading in inappropriate forms such as bundles of leather books held by a strap, lizard-skin bags, china Toby jugs, golf bags with clubs or logs of wood'.

195 Phyllis Barron. Hand block-printed fabric.

196 *La Vie au Grand Air*. Printed in monochrome on cotton by Scheurer, Lauth et Cie, from a design by André Marty. Marty was a fashion artist and the illustrator of many books; he was associated with Sue et Mare in the design of exhibits for the 1925 Exhibition where this panel, intended to be mounted as a screen, was presented.

197 *The Studio.* Cover design by E. McKnight Kauffer.

198 Simon Bussy. Poster for the London and North Eastern Railway.

199 E. McKnight Kauffer. Royal Wilton carpet. 1928. McKnight Kauffer, husband of Marion Dorn, designed a number of carpets but was more noted for his graphic work. The numerous posters he designed for the London Underground played a great part in making cubism acceptable to the general public.

200 *It.* Printed silk by Ruzzie Green for the Stehli Silk Co. N.Y., 1928. An early example of the use of typographic elements as a basis for design of fabrics; compare the contemporary design by Foujita which uses Chinese ideograms (plate 85). 'It' was the name invented to denote sex-appeal by the novelist Elinor Glyn and the publicity department of the film studio which had her under contract to adapt her novel *Three Weeks.* Clara Bow, a vivacious film star also under contract to the same studio was known as the 'It Girl' and, until the advent of the talkies, made a successful career more from her reputed possession of 'It' than any acting ability.

201 Tom Purvis. Poster for Austin Reed. Purvis was a well known poster artist in the late 'twenties and early 'thirties and his work was distinguished by a use of flat simplified areas of colour and well designed legible lettering.

202 Jean d'Ylen. Poster for Sandeman's.

203 Aubrey Hammond. Poster for the Folkestone Theatre. 1927. Hammond was a prolific and successful graphic artist who also designed the scenery and costumes for a number of theatrical productions.

204 Delis. Lithographed poster for Clotilde and Alexandre Sakharoff. 1923. Many of the best designers of the period were commissioned by the Sakharoffs to design posters for their recitals of combined mime and dance, recitals which they gave with great success all over the world before their retirement in 1953 after a career which in the case of Alexandre Sakharoff had begun in 1911.

205 Pico. Poster for the Folies Bergère. Prior to 1928. The distortions of Negro sculpture had become sufficiently accepted by the general public for them to be applied to an advertisement for a production which traditionally featured female beauty.

206 Jean Dupas. Poster in colours for Arnold Constable. *c.* 1926.

207 *Monte Carlo.* Poster designed by Michel Bouchaud. 1929.

208 Poster for the Paris dressmakers' ball. Anonymous.

209 Press advertisement for Worth scent. 1928. About 1927, photography began to be increasingly used in advertising; hitherto it had been rarely used, preference being given to line or wash drawings of the products but advertising studios, influenced by European examples, began to realize the visual appeal of photographs incorporated into a composition. The simple but elegant lettering plays an important part, the exaggerated 'O' in Worth echoing the shape of the scent bottle.

210 Carlègle. Housemark for Léon Pichon. Prior to 1924.

Source books

After All, Elsie de Wolfe; Heinemann, London; and Harper & Brothers, New York, 1935

Antoine by Antoine, Cierplikowski Antoine; W.H. Allen, London, 1946; and Prentice-Hall, New York, 1945

A Survey of British Industrial Arts, Henry G. Dowling; F. Lewis, Leigh-on-Sea, Essex, 1935

Colour and Interior Decoration, Basil Ionides; Country Life, London, 1926

Costume Design and Illustration, Ethel Traphagen; John Wiley & Sons, New York, 1918

Design in Modern Industry; Benn, London, 1922

Design in Modern Life and Industry, 1924-5; Benn, London, 1925

Discretions and Indiscretions, Lady Duff Gordon; Jarrolds, London, 1932

Encyclopédie des Arts Décoratifs et Industriels Moderns; Office Central d'Editions et de Librairie, Paris, 1925

Floral Art, Decoration and Design, H. David Richter; Batsford, London, 1932

Hammersmith Hoy, Nigel Playfair; Faber, London, 1930

Intérieurs au Salon des Artistes-Décorateurs; Editions d'Art Ch. Moreau, Paris, 1929

La Ferronnerie Moderne, H. Clouzot; Editions d'Art. Ch. Moreau, Paris, 1925

L'Art Décoratif Français, 1918-1925; Editions Albert Levy, Paris, 1925

La Sculpture Décorative Moderne, H. Rapin; Editions d'Art Ch. Moreau, Paris, 1925

Le Arti d'Oggi, Roberto Papini; Casa Editrice d'Arte Bestetti & Jumminelli, Rome and Milan, 1925

Le Luminaire, Guillaume Janneau, Editions d'Art Ch. Moreau, Paris, 1925

Les Années ' 25 ': Art Déco/Bauhaus/Stijl/Esprit Nouveau; Musée des Arts Décoratifs, Paris, 1966

Lo Stile 1925, Yvonne Brunhammer; Fratelli Fabbri Editori, Milan, 1966

Modern Decorative Art, Maurice Adams; Batsford, London, 1930

Modern English Furniture, J.C. Rogers; Country Life, London, 1930

Modern French Decoration, Katherine Morrison Kahle; The Knickerbocker Press, New York, 1930

Modern French Decorative Art; The Architectural Press, London, 1930

Modern Plywood, Shirley P. Wainwright; Benn, London, 1927

My First Fifty Years, Paul Poiret; Gollancz, London; and (as *King of Fashion*: *the autobiography of Paul Poiret*) J.B. Lippincott, Philadelphia, 1931

New Dimensions, Paul T. Frankl; Payson & Clarke, New York, 1928

Répertoire du Goût Modern; Editions Albert Levy, Paris, 1929

Report on the Industrials Arts, ' International Exhibition, Paris 1925 '; Department of Overseas Trade, London, 1925

Simple Schemes for Decoration, John Gloag; Duckworth, London, 1922

Studies in Art, Architecture and Design, vol. II, Pevsner; Thames & Hudson, London, 1968

Style and Design, 1909-1929, Veronesi; Braziller, New York, 1968

The Beggar's Opera, John Gay; Heinemann, London, 1921

The Duenna, Richard Brinsley Sheridan; Constable, London, 1925
The New Interior Decoration, Dorothy Todd and Raymond Mortimer; Batsford,
London; and Charles Scribner's Sons, New York, 1929
The Royal Academy Illustrated; Walter Judd, London, 1920-1930
The Studio Year Books of Decorative Art; The Studio, London, 1906-1932

Important magazines of the period
The Studio (London); *Vogue* (London, New York, Paris);
House and Garden (London, New York); *Our Homes and Gardens* (London);
L'Amour de l'Art (Paris); *Les Feuillets d'Art* (Paris).

Index